The new BIG BOOK of LOGOS

David E. Carter editor

book design
Suzanna M.W.

layout & production
Graham Allen
Christa Carter

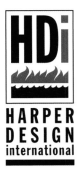

HDi

HARPER
DESIGN
international

An Imprint of HarperCollins*Publishers*

THE NEW BIG BOOK OF LOGOS (paperback)
Copyright (c) 2000 HBI and David E. Carter

First published in hardcover in 2000 by:
HBI, an imprint of HarperCollinsPublishers
10 East 53rd Street
New York, NY 10022

First paperback edition published in 2003 by:
Harper Design International,
an imprint of HarperCollinsPublishers
10 East 53rd Street
New York, NY 10022

Distributed throughout the world by:
HarperCollins International
10 East 53rd Street
New York, NY 10022
Fax: (212) 207-7654

HarperCollins books may be purchased for educational, business, or sales promotional use. For information, please write: Special Markets Department, HarperCollins Publishers Inc., 10 East 53rd Street, New York, NY 10022.

Library of Congress Cataloging-in-Publication Data

The new big book of logos / David E. Carter.
                    p. cm.
     Includes index.
     ISBN 0-06-056755-4 (pb)
          1. Logos (Symbols)—United States—History—20th century—Catalogs. 2. Commercial art—United States—History—20th century—Catalogs. I. Title: Big book of logos. II. Carter, David E.

NC1002.L63N48 2003
929.9'5'0973—dc21
                                                            2003047807

All images in this book have been reproduced with the knowledge and prior consent of the individuals concerned. No responsibility is accepted by producer, publisher, or printer for any infringement of copyright or otherwise arising from the contents of this publication. Every effort has been made to ensure that credits accurately comply with information supplied.

Printed in Hong Kong by Everbest Printing Company through Four Colour Imports, Louisville, Kentucky.

Third paperback printing, 2004

Once upon a time, there was a big book.

A **Big Book of Logos**. It became a major seller. Well, not by John Grisham or Stephen King standards, but in the world of graphics, it was huge. It actually cracked the circle of the top 3% of ALL books sold on Amazon.com.

Graphic designers really, really liked this book. And when a book is that successful, **you know what happens**: a sequel.

So, the publishers huffed, and they puffed, and they convinced David Carter to do another Big Book of Logos. (He wanted to call the book "Green Eggs and Ham", but that title was already taken.) **THIS is THAT book**.

And, oh yes, they reminded him that this sequel had to be just as good as—or better than—the original. Someone said something about "an offer you can't turn down."

We listened carefully, and selected about 2,500 outstanding logos that had been designed in the last three years. And, once again, **The NEW Big Book of Logos** will go into the design world and say "We've done it again."

This book, combined with its predecessor, contains well over 5,000 great logo designs. This may be one of the best sources of logo design ideas ever assembled. (Or maybe not. That's for you to judge. But we think you'll find this great collection to be inspirational.)

To paraphrase W.P. Kinsella, "Publish it and they will buy."

David E. Carter

1.

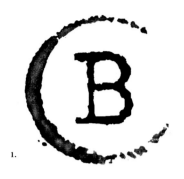

2. PRETTY GOOD PRIVACY™

3. avenue a™

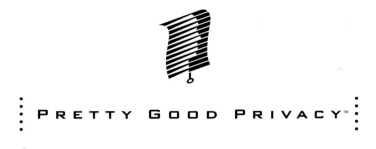

4. ALTA

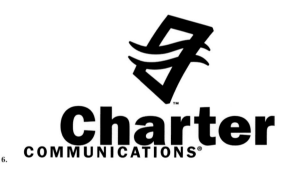

5. ATRéVA™

6. Charter
COMMUNICATIONS®

A WIRED WORLD COMPANY

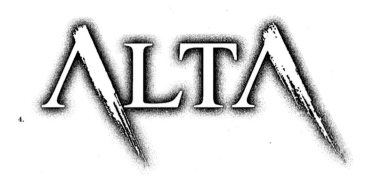

7. blue nile

8. grape finds℠

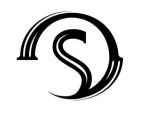

STEWART CAPITAL MANAGEMENT

10.

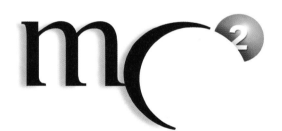

9.

innoVentry™

11.

rpm

12.

mc²

13.

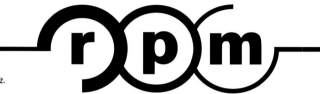

14.

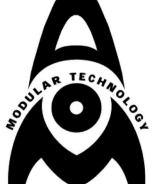

15.

(all)

Design Firm Hornall Anderson Design Works

1. Client   Best Cellars
   Designers   Jack Anderson, Lisa Cerveny,
              Jana Wilson Esser, David Bates,
              & Nicole Bloss

2. Client   (PGP) Pretty Good Privacy
   Designers   Jack Anderson, Debra
              McCloskey, Michael Brugman,
              Heidi Favour, Jana Wilson Esser,
              & Katha Dalton

3. Client   Avenue A
   Designers   Jack Anderson, Debra
              McCloskey, Tobi Brown,
              Henry Yiu, James Tee,
              & Gretchen Cook

4. Client   Alta Beverage Company
   Designers   Jack Anderson, Larry Anderson,
              & Julie Keenan

5. Client   Wells Fargo "Atreva"
   Designers   Jack Anderson, Kathy Saito,
              Alan Copeland, Cliff Chung,
              & Chris Sallquist

6. Client   Charter Communications
   Designers   Jack Anderson, Lisa Cerveny,
              Jana Wilson Esser, Mike Calkins,
              David Bates, Julia LaPine,
              & Sonja Max

7. Client   Blue Nile
   Designers   Jack Anderson, Bruce Stigler,
              Gretchen Cook, Henry Yiu,
              & Sonja Max

8. Client   grapefinds
   Designers   Jack Anderson, Lisa Cerveny,
              Gretchen Cook, Jana Wilson
              Esser, & Mary Chin Hutchison

9. Client   SaviShopper.com
   Designers   Jack Anderson, Ryan Wilkerson,
              Naomi Davidson
              & Margaret Long

10. Client   Stewart Capital Management
    Designers Jack Anderson, Debra
               McCloskey, David Bates,
               & Lisa Cerveny

11. Client   Wells Fargo "innoVentry"
    Designers Jack Anderson, Kathy Saito,
               Sonja Max, & Alan Copeland

12. Client   (RPM) Wells Fargo
    Designers Jack Anderson, Kathy Saito,
               Sonja Max, & Alan Copeland

13. Client   MC²
    Designers Jack Anderson & Margaret Long

14. Client   Healthshop.com
    Designers Jack Anderson, Mary Hermes,
               Mike Calkins, David Bates,
               & Holly Finlayson

15. Client   K2 Corporation
    Designers Jack Anderson, Andrew Smith,
               Taro Sakita, & Mary Chin
               Hutchison

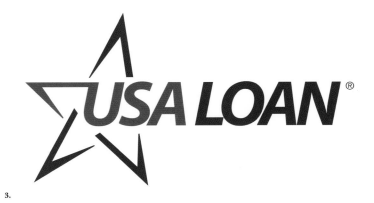

1.

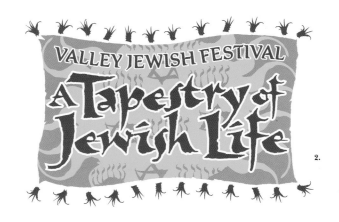

2.

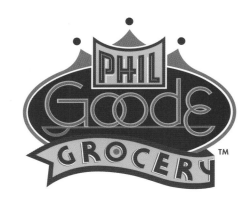

3.

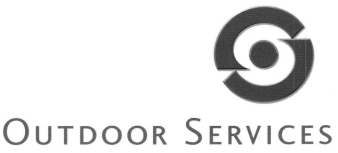

OUTDOOR SERVICES

4.

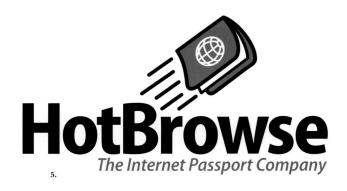

HotBrowse

The Internet Passport Company

5.

BroadStream

6.

V

VARNA
PLATINUM

7.

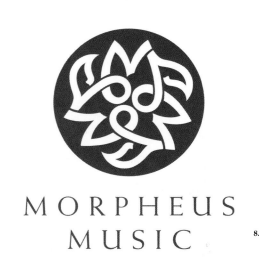

MORPHEUS
MUSIC

8.

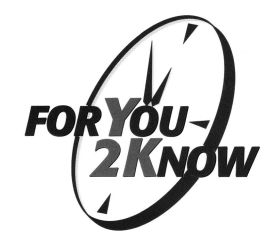

9.

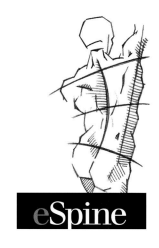

eSpine

10.

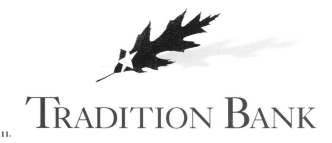

11.

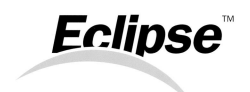

12.

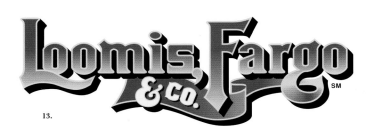

13.

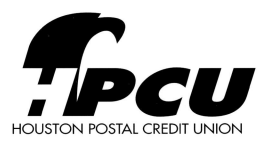

14.

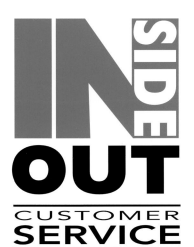

15.

1		
	Design Firm	Sayles Graphic Design
2 - 10		
	Design Firm	Glyphix Studio
11 - 15		
	Design Firm	The Focus Group
1.	Client	Phil Goode Grocery
	Designer	John Sayles
2.	Client	The Jewish Federation/ Valley Alliance
	Designer	Paul Ruettgers
3.	Client	USA Loan
	Designer	Brad Wilder
4.	Client	Outdoor Services
	Designer	Brad Wilder
5.	Client	HotBrowse
	Designer	Brad Wilder
6.	Client	Broadstream
	Designer	Brad Wilder

7.	Client	Varna Platinum
	Designer	Brad Wilder
8.	Client	Morpheus Music
	Designer	Brad Wilder
9.	Client	City of Los Angeles
	Designer	Brad Wilder
10.	Client	eSpine
	Designers	Eric Sena & Brad Wilder
11.	Client	Tradition Bank
	Designer	Kirk Davis
12.	Client	TeleCheck
	Designers	Dan Feder & Kelly Johnson
13.	Client	Loomis, Fargo & Co.
	Designer	Kirk Davis
14.	Client	Houston Postal Credit Union
	Designer	Kelly Johnson
15.	Client	Solvay Polymers
	Designer	Kelly Johnson

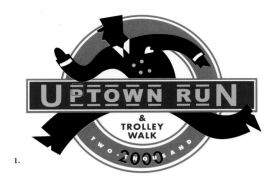

1.

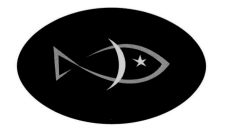

2.

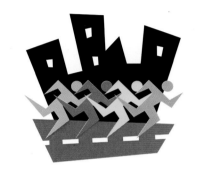

DEEP ELLUM DASH

3.

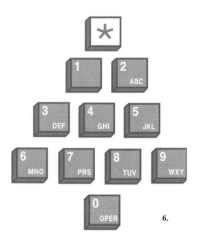

4.

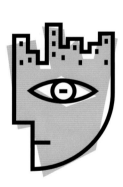

DEEP ELLUM

5.

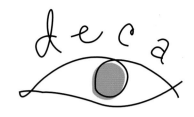

6.

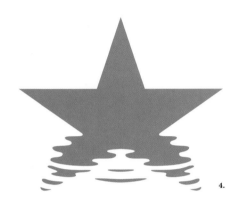

7.

1 - 7

Design Firm Squires & Company

1. Client   Uptown Run, Annual 5K,
                10K Run
    Designer   Christie Grotheim

2. Client   DECA Art Gallery
                Featuring Local Artists
    Designer   Christie Grotheim

3. Client   Deep Ellum Dash '97
                10K Fun Run
    Designer   Paul Black

4. Client   Aqua Star, Pools and Spa
    Designer   Paul Black

5. Client   Deep Ellum Association
                An Historic Industrial
                Area of Dallas
    Designer   Paul Black

6. Client   Communigroup
    Designers   Amy Chang & Brandon Murphy

7. Client   Sushi Nights, Restaurant and Bar
    Designer   Christie Grotheim

(opposite)
Design Firm Dixon & Parcels Associates, Inc.

    Client   Eggland's Best, Inc.

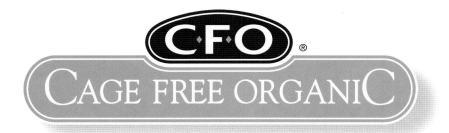

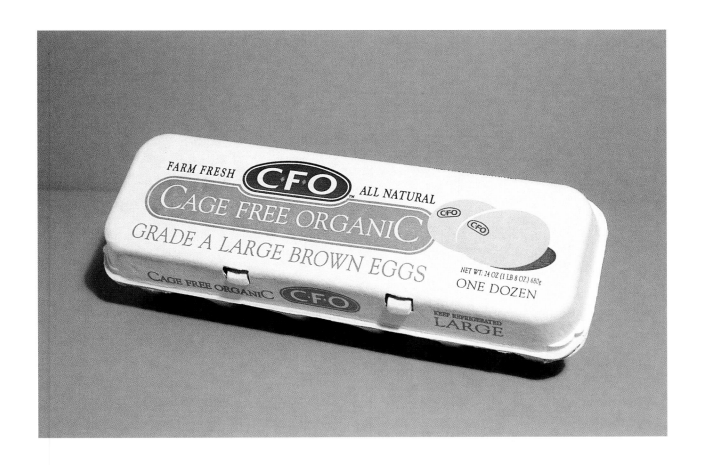

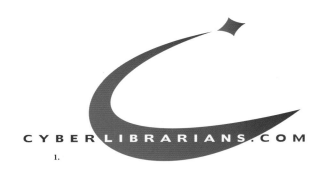

CYBERLIBRARIANS.COM

1.

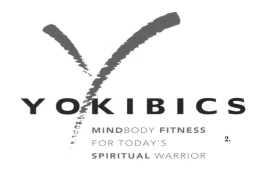

YOKIBICS

MINDBODY FITNESS
FOR TODAY'S
SPIRITUAL WARRIOR

2.

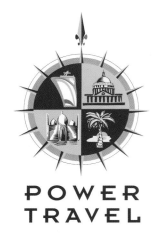

POWER
TRAVEL

3.

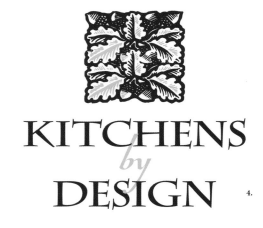

KITCHENS
by
DESIGN

4.

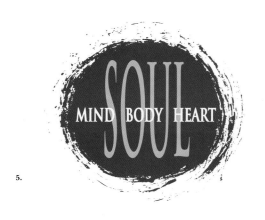

SOUL
MIND BODY HEART

5.

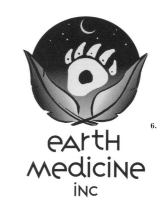

eARtH
Medicine
iNC

6.

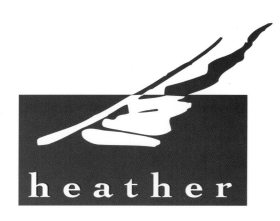

heather

7.

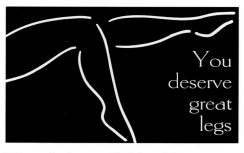

You
deserve
great
legs

Dr. Julius W. Garvey

8.

10

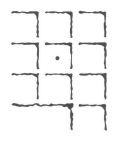

mark d. bennett, cpa

9.

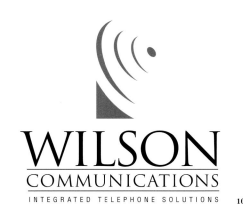

WILSON
COMMUNICATIONS
INTEGRATED TELEPHONE SOLUTIONS

10.

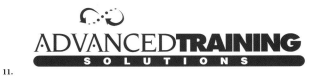

11.

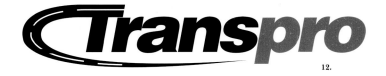

12.

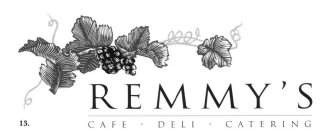

R E M M Y ' S
CAFE · DELI · CATERING

13.

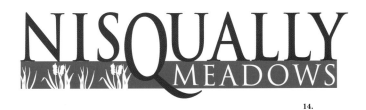

14.

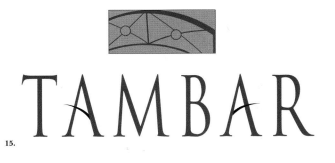

TAMBAR

15.

1 - 8
Design Firm Guarino Graphics
**   & Design Studio**

9 - 15
Design Firm Graphic Technologies

1. Client	Cyberlibrarians.com	
Designer	Jan Guarino	
2. Client	Yokibics	
Designer	Jan Guarino	
3. Client	Power Travel	
Designer	Jan Guarino	
4. Client	Kitchens by Design	
Designer	Jan Guarino	
5. Client	Soul•Mind•Body•Heart	
Designer	Jan Guarino	
6. Client	Earth Medicine	
Designer	Jan Guarino	
7. Client	Heather	
Designer	Jan Guarino	

8. Client	Dr. Julius Garvey
Designer	Jan Guarino
9. Client	Mark Bennett, CPA
Designer	Gary Thompson
10. Client	Wilson Communications
Designer	Gary Thompson
11. Client	Advanced Training Solutions
Designer	Gary Thompson
12. Client	Transpro
Designer	Gary Thompson
13. Client	Remmy's
Designer	Gary Thompson
14. Client	Nisqually
Designer	Gary Thompson
15. Client	Tambar
Designer	Gary Thompson

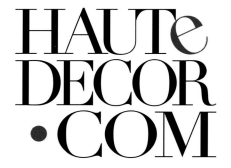

1.

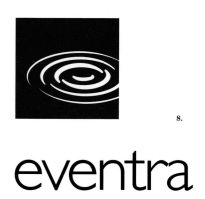

2.

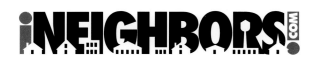

3.

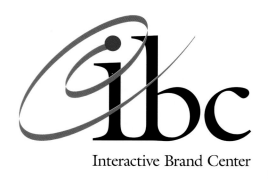

4.

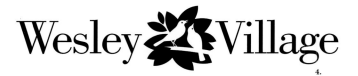

5.

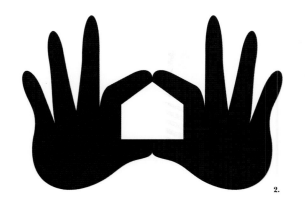

6.

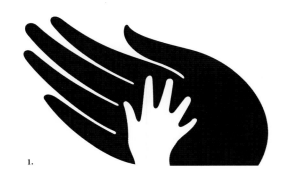

7.

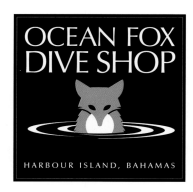

8.

eventra

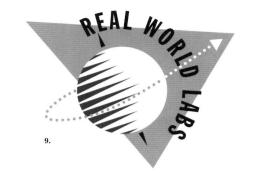

9.

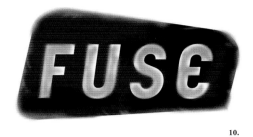

10.

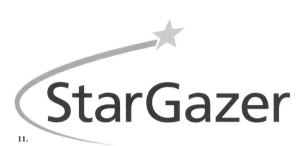

11.

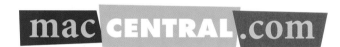

12.

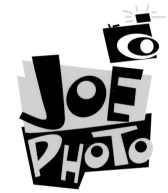

13.

NETWORK

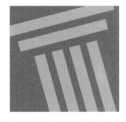

SOCIETY™ 14.

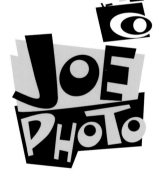

THE RIDGE
COMMUNITY CHURCH

15.

1 - 8
Design Firm Tom Fowler, Inc.
9, 12, 14
Design Firm Edmonds Design
10, 11, 13
Design Firm Fuse, Inc.
15
Design Firm Graphic Technologies

1. Client   Ross Products Division/
           Abbott Laboratories
   Designer   Thomas G. Fowler

2. Client   St. Luke's LifeWorks
   Designer   Karl S. Maruyama

3. Client   Reynolds and Rose
   Designer   Karl S. Maruyama

4. Client   United Methodist Homes
   Designers   Thomas G. Fowler
            & Karl S. Maruyama

5. Client   Haute Decor.com
   Designers   Thomas G. Fowler
            & Elizabeth P. Ball

6. Client   IBC
   Designer   Elizabeth P. Ball

7. Client   Ocean Fox Dive Shop
   Designer   Thomas G. Fowler

8. Client   Eventra
   Designer   Karl S. Maruyama

9. Client   Network Computing Magazine
   Designer   Nancy Edmonds

10. Client   Fuse, Inc.
    Designer   Russell Pierce

11. Client   PairGain—StarGazer
    Designer   Russell Pierce

12. Client   Mac Publishing/MacWorld
    Designer   Nancy Edmonds

13. Client   Joe Photo
    Designer   Russell Pierce

14. Client   Network Computing Magazine
    Designer   Nancy Edmonds

15. Client   The Ridge Community Church
    Designer   Gary Thompson

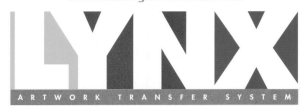

Chesebrough-Pond's USA Co.
LYNX
ARTWORK TRANSFER SYSTEM

1.

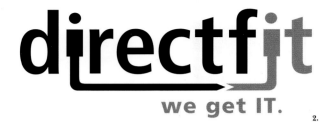

directfit
we get IT.

2.

centricity

3.

pairgain
THE POWER OF DSL ACCESS

4.

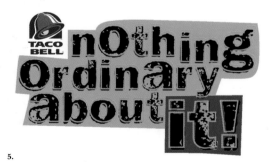

5.

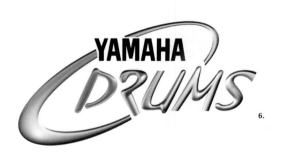

YAMAHA DRUMS

6.

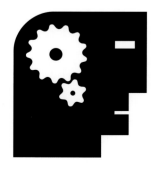

7.

1
Design Firm Tom Fowler, Inc.
2 - 6
Design Firm Fuse, Inc.
7
Design Firm Squires & Company

1. Client	Chesebrough-Ponds USA Co	
Designer	Elizabeth P. Ball	
2. Client	DirectFit	
Designers	Matthew Stainner	
	& Mike Esperanza	
3. Client	Centricity	
Designer	Russell Pierce	
4. Client	PairGain	
Designer	Mike Esperanza	

5. Client	Taco Bell—Nothing Ordinary About It
Designer	Russell Pierce
6. Client	Yamaha Corporation of America
Designer	Kristi Kamei
7. Client	I Think, Inc.
Designers	Clark Bystrom & Paul Black

(opposite)
Design Firm Miriello Grafico Inc.

Client	Eastpack
Designer	Ron Miriello

14

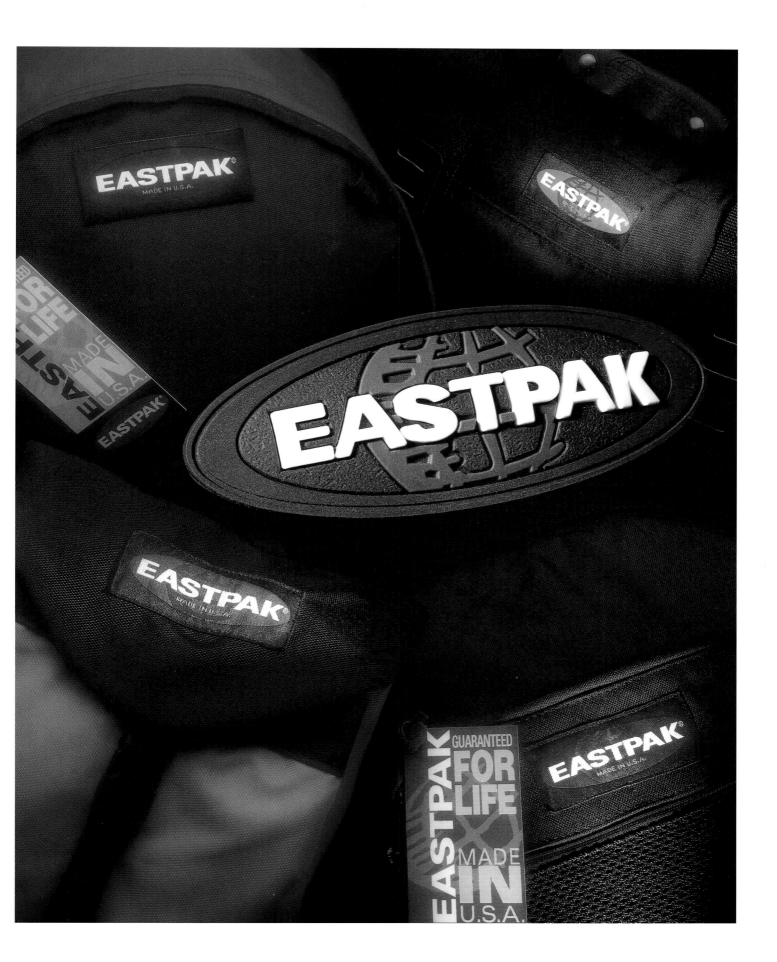

15

K 1 D **C** O N C E P T S

1.

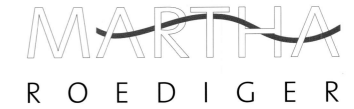

2.

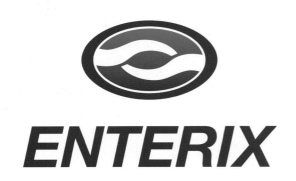

3.

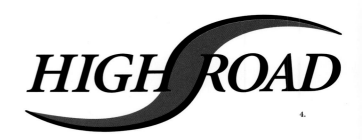

4.

ENTERIX

5.

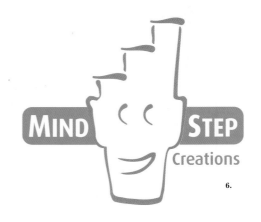

6.

ASSET
PR⌂TECTION
A S S O C I A T E S

PROTECTING WHAT YOU HAVE EARNED

FOR THE REST OF YOUR LIFE

7.

TECHNIUM

8.

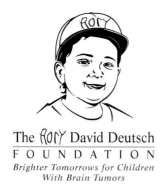

The *Rory* David Deutsch
F O U N D A T I O N
*Brighter Tomorrows for Children
With Brain Tumors*

9.

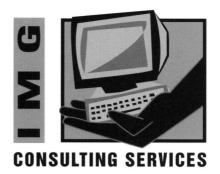

CONSULTING SERVICES

10.

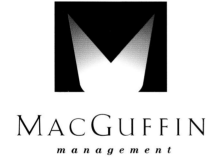

GEORGE ORLOFF, M.D.

11.

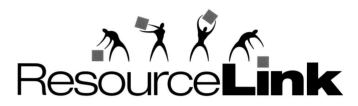

ResourceLink

12.

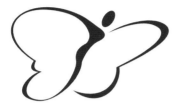

MACGUFFIN
management

13.

DEEP ELLUM
Arts Festival

14.

JENSEN
MAGIC

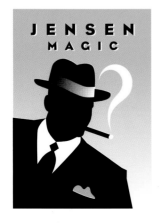

15.

1 - 6
**Design Firm   Thibault Paolini
Design Associates**
7 - 10
Design Firm   Design Moves, Ltd.
11 - 12
Design Firm   Glyphix Studio
13 - 15
Design Firm   Squires & Company

1. Client   Kid Concepts
    Designers   Renée Fournier
                 & Sue Schenning

2. Client   Martha Roediger
    Designer   Renée Fournier

3. Client   Tom McPherson Photography
    Designer   Renée Fournier

4. Client   Talus
    Designer   Sue Schenning

5. Client   Enterix
    Designers   Judy Paolini & Sue Schenning

6. Client   Mind Step Creations
    Designer   Sue Schenning

7. Client   Asset Protection Associates
    Designers   Laurie Freed, Bill Sprowl,
                 & Jennifer Rayburn

8. Client   Technium, Inc.
    Designers   Laurie Freed, Bill Sprowl,
                 & Jennifer Rayburn

9. Client   Rory David Deutsch Foundation
    Designers   Laurie Medeiros Freed,
                 Eric Halloran, Jennifer Rayburn,
                 & Bill Sprowl

10. Client   Information Management
                Group
    Designers   Laurie Freed, Jennifer Rayburn,
                 Bill Sprowl, & Amy Forbes

11. Client   George Orloff, M.D.
    Designer   Eric Sena

12. Client   ResourceLink
    Designer   Eric Sena

13. Client   MacGuffin
    Designer   Christie Grotheim

14. Client   Deep Ellum Arts Festival
    Designers   Thomas Vasquez & Paul Black

15. Client   Jenson
    Designer   Paul Black

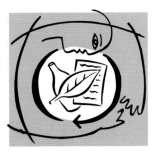

Palo Alto
Recycling
Program

1.

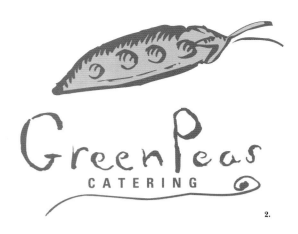

GreenPeas
CATERING

2.

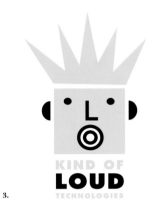

KIND OF
LOUD
TECHNOLOGIES

3.

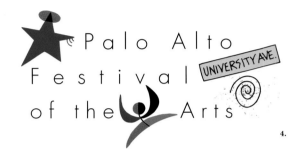

Palo Alto
Festival
of the   Arts

UNIVERSITY AVE.

4.

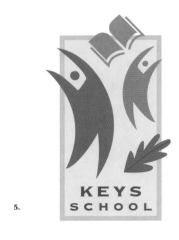

KEYS
SCHOOL

5.

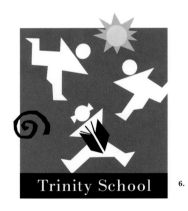

Trinity School

6.

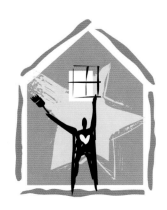

7.

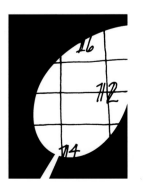

8.

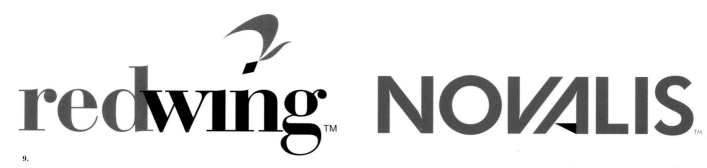

redwing™

NOVALIS™

9.

10.

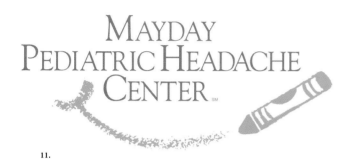

MAYDAY
PEDIATRIC HEADACHE
CENTER℠

11.

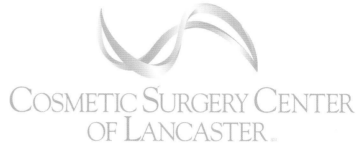

COSMETIC SURGERY CENTER
OF LANCASTER℠

at Lancaster General Hospital Health Campus

12.

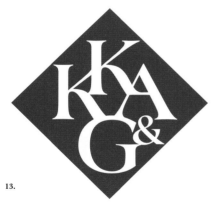

13.

DA

technology
solutions, LLC

14.

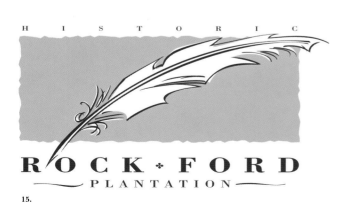

HISTORIC

ROCK♦FORD
PLANTATION

15.

1 - 8		
Design Firm	**Artefact Design**	
9 - 15		
Design Firm	**Albert/Bogner**	
	Design Communications	
1. Client	City of Palo Alto Recycling Program	
Designers	Artefact Design	
2. Client	Green Peas Catering	
Designers	Artefact Design	
3. Client	Kind of Loud Technologies	
Designers	Artefact Design	
4. Client	Palo Alto Festival of the Arts	
Designers	Artefact Design	
5. Client	Keys School	
Designer	Kim Schwede	
6. Client	Trinity School	
Designer	Artefact Design	
7. Client	Christmas in April— Mid Peninsula	
Designer	Artefact Design	

8. Client	Tom Richman & Associates
Designer	Artefact Design
9. Client	Red Wing
Designers	Kelly Albert, & Marie Elaina Miller
10. Client	Novalis
Designer	Marie Elaina Miller
11. Client	Maday Pediatric Headache Center
Designer	Kelly Albert
12. Client	Cosmetic Surgery Center of Lancaster
Designer	Kelly Albert
13. Client	Kegel, Kelin, Almy, Grimm
Designer	Marie Elaina Miller
14. Client	DA Technology Solutions
Designer	Marie Elaina Miller
15. Client	Historic Rockford Plantation
Designers	Kelly Albert, & Marie Elaina Miller

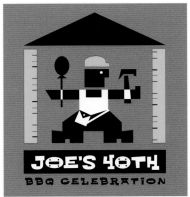

1.

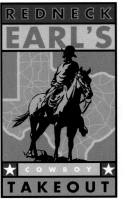

2.

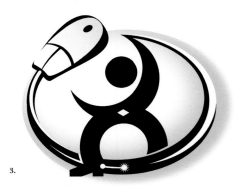

3.

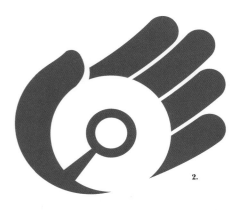

MOTORWEB

4.

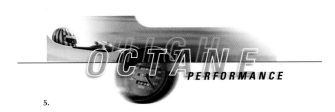

OCTANE
PERFORMANCE

5.

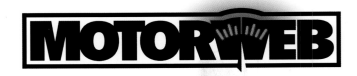

6.

JOE'S 40TH
BBQ CELEBRATION

7.

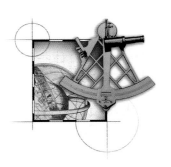

REDNECK
EARL'S
COWBOY
TAKEOUT

8.

20

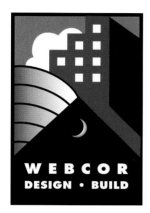

CORTANA

9.

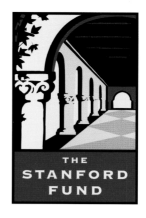

10.

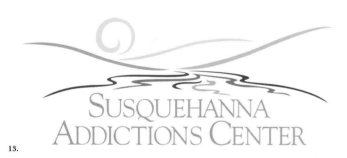

11.

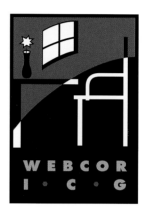

12.

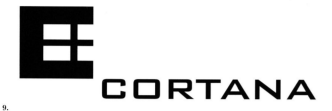

SUSQUEHANNA
ADDICTIONS CENTER

13.

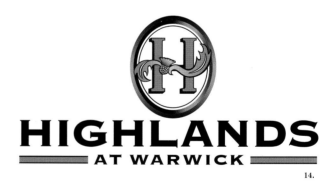

14.

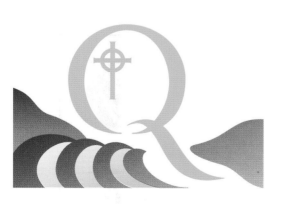

15.

1, 3, 4			
Design Firm	Ross West Design		
2, 5, 6			
Design Firm	GA Design		
7 - 12			
Design Firm	Artefact Design	8. Client	Redneck Earl's Cowboy Takeout
13 - 15		Designer	Artefact Design
Design Firm	Albert/Bogner Design		
	Communications	9. Client	Cortana Corporation
		Designers	Artefact Design, Kim Schwede
1. Client	Dr. Andrew J. Kapust DDS		
Designer	Ross West	10. Client	The Stanford Fund
		Designer	Artefact Design
2. Client	Microsoft		
Designer	Ross West	11. Client	Webcor Builders, Inc.
		Designer	Artefact Design
3. Client	Ross West Design		
Designer	Ross West	12. Client	Webcor Builders, Inc.
		Designer	Artefact Design
4. Client	Microsoft		
Designer	Ross West	13. Client	Susquehanna Addictions Center
		Designers	Kelly Albert
5. Client	Washington Mutual		& Marie Elaina Miller
Designer	Ross West		
		14. Client	Highlands at Warwick
6. Client	Microsoft	Designer	Kelly Albert
Designer	Ross West		
		15. Client	Quarryville Retirement
7. Client	Joe's 40th Birthday		Community
Designer	Kim Schwede	Designers	Kelly Albert
			& Marie Elaina Miller

21

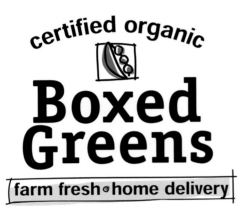 **UniSource Energy**

1.

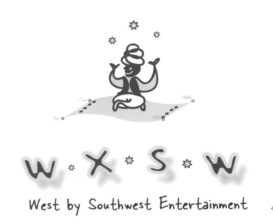 **DakotaCom.net**

2.

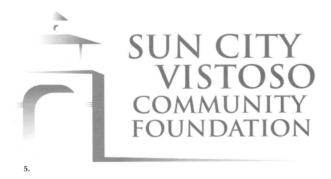

3.

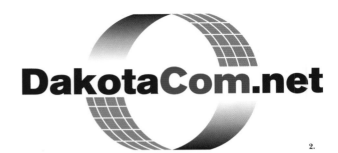

West by Southwest Entertainment

4.

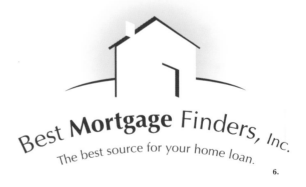 SUN CITY VISTOSO COMMUNITY FOUNDATION

5.

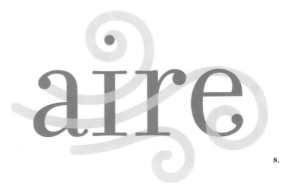

6.

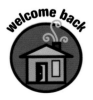 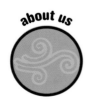 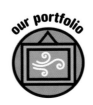

7.

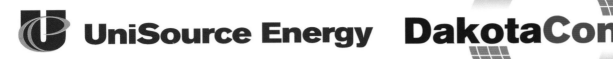

8.

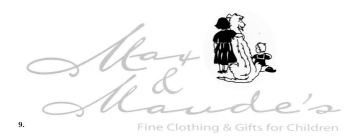

9.

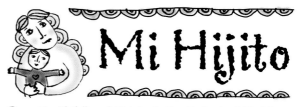

Favorite Childhood Originals for Infants & Toddlers

10.

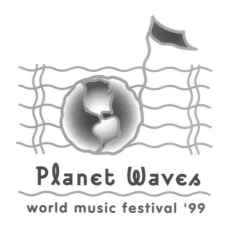

11.

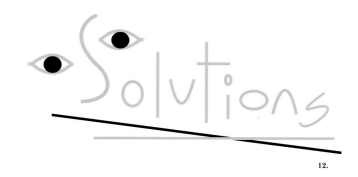

12.

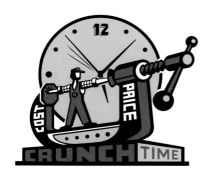

13.

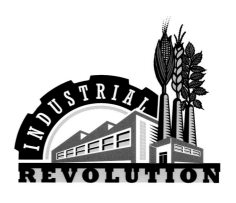

14.

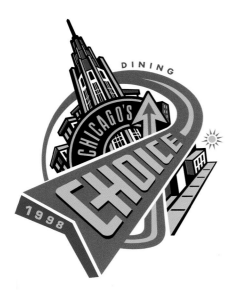

15.

HORVATH

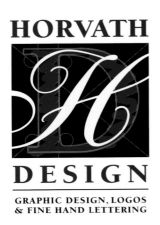

D E S I G N

GRAPHIC DESIGN, LOGOS
& FINE HAND LETTERING

1.

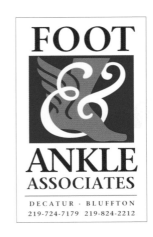

FOOT

ANKLE
ASSOCIATES

DECATUR · BLUFFTON
219-724-7179 219-824-2212

2.

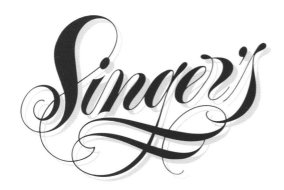

Baggerie

K A N S A S   C I T Y

3.

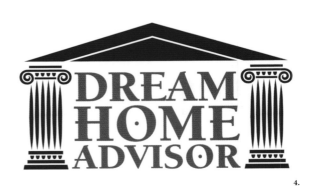

DREAM
HOME
ADVISOR

4.

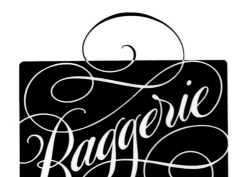

Singer's

5.

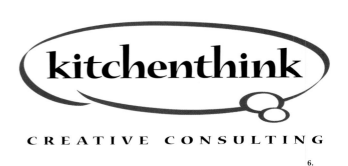

kitchenthink

C R E A T I V E   C O N S U L T I N G

6.

HARRINGTON

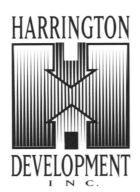

DEVELOPMENT
I N C.

7.

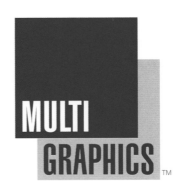

MULTI
GRAPHICS ™

8.

OMAN

9.

ENNISKNUPP

10.

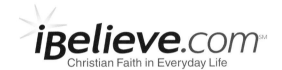

iBelieve.comSM
Christian Faith in Everyday Life

11.

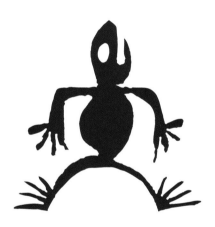

iflourishsm
My Active Living Resource

12.

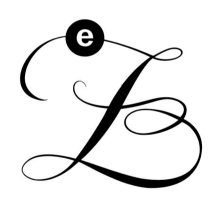

13.

14.

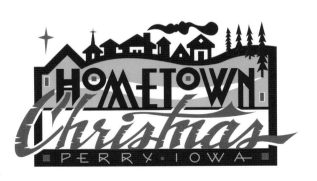
HOMETOWN Christmas
- PERRY · IOWA -

15.

1 - 7		
Design Firm	**Horvath Design**	
8 - 14		
Design Firm	**Liska + Associates, Inc.**	
15		
Design Firm	**Sayles Graphic Design**	

No.			No.		
1.	Client	Horvath Design	8.	Client	Multigraphics
	Designer	Kevin Horvath		Designer	Andrea Wener
2.	Client	Foot & Ankle Clinic	9.	Client	Oman Photography
	Designer	Kevin Horvath		Designer	Steve Liska
3.	Client	Baggerie	10.	Client	EnnisKnupp & Associates
	Designer	Kevin Horvath		Designer	Liska + Associates, Inc.
4.	Client	Dream Home Advisor	11.	Client	iBelieve.com
	Designer	Kevin Horvath		Designer	Liska + Associates, Inc.
5.	Client	Singers Restaurant	12.	Client	iFlourish.com
	Designer	Kevin Horvath		Designer	Liska + Associates, Inc.
6.	Client	Kitchen Think	13.	Client	Elizabeth Zeschin Photography
	Designer	Kevin Horvath		Designer	Bonnie Giard
7.	Client	Harrington Development	14.	Client	Reptile Artists Agents
	Designer	Kevin Horvath		Designer	Holle Andersen
			15.	Client	Patee Enterprises "Hometown Christmas"
				Designer	John Sayles

< P O P U L I >

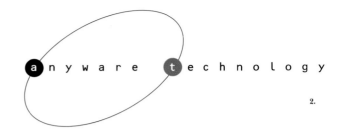

1.

2.

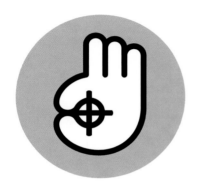

3.

4.

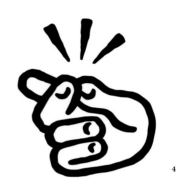

5.

6.

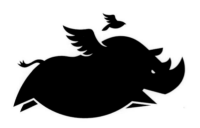

7.

1 - 9
Design Firm Squires & Company

1. Client   Populi
    Designers   Brandon Murphy & Amy Chang

2. Client   Anyware Technology
    Designer   Brandon Murphy

3. Client   Pro Color Imaging
    Designers   Kristine Murphy
                       & Brandon Murphy

4. Client   Loomis Productions
    Designer   Kristine Murphy

5. Client   Black Rhino Graphics
    Designers   Kristine Murphy
                       & Brandon Murphy

6. Client   Hill Country Equestrian Lodge
    Designers   Bryan Hynecek
                       & Brandon Murphy

7. Client   Moving Pictures Editorial
    Designers   Kristine Murphy
                       & Brandon Murphy

(opposite)
Design Firm Squires & Company

8. Client   Deep Ellum Dash '98,
                       Annual Fun Run
    Designer   Christie Grotheim

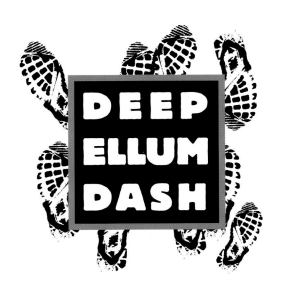

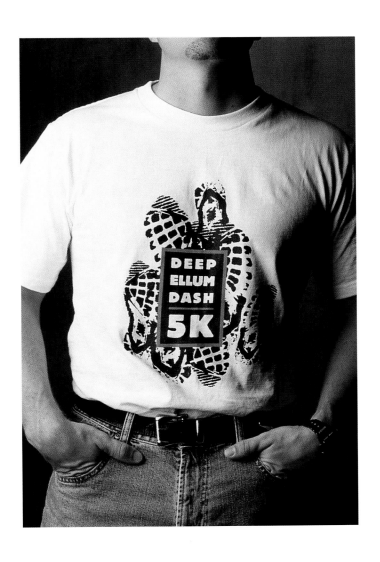

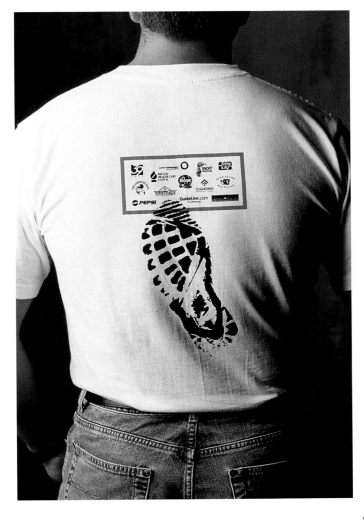

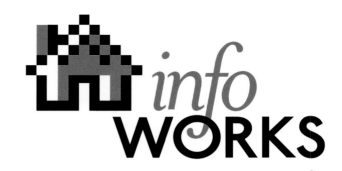

SHAMAN

Good Medicine For Technology

1.

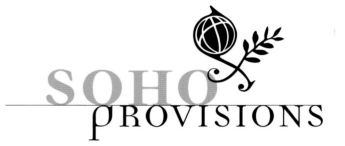

info **WORKS**

2.

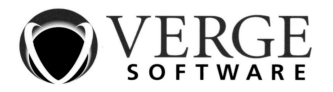

accompany

3.

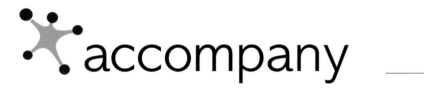

SOHO
ρROVISIONS

4.

VERGE
SOFTWARE

5.

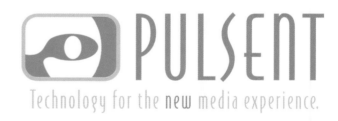

PULSENT

Technology for the new media experience.

6.

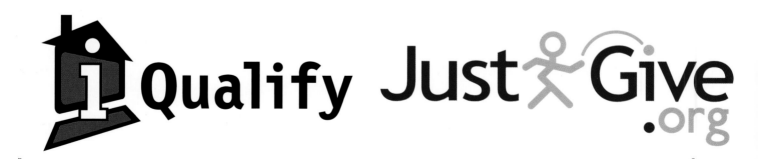

Qualify

7.

Just Give
.org

8.

28

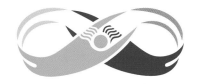

SAMBA

9.

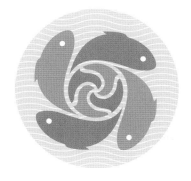

10.

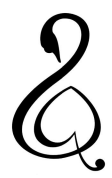

11.

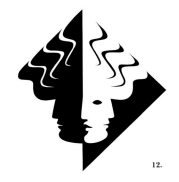

12.

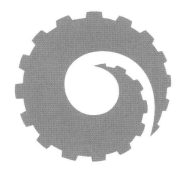

13.

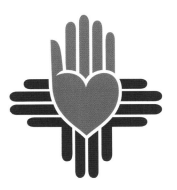

14.

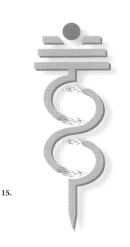

15.

1 - 8		
Design Firm	Diesel Design	
9 - 15		
Design Firm	Macnab Design	
	Visual Communication	

1.	Client	Shaman	8.	Client	Just Give.org
	Designer	Amy Bainbridge		Designers	Amy Bainbridge
					& Luis Dominguez
2.	Client	Info Works	9.	Client	Samba
	Designer	Aaron Morton		Designer	Maggie Macnab
3.	Client	Accompany	10.	Client	Truchas Hydrologic Associates
	Designer	Aaron Morton		Designer	Maggie Macnab
4.	Client	Soho Provisions	11.	Client	Swan Songs
	Designer	Pam Purser		Designer	Maggie Macnab
5.	Client	Verge Software	12.	Client	MUSE Technologies Inc.
	Designer	Luis Dominguez		Designer	Maggie Macnab
6.	Client	Pulsent	13.	Client	CSI Technologies Inc.
	Designer	Luis Dominguez		Designer	Maggie Macnab
7.	Client	iQualify	14.	Client	Heart Hospital of New Mexico
	Designer	Heather Bodlak		Designer	Maggie Macnab
			15.	Client	Oriental Medicine Consultants
				Designer	Maggie Macnab

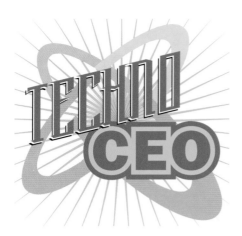

1.

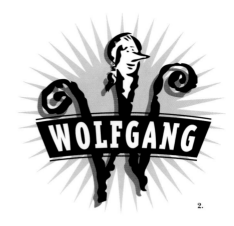

2.

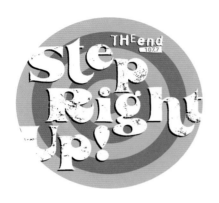

3.

ENDFEST!
ALL STAR ROCK & ROLL GRUDGE MATCH

4.

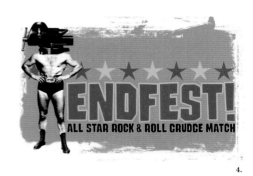

5.

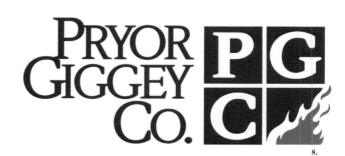

6.

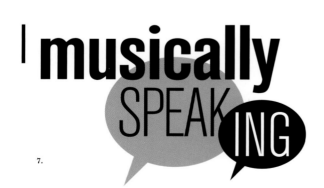

7.

PRYOR
GIGGEY
Co.

PG
C

8.

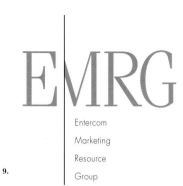

Entercom
Marketing
Resource
Group

9.

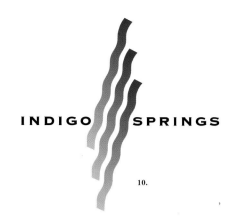

10.

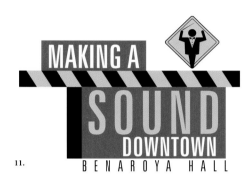

11.

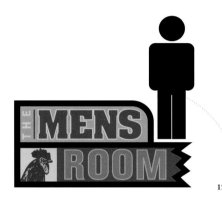

12.

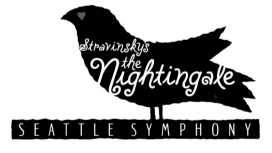

13.

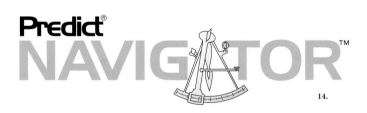

14.

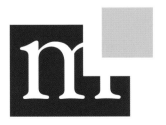

Michael Luis & Associates

15.

1 - 15
Design Firm Art O Mat Design

1. Client		Technology Alliance
	Designers	Jacki McCarthy & Mark Kaufman
2. Client		Seattle Symphony—Wolfgang
	Designers	Jacki McCarthy & Mark Kaufman
3. Client		107.7 The End—Step Right Up
	Designers	Jacki McCarthy & Mark Kaufman
4. Client		107.7 The End—Endfest 3
	Designers	Jacki McCarthy & Mark Kaufman
5. Client		107.7 The End—Endfest 1
	Designers	Jacki McCarthy & Mark Kaufman
6. Client		107.7 The End— Deck the Hall Ball
	Designers	Jacki McCarthy & Mark Kaufman
7. Client		Seattle Symphony— Musically Speaking
	Designers	Jacki McCarthy & Mark Kaufman

8. Client		Pryor Giggey Co.
	Designers	Jacki McCarthy & Mark Kaufman
9. Client		Entercom Marketing Resource Group
	Designers	Jacki McCarthy & Mark Kaufman
10. Client		Indigo Springs
	Designers	Jacki McCarthy & Mark Kaufman
11. Client		Seattle Symphony— Make a Sound Downtown
	Designers	Jacki McCarthy & Mark Kaufman
12. Client		Mens Room
	Designers	Jacki McCarthy & Mark Kaufman
13. Client		Seattle Symphony—Nightingale
	Designers	Jacki McCarthy & Mark Kaufman
14. Client		Predict Navigator
	Designers	Jacki McCarthy & Mark Kaufman
15. Client		Michael Luis & Associates
	Designers	Jacki McCarthy & Mark Kaufman

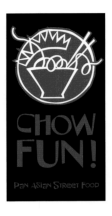

1.

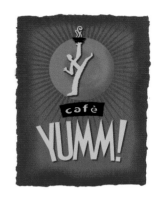

2.

Chambers
Cable

3.

Chambers
P R O D U C T I O N S

4.

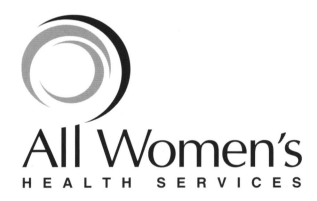

5.

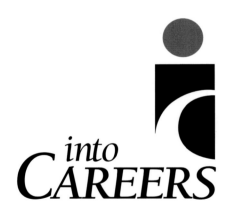

6.

PARK 5

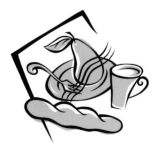

BISTRO

7.

1 - 7
Design Firm Funk and Associates

1. Client   Stephanie Pearl Kimmel
    Designer   Beverly Soasey

2. Client   Café Yumm
    Designer   Christopher Berner

3. Client   Chambers
                Communication, Copp.
    Designers   Kathleen Heinz, Christopher
                Berner, & David Funk

4. Client   Chambers
                Communication, Copp.
    Designers   Kathleen Heinz, Christopher
                Berner, & David Funk

5. Client   All Women's Health Services
    Designer   Joan Gilbert Madsen

6. Client   Career Information System
    Designers   Beverly Soasey
                & Kathleen Heinz

7. Client   Epping
    Designer   Beverly Soasey

(opposite)
Design Firm Pace Design Group

    Client   Providian Financial Corporation
    Designer   Evan Deterling

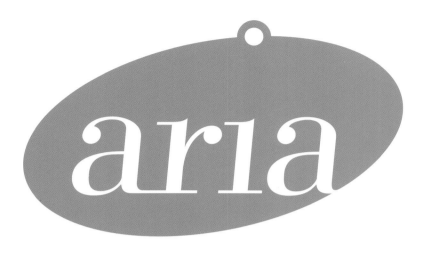

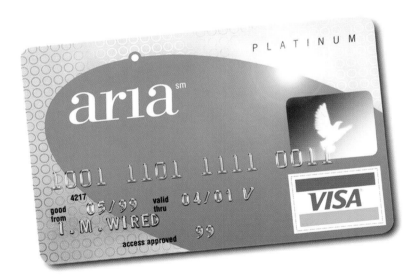

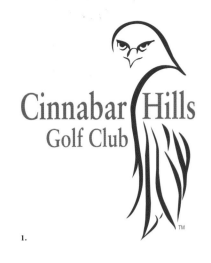

Cinnabar Hills
Golf Club

1.

HAMPTON
FINANCIAL
PARTNERS

2.

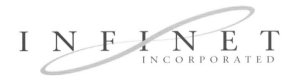

INFINET
INCORPORATED

3.

VERIDA

4.

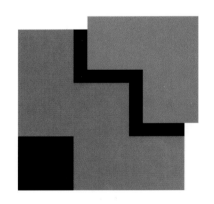

5.

Point Connect

6.

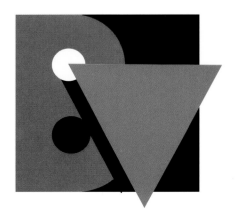

7.

1
Design Firm Bauer Holland Design

3
Design Firm Cathey Associates, Inc.

2, 4 - 7
Design Firm Triad, Inc.

1. Client   Cinnabar Hills Golf Club
   Designers   Julie Holland & Suzanne Bauer

2. Client   Hampton Financial Partners
   Designer   Michael Dambrowski

3. Client   InfiNet, Inc.
   Designer   Gordon Cathey

4. Client   Verida Internet Corp.
   Designer   Diana Kollanyi

5. Client   PointConnect Inc.
   Designer   Michael Dambrowski

6. Client   PointConnect Inc.
   Designer   Diana Kollanyi

7. Client   PointConnect Inc.
   Designer   Michael Dambrowski

(opposite)
Design Firm Donovan and Green

   Client   Faroy
   Designers   Janet Johnson & Ryan Paul

FAROY

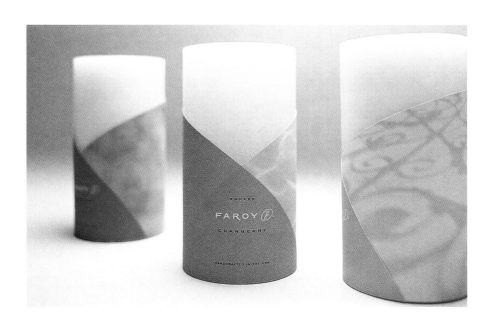

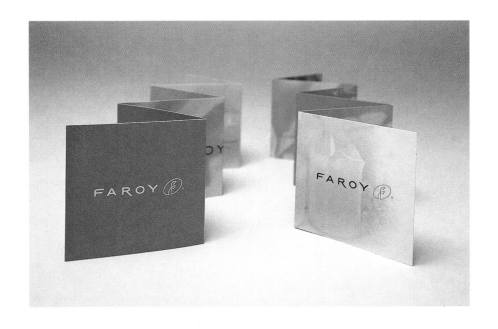

M@llNet™

1.

Unifications
Custom Rug Design

2.

PRO**TAB**

3.

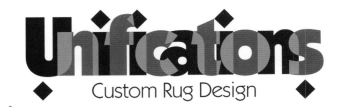

OneSource
Communications, Inc.

4.

state of mind

5.

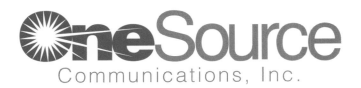

6.

LE∆P

7.

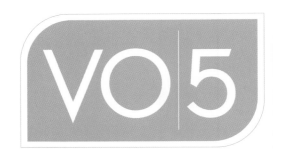

BioNexus Foundation
Connecting
Global Life Science

8.

ATCC

electric stock

Jet Silver

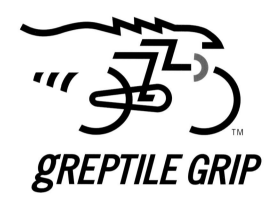

GREPTILE GRIP™

9.

10.

11.

12.

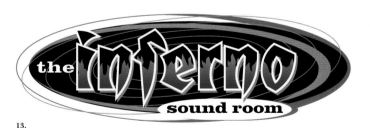

the **inferno** sound room

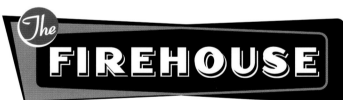

The **FIREHOUSE**

13.

14.

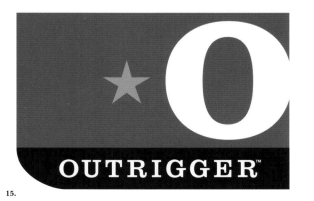

★**O** **OUTRIGGER**™

15.

1
Design Firm Donovan and Green
2 - 4
Design Firm Cathey Associates, Inc.
5 - 7
Design Firm Desgrippes Gobé
8 - 10
Design Firm Stephen Loges Graphic Design
11 - 15
Design Firm Phoenix Creative

1. Client   MallNet
   Designer   Janet Johnson

2. Client   Unifications
   Designer   Gordon Cathey

3. Client   ProTab
   Designer   Gordon Cathey

4. Client   One Source
             Communications, Inc.
   Designer   Matt Westapher

5. Client   CBI Laboratory
   Designers Susan Berson & Deirdre Tighe

6. Client   Unisunstar B.V., Inc.
   Designers Phyllis Aragaki & Deirdre Tighe

7. Client   Leap Energy and Power Corp.
   Designers Phyllis Aragaki & Natalie Jacobs

8. Client   BioNexus Foundation
   Designer   Stephen Loges

9. Client   ATCC
   Designer   Stephen Loges

10. Client   Electric Stock
    Designer Stephen Loges

11. Client   Edison Brothers Stores (5•7•9)
    Designer Danielle John

12. Client   Pearl Izumi/Greptile Grip
    Designer Steve Wienke

13. Client   The Inferno Sound Room
    Designer Kathy Wilkinson

14. Client   The Firehouse
    Designer Kathy Wilkinson

15. Client   Edison Brothers Stores/
             Outrigger
    Designer Jenny Anderson

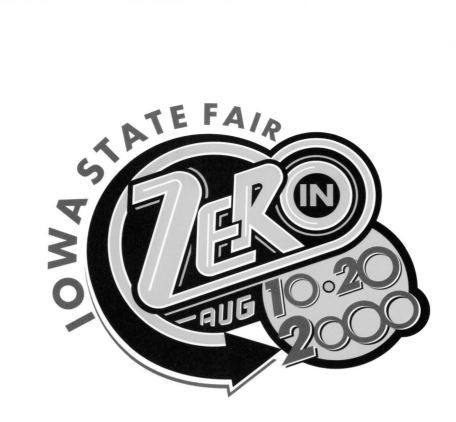

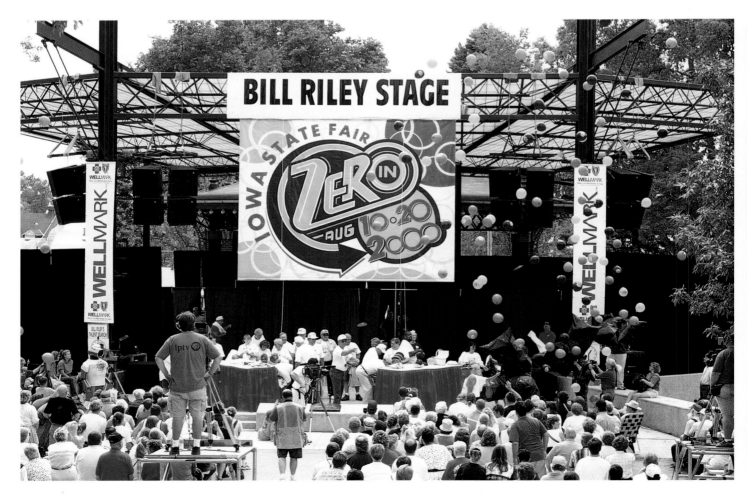

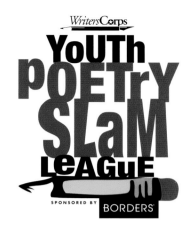

1.

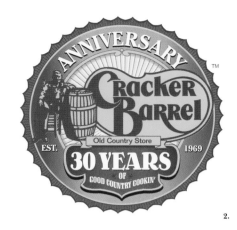

2.

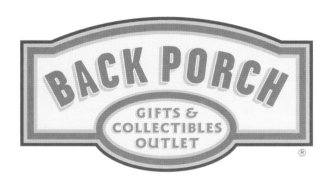

3.

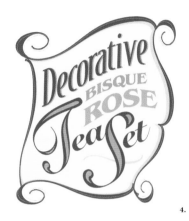

4.

5.

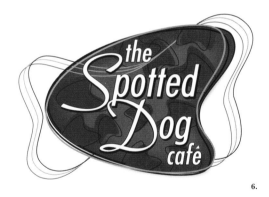

6.

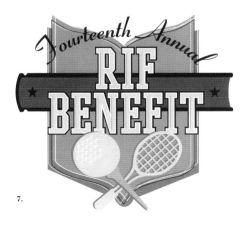

7.

(opposite)
Design Firm	**Sayles Graphic Design**		
Client	2000 Iowa State Fair "Zero In On Fun"		
Designer	John Sayles		

1 - 7
Design Firm Phoenix Creative

1. Client — Borders/Youth Poetry Slam
   Designers — Deborah Finkelstein & Jenny Anderson

2. Client — Cracker Barrel Old Country Store (30th Anniversary)
   Designer — Paul Jarvis

3. Client — Cracker Barrel Old Country Store/Back Porch
   Designer — Kathy Wilkinson

4. Client — Cracker Barrel Old Country Store (Tea Set)
   Designer — Curtis Potter

5. Client — Borders/Living Through Books
   Designer — Kathy Wilkinson

6. Client — The Spotted Dog Café
   Designer — Kathy Wilkinson

7. Client — WaldenBooks/RIF Benefit
   Designer — Tyler Small

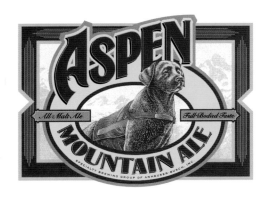

1.

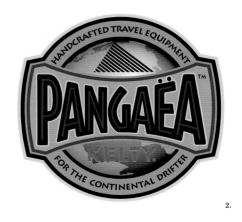

2.

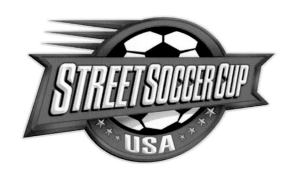

3.

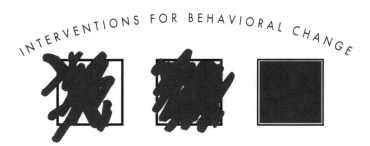

4.

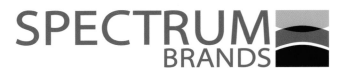

5.

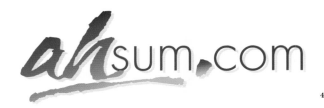

6.

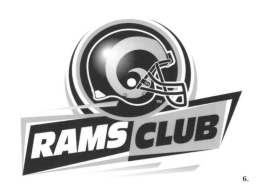

7.

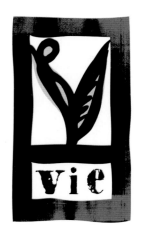

8.

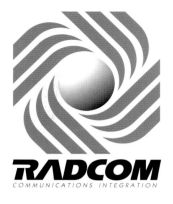

9.

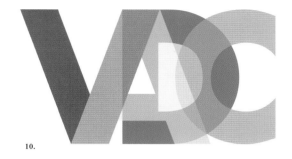

10.

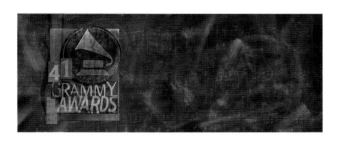

11.

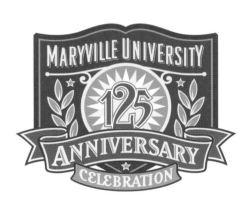

12.

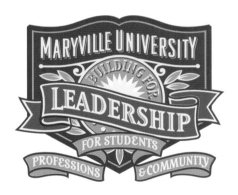

13.

14.

15.

1 - 3, 5 - 8, 10 - 15
Design Firm Phoenix Creative
4, 9
Design Firm Cathey Associates, Inc.

1. Client   Anheuser-Busch/Aspen Ale
    Designer   Kathy Wilkinson

2. Client   Kelty/Pangãea
    Designer   Kathy Wilkinson

3. Client   Spectrum Brands
    Designer   Tyler Small

4. Client   ahsum.com
    Designer   Matt Westapher

5. Client   Think Tank/
                Street Soccer Cup USA
    Designer   Steve Hicks

6. Client   St. Louis Rams
    Designer   Kathy Wilkinson

7. Client   Interventions for
                Behavioral Change
    Designer   Steve Morris

8. Client   Vie
    Designer   Jenny Anderson

9. Client   Radcom Communications
                Integration
    Designers   Matt Westapher
                & Gordon Cathey

10. Client   Washington University
                Visual Arts and Design Center
    Designer   Deborah Finkelstein

11. Client   Borders/National Association
                of Recording Merchandisers
    Designers   Deborah Finkelstein
                & Scott Ferguson

12. Client   Anne Ibur Creations
    Designer   Deborah Finkelstein

13, 14
    Client   Maryville University of St. Louis
    Designer   Ed Mantels-Seeker

15. Client   Moses.com
    Designer   Elizabeth Williams

Freire *Charter School*

1.

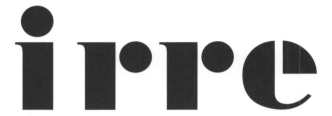

2.

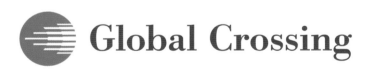

Arnosti
Consulting

3.

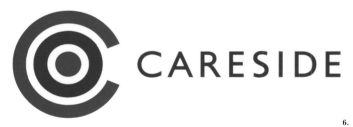

**Institute for
Research and Reform
in Education**

4.

Global Crossing

5.

CARESIDE

6.

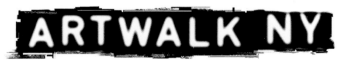

7.

1 - 4
Design Firm Joel Katz Design Associates
5 - 7
Design Firm Studio Morris

1. Client   Freire Charter School
   Designers   Mary Torrieri & Joel Katz

2. Client   Ringing Rocks Foundation
   Designers   Leslie Conner-Newbold
                   & Jennifer Long

3. Client   Arnosti Consulting
   Designer   Joel Katz

4. Client   Institute for Research
                   and Reform in Education
   Designers   Dave Schpok & Joel Katz

5. Client   Global Crossing
   Designer   Jeff Morris

6. Client   Careside
   Designer   Hyun Lee

7. Client   Coalition for The Homeless
   Designers   Jeff Morris & Kaoru Sato

(opposite)
Design Firm Lawson Design

   Client   Rubin Postaer & Assoc. for
                   American Century
   Designers   Jeff Lawson & Bob Francis

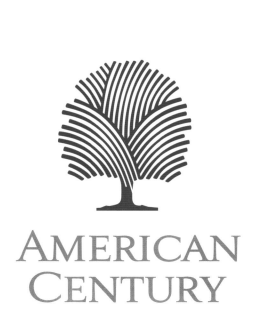

AMERICAN CENTURY

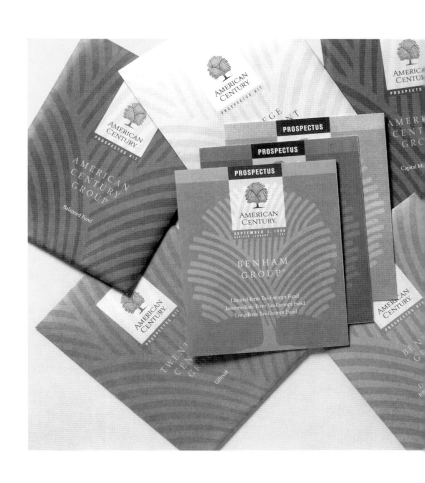

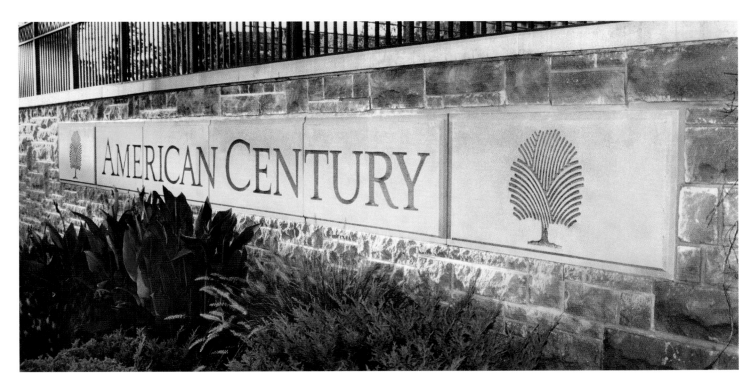

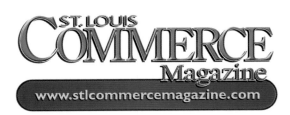

1.

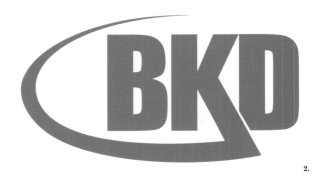

2.

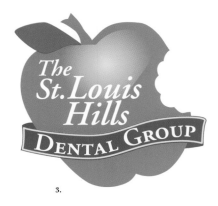

3.

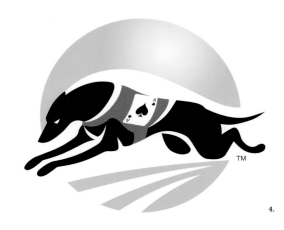

4.

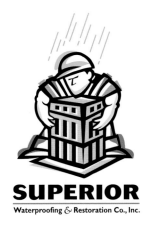

5.

6.

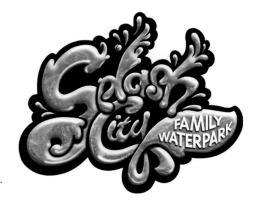

7.

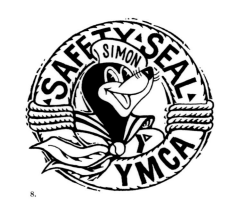

8.

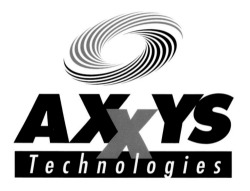

9.

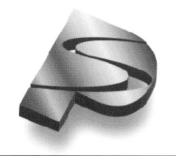

THE PRINTING SOURCE INC.

10.

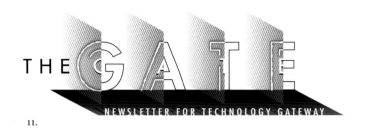

11.

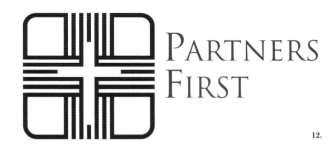

12.

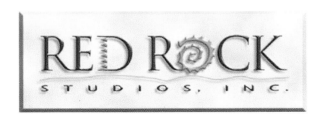

13.

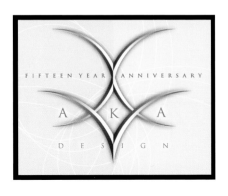

14.

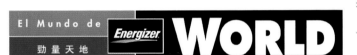

15.

1 - 8, 10 - 15
Design Firm   AKA Design, Inc.
9
Design Firm   Cathey Associates, Inc.

1.	Client Designer	Commerce Magazine Stacy Lanier	8.	Client Designer	YMCA of Greater St. Louis John Ahearn
2.	Client Designers	Baird, Kurtz & Dobson Stacy Lanier & John Ahearn	9.	Client Designer	Axxys Technologies Matt Westapher
3.	Client Designers	St. Louis Hills Dental Group Jim Jarvis & John Ahearn	10.	Client Designer	The Printing Source Richie Murphy
4.	Client Designer	Object Computing Inc. Mike Mullen	11.	Client Designer	Technology Gateway Virginia Schneider
5.	Client Designer	Superior Waterproofing & Construction Related Restoration John Ahearn	12.	Client Designer	Partners First Craig Martin Simon
6.	Client Designer	Parkcrest Surgical Associates Virginia Schneider	13.	Client Designer	Red Rock Studios Richie Murphy
7.	Client Designers	Splash City Waterpark Craig Martin Simon & Mike Mullen	14.	Client Designer	AKA Design, Inc. Richie Murphy
			15.	Client Designer	Energizer World Mike Mullen

45

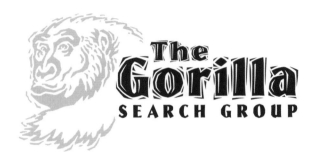

1.

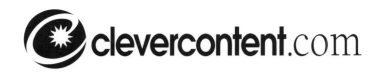

2.

Alchemedia

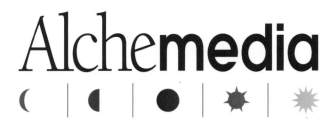

3.

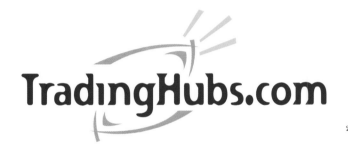

4.

ASTROBIOLOGY

5.

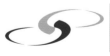 Supply-Line.com

6.

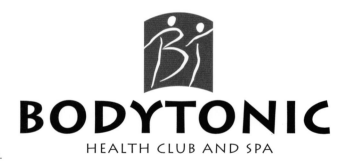

7.

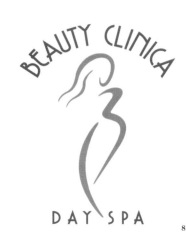

8.

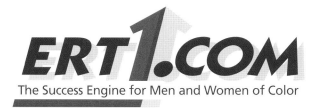

The Success Engine for Men and Women of Color

9.

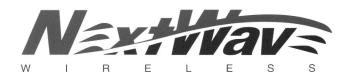

10.

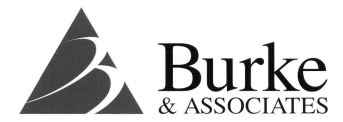

11.

12.

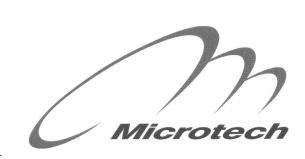

13.

Trail
Ridge
Retirement
Community

14.

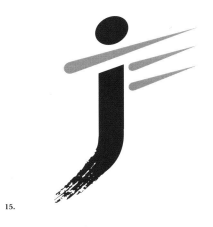

15.

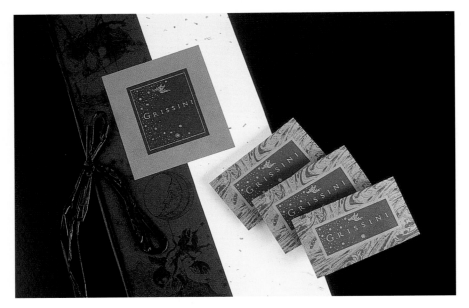

1.

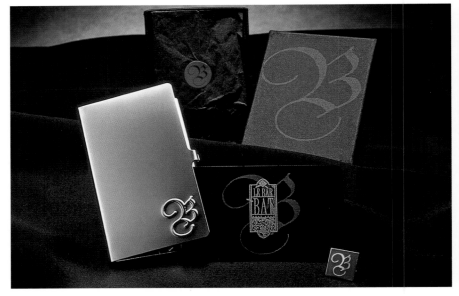

2.

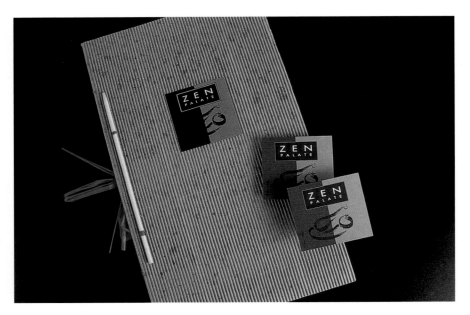

3.

4.

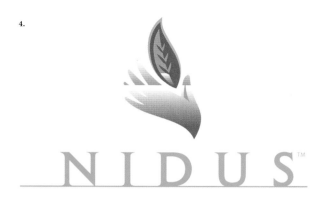

5.

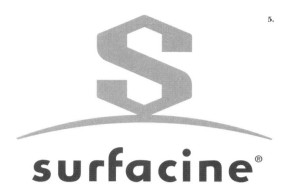

6.

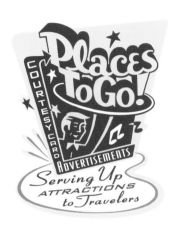

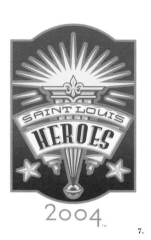

7.

8.

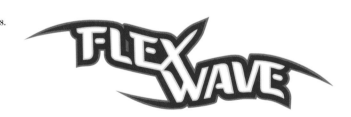

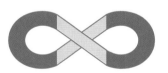

9.

10.

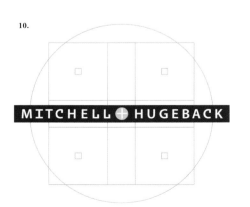

1 - 3
**Design Firm Louey/Rubino
Design Group, Inc.**

4 - 10
Design Firm Phoenix Creative

1. Client	Grissini	
Designer	Robert Louey	
2. Client	Le Bar Bat	
Designer	Robert Louey	
3. Client	Zen Palate	
Designer	Robert Louey	
4. Client	Monsanto Company/ Nidus Center	
Designer	Ed Mantels-Seeker	
5. Client	Surfacine Development Company	
Designer	Ed Mantels-Seeker	

6. Client	Places To Go	
Designer	Ed Mantels-Seeker	
7. Client	Saint Louis Heroes/ St. Louis 2004	
Designer	Ed Mantels-Seeker	
8. Client	St. Louis Music/ FlexWave Amplifiers	
Designers	Ed Mantels-Seeker & Luke Partridge	
9. Client	Conceptual Capital	
Designer	Ed Mantels-Seeker	
10. Client	Mitchell and Hugeback Architects	
Designer	Ed Mantels-Seeker	

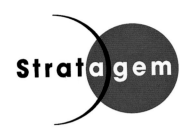

1.

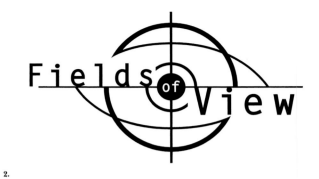

2.

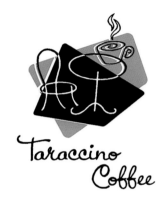

3.

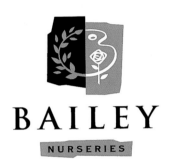

4.

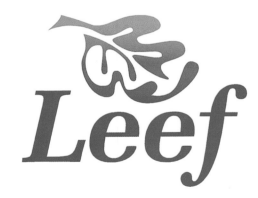

5.

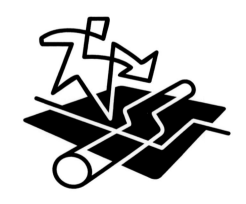

6.

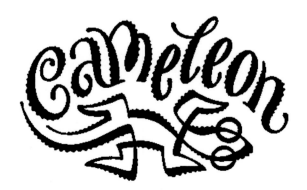

7.

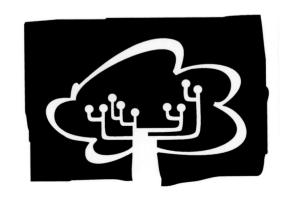

8.

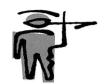

Systems Consulting Group, Inc.

9.

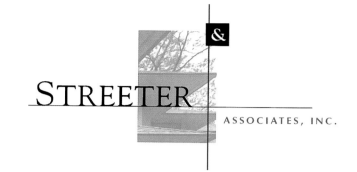

STREETER

&

ASSOCIATES, INC.

10.

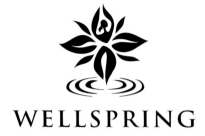

WELLSPRING

The Source for
Women's Health
and Fitness

11.

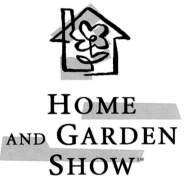

HOME
AND GARDEN
SHOW℠

12.

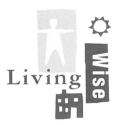

Living WISE

Choices *for*
Your Health

13.

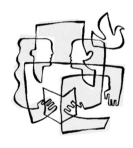

14.

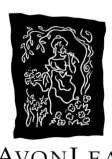

AVONLEA

FLORAL ARTS

15.

(all)

Design Firm Design Center

1. Client — Strategem
   Designers — John Reger
   Design Director:
   Sherwin Schwartzrock

2. Client — Fields of View
   Designers — John Reger & Cory Dockew

3. Client — Taraccino Coffee
   Designers — John Reger & Todd Spichke

4. Client — Baileys Nursery
   Designers — John Reger
   & Sherwin Schwartzrock

5. Client — Leef
   Designers — John Reger
   & Sherwin Schwartzrock

6. Client — Noram
   Designers — John Reger
   & Sherwin Schwartzrock

7. Client — Cameleon
   Designers — John Reger
   & Sherwin Schwartzrock

8. Client — Oak Systems
   Designers — John Reger & Jon Erickson

9. Client — System Consulting Group
   Designers — John Reger, Sherwin
   Schwartzrock & Jon Erickson

10. Client — Streeter & Associates
    Designers — John Reger
    & Sherwin Schwartzrock

11. Client — Wellspring
    Designers — John Reger
    & Sherwin Schwartzrock

12. Client — Home and Garden Show
    Designers — John Reger
    & Sherwin Schwartztock

13. Client — Living Wise
    Designers — John Reger
    & Sherwin Schwartzrock

14. Client — Resurrection Life Church
    Designers — John Reger
    & Sherwin Schwartzrock

15. Client — Avonlea
    Designers — John Reger
    & Sherwin Schwartzrock

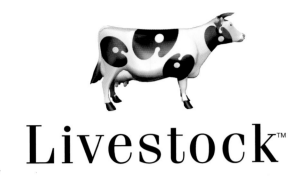

Livestock™

1.

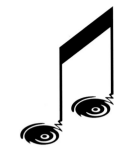

RIVERFRONT
CONCERTS

2.

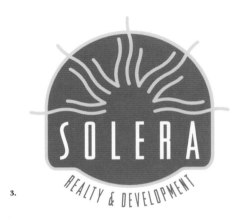

3.

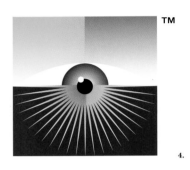

™

4.

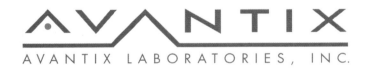

5.

6.

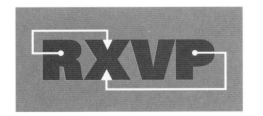

7.

1 - 7			5.	Client	Avantix Laboratories, Inc.
	Design Firm	**Orbit Integrated**		Designer	Jack Harris
1.	Client	Livestock	6.	Client	Verity
	Designer	Jack Harris		Designer	Jack Harris
2.	Client	Delaware Theatre Company	7.	Client	RXVP
				Designer	Jack Harris
3.	Client	Solera Realty + Development	**(opposite)**		
	Designer	Mark Miller		**Design Firm**	**Squires & Company**
4.	Client	New Media Insight		Client	Everlink
	Designer	Jack Harris		Designer	Anna Magruder

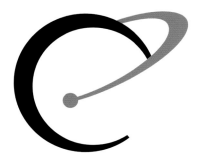

EverLink™

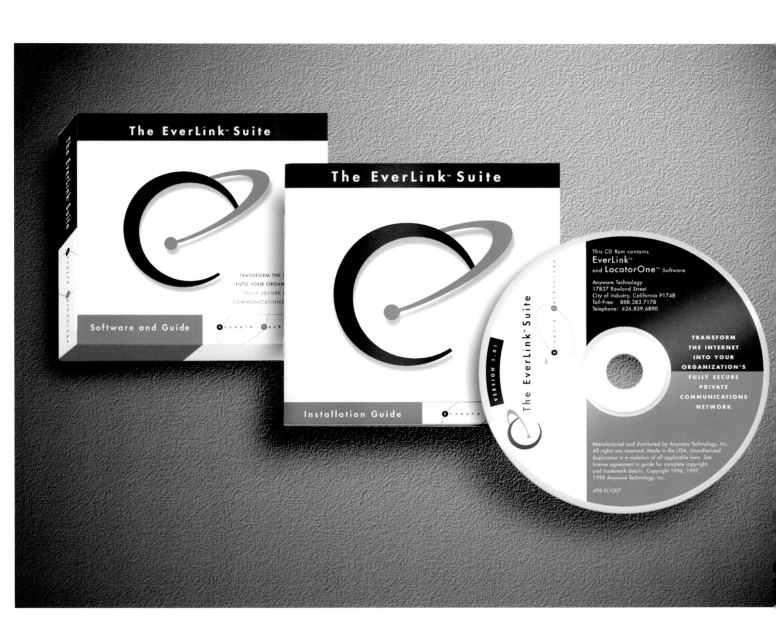

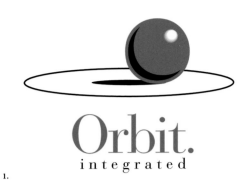

1.

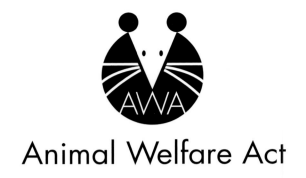

2.

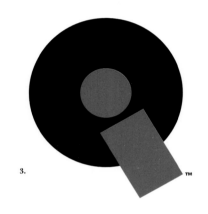

3.

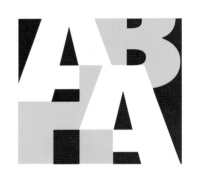

4.

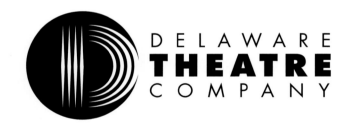

5.

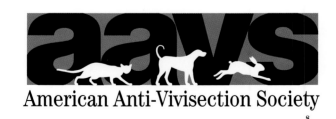

6.

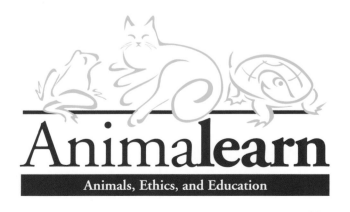

7.

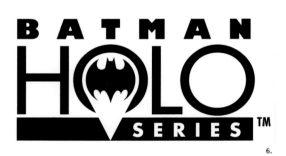

8.

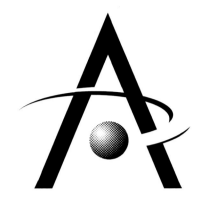

9.

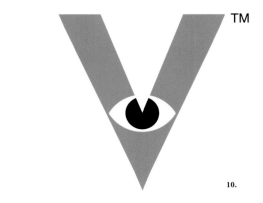

TM

10.

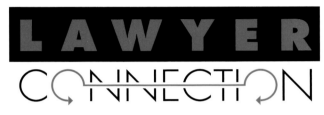

OF GREATER PHILADELPHIA

11.

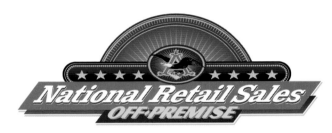

12.

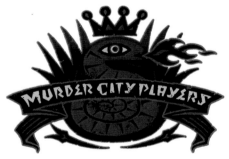

13.

14.

15.

1 - 11
Design Firm Orbit Integrated
12 - 14
Design Firm Phoenix Creative, St. Louis
15
Design Firm Studio Morris

1. Client	Orbit Integrated	
Designer	Jack Harris	
2. Client	American Anti-Vivisection Society	
Designer	Jack Harris	
3. Client	Orbit Integrated	
Designer	Jack Harris	
4. Client	ABHA	
Designer	Jack Harris	
5. Client	Delaware Theatre Company	
Designer	Jack Harris	
6. Client	DC Comics	
Designer	Jack Harris	
7. Client	American Anti-Vivisection Society	
Designer	Jack Harris	

8. Client	American Anti-Vivisection Society	
Designer	Jack Harris	
9. Client	Environmental Alliance	
Designer	Jack Harris	
10. Client	Visual Logic	
Designer	Jack Harris	
11. Client	Lawyer Connection of Gr. Philadelphia	
Designer	Jack Harris	
12. Client	Anheuser-Busch National Retail Sales	
Designer	Ed Mantels-Seeker	
13. Client	Murder City Players	
Designer	Ed Mantels-Seeker	
14. Client	Big Brothers Big Sisters of Greater St. Louis	
Designer	Deborh Finkelstein	
15. Client	Homespace	
Designer	Hyun Lee	

1.

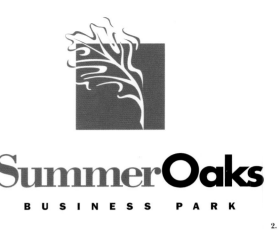

2.

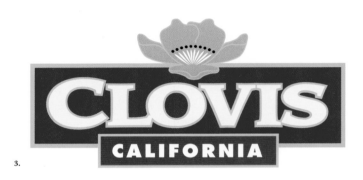

3.

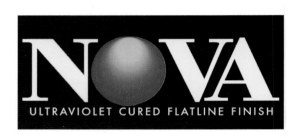

4.

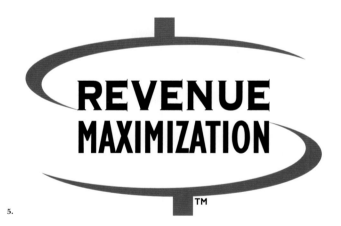

5.

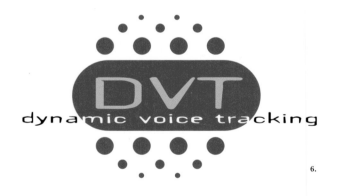

6.

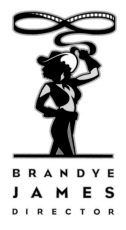

7.

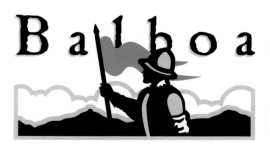

8.

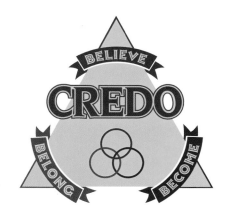

9.

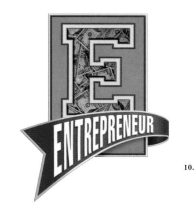

10.

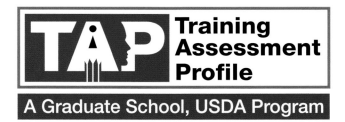

11.

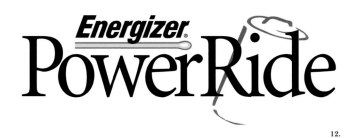

12.

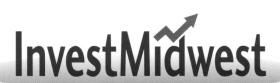

13.

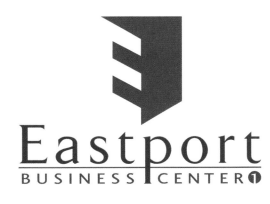

14.

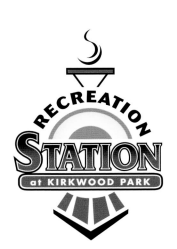

15.

1 - 6
Design Firm Funk and Associates
7 - 8
Design Firm Squires & Company
9 - 15
Design Firm AKA Design, Inc.

1. Client   Eugene Public
         Library Foundation
   Designers   Beverly Soasey
         & Kathleen Heinz

2. Client   Dan Tucci
   Designers   Beverly Soasey
         & Christopher Berner

3. Client   City of Clovis, CA
   Designer   Christopher Berner

4. Client   States Industries
   Designer   Christopher Berner

5. Client   CBSI (Revenue Maximization)
   Designer   Krista Lippert

6. Client   CBSI (DVT)
   Designer   Krista Lippert

7. Client   Brandye James
   Designer   Paul Black

8. Client   Balboa
   Designer   Paul Black

9. Client   Credo
   Designers   John Ahearn & Sara Gries

10. Client   Collegiate Entrepreneur
         of the Year
   Designers   Richie Murphy & John Ahearn

11. Client   Graduate School, USDA
   Designer   Mike Mullen

12. Client   Energizer
   Designer   Richie Murphy

13. Client   Invest Midwest
   Designer   Richie Murphy

14. Client   Eastport Business Center
   Designers   Virginia Schneider
         & John Ahearn

15. Client   Recreation Station
   Designers   Stacy Lanier
         & Craig Martin Simon

57

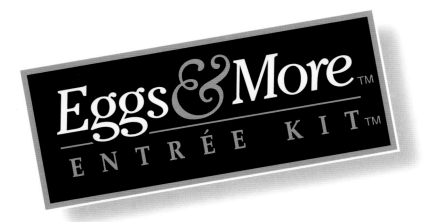

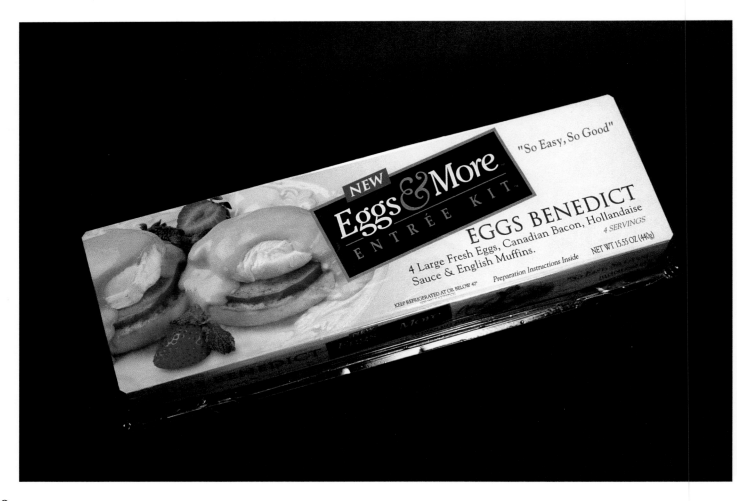

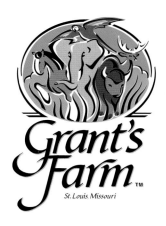

1.

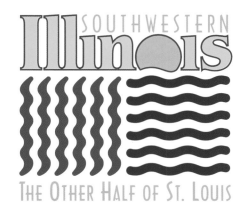

2.

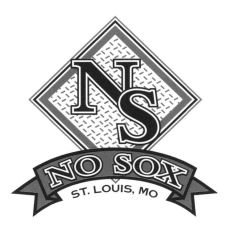

3.

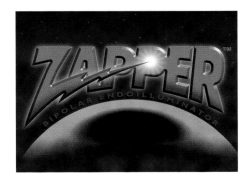

4.

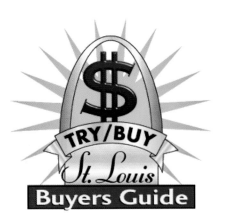

5.

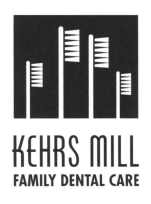

6.

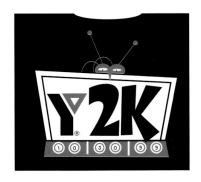

7.

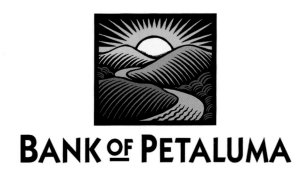

1.

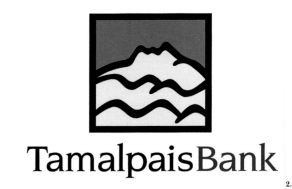

2.

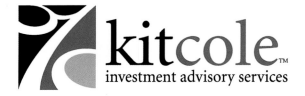

3.

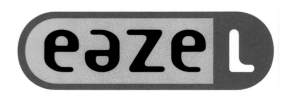

4.

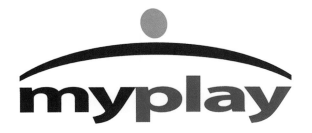

5.

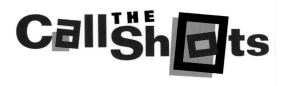

6.

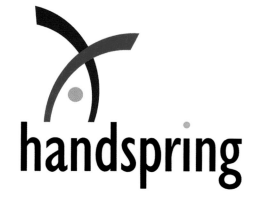

7.

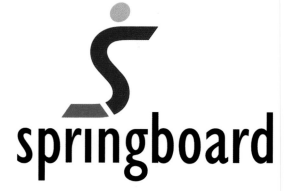

8.

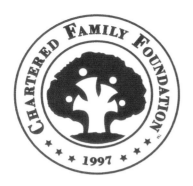

9.

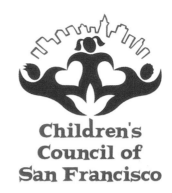

Children's
Council of
San Francisco

10.

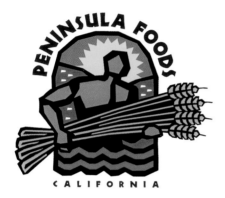

11.

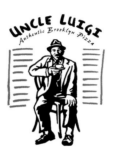

12.

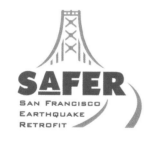

13.

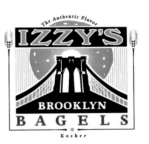

14.

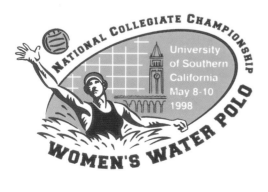

15.

1 - 8				7. Client	Handspring
Design Firm	**Mortensen Design**			Designers	PJ Nidecker
9 - 15					& Gordon Mortensen
Design Firm	**The Visual Group**			8. Client	Handspring, Inc.
				Designers	PJ Nidecker
1. Client	Bank of Petaluma				& Gordon Mortensen
Designers	Gordon Mortensen,			9. Client	Peninsula Community
	Wendy Chon, & Chris Gall				Foundation
2. Client	Tamalpais Bank			Designers	Lim Ng & Ark Stein
Designers	Wendy Chon			10. Client	Children Council
	& Gordon Mortensen				of San Francisco
3. Client	Kit Cole Investment			Designer	Ark Stein
	Advisory Services			11. Client	Peninsula Foods
Designers	Gordon Mortensen			Designer	Ark Stein
	& Wendy Chon			12. Client	Uncle Luigi Pizza
4. Client	Eazel			Designer	Ark Stein
Designers	PJ Nidecker			13. Client	Caltrans
	& Gordon Mortensen			Designer	Ark Stein
5. Client	MyPlay, Inc.			14. Client	Izzy's Brooklyn Bagels
Designers	PJ Nidecker			Designers	Bill Mifsud & Ark Stein
	& Gordon Mortensen			15. Client	USC
6. Client	CallTheShots			Designer	Ark Stein
Designers	Gordon Mortensen				
	& Wendy Chon				

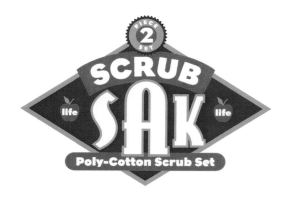

1.

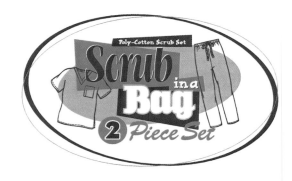

2.

NORTHSTAR

3.

SetRite™

4.

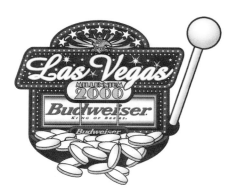

5.

IZZY'S
BROOKLYN
BAGELS
Kosher

6.

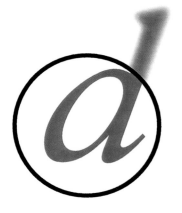

7.

(all)
Design Firm CUBE Advertising & Design

1. Client   Life Uniform
   Designer   David Chiow

2. Client   Life Uniform
   Designer   David Chiow

3. Client   Northstar Management Co.
   Designers   David Chiow & Matt Marino

4. Client   Crown Theraputics, Inc.
   Designer   David Chiow

5. Client   Anheuser-Busch, Inc.
   Designers   David Chiow & Kevin Hough

6. Client   The Natural Way
   Designer   David Chiow

7. Client   dreyfus + associates photography
   Designer   David Chiow

(opposite)
Design Firm CUBE Advertising & Design

   Client   St. Louis Zoo
   Designer   David Chiow

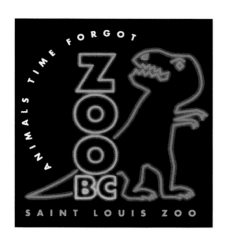

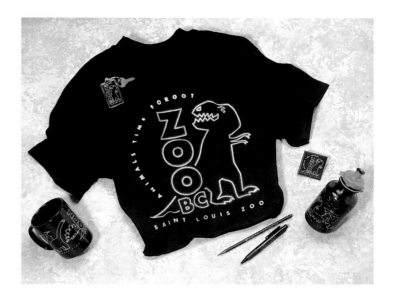

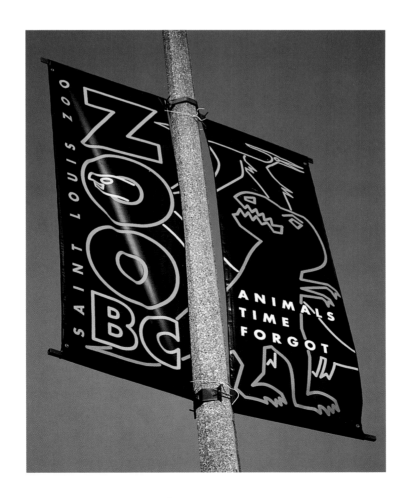

TRANSCORE

1.

bailey design group inc

2.

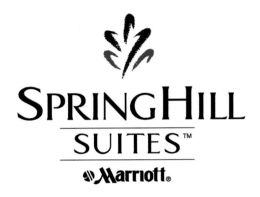

SPRINGHILL SUITES™

Marriott®

3.

EXECUSTAY
CORPORATE HOUSING SOLUTIONS
Marriott®

4.

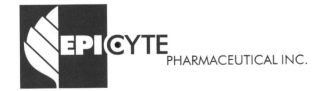

EPICYTE
PHARMACEUTICAL INC.

5.

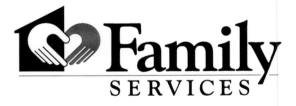

Family
SERVICES

6.

S·P·I·R·I·T

7.

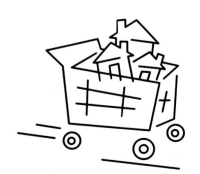

8.

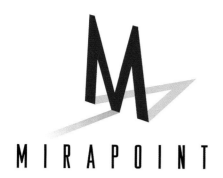

MIRAPOINT

9.

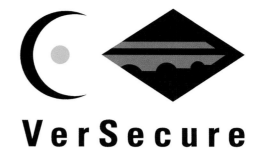

VerSecure

10.

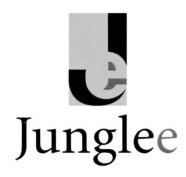

Junglee

11.

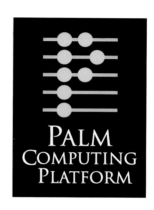

PALM COMPUTING PLATFORM

12.

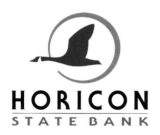

HORICON STATE BANK

13.

GROWTH NETWORKS

14.

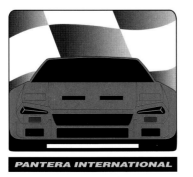

PANTERA INTERNATIONAL

15.

1 - 8
Design Firm Bailey Design Group, Inc.
9 - 14
Design Firm Mortensen Design
15
Design Firm Theodore C. Alexander, Jr.

1. Client Transcore
   Designer Laura Markley

2. Client Bailey Design Group, Inc.
   Designer Gary LaCroix

3. Client Marriott Corporation
   Designers Wendy Slavish & Steve Perry

4. Client Marriott Corporation
   Designer David Fiedler

5. Client Epicyte Pharmaceutical
   Designer Steve Perry

6. Client Family Services
   Designer Steve Perry

7. Client Spirit
   Designer David Fiedler

8. Client Annabelle Properties
   Designer Steve Perry

9. Client Mirapoint, Inc.
   Designers PJ Nidecker
   & Gordon Mortensen

10. Client Hewlett-Packard
    Designers Diana Kauzlarich
    & Gordon Mortensen

11. Client Junglee Corporation
    Designers Diana Kauzlarich
    & Gordon Mortensen

12. Client Palm Computing
    Designers Gordon Mortensen
    & Wendy Chon

13. Client Horicon Bank
    Designers Wendy Chon
    & Gordon Mortensen

14. Client Growth Networks
    Designers Wendy Chon
    & Gordon Mortensen

15. Client Pantera International
    Designer Theodore C. Alexander

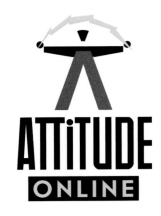

1.

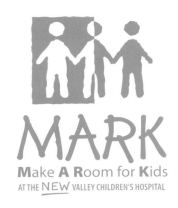

2.

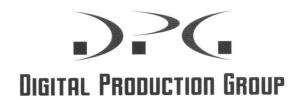

3.

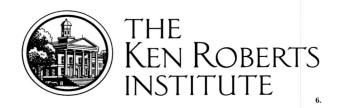

4.

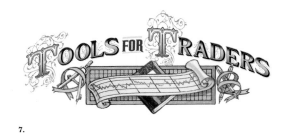

5.

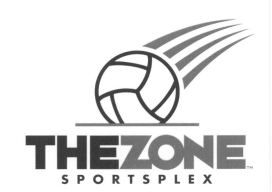

6.

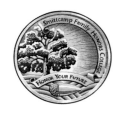

7.

8.

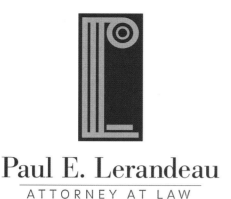

Paul E. Lerandeau
ATTORNEY AT LAW

9.

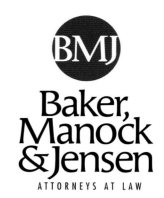

Baker, Manock &Jensen
ATTORNEYS AT LAW

10.

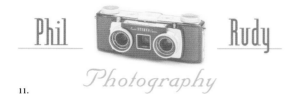

11.

THE KEN ROBERTS Gallery

12.

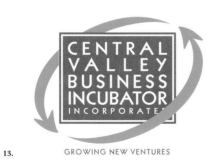

13.

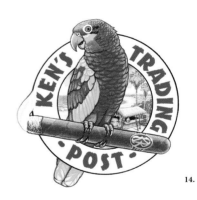

14.

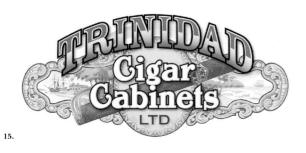

15.

(all)

Design Firm Shields Design

1.	Client	Attitude Online
	Designers	Juan Vega & Charles Shields
2.	Client	Valley Children's Hospital
	Designers	Laura Thornton
		& Charles Shields
3.	Client	Digital Production Group
	Designers	Thomas Kimmelman
		& Charles Shields
4.	Client	Heberger & Company
	Designers	Charles Shields
		& Stephanie Wong
5.	Client	Smittcamp Family
		Honors College
	Designers	Charles Shields
		& Stephanie Wong
6.	Client	The Ken Roberts Company
	Designer	Charles Shields
7.	Client	Great Pacific Trading Company
	Designer	Charles Shields

8.	Client	The Zone Sportsplex
	Designers	Charles Shields
		& Stephanie Wong
9.	Client	Paul E. Lerandeau
	Designers	Thoms Kimmelman
		& Charles Shields
10.	Client	Baker, Manock & Jensen
	Designer	Charles Shields
11.	Client	Phil Rudy Photography
	Designer	Charles Shields
12.	Client	The Ken Roberts Company
	Designer	Charles Shields
13.	Client	Central Valley Business Incubator
	Designer	Charles Shields
14.	Client	The Ken Roberts Company
	Designer	Charles Shields
15.	Client	The Ken Roberts Company
	Designer	Charles Shields

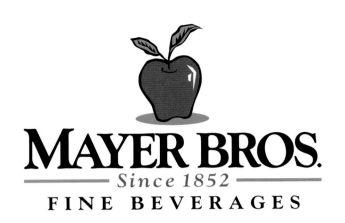

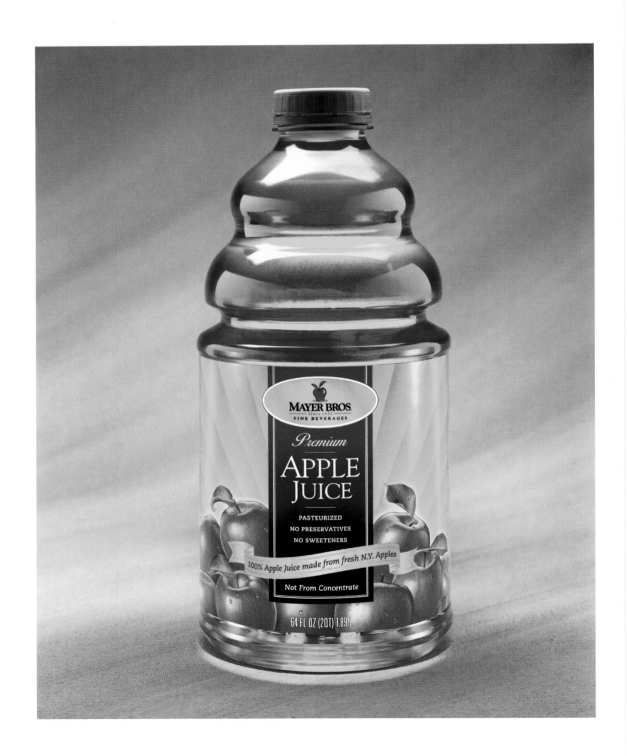

1.

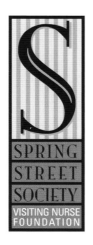

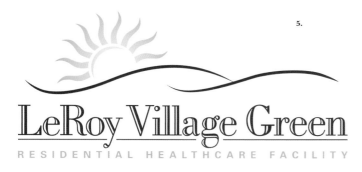

Premium Dried Fruit

2.

3.

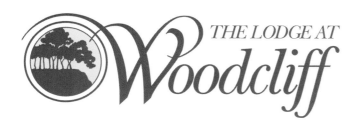

THE LODGE AT Woodcliff

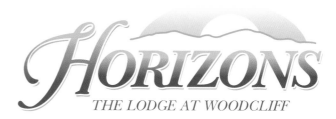

THE LODGE AT WOODCLIFF

4.

5.

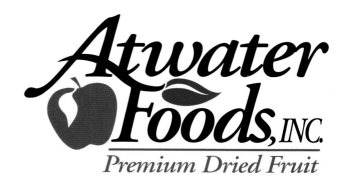

LeRoy Village Green

RESIDENTIAL HEALTHCARE FACILITY

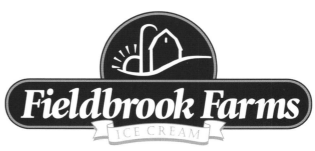

6.

7.

S

SPRING STREET SOCIETY

VISITING NURSE FOUNDATION

(opposite)
Design Firm McElveney & Palozzi
            Design Group, Inc.

Client   Mayer Bros.
Designers   William McElveney
            & Lisa Parenti

1 - 7
Design Firm McElveney & Palozzi
             Design Group, Inc.

1. Client   Fowler Farms
    Designers   William McElveney, Matt
                Nowicki, & Jan Marie Gallagher

2. Client   Atwater Foods Inc.
    Designers   Bill McElveney
                & Lisa Williamson

3. Client   The Lodge at Woodcliff
    Designers   William McElveney
                & Ellen Johnson

4. Client   The Lodge at Woodcliff
    Designers   William McElveney
                & Ellen Johnson

5. Client   LeRoy Village Green
    Designers   William McElveney, Lisa Parenti,
                & Jan Marie Gallagher

6. Client   Fieldbrook Farms Inc.
    Designers   William McElveney
                & Ellen Johnson

7. Client   Spring Street Society
    Designer   Steve Palozzi

ℰ

THE ELLIOTT

1.

palouse

2.

 Starting Early
STARTING SMART

3.

ESM CONSULTING ENGINEERS

4.

redley

5.

iridio •••

6.

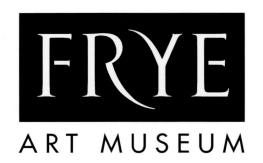 **FRYE**
ART MUSEUM

7.

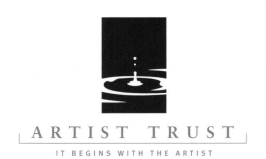 **ARTIST TRUST**
IT BEGINS WITH THE ARTIST

8.

NewHolly

9.

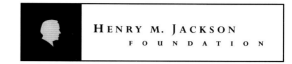

10.

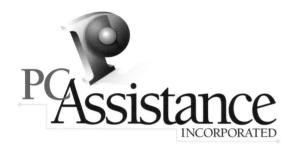

11.

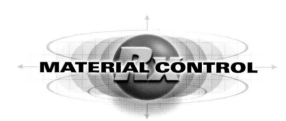

12.

Walter Dyer's
SHOES & LEATHER

13.

Alliance
BY FACTURA ™

14.

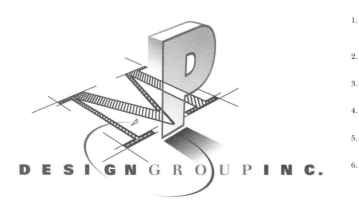

15.

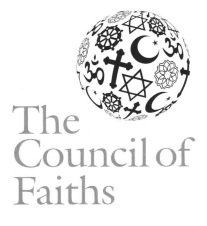

The Council of Faiths

1.

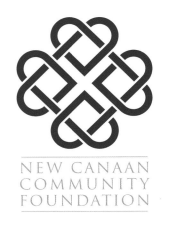

NEW CANAAN COMMUNITY FOUNDATION

2.

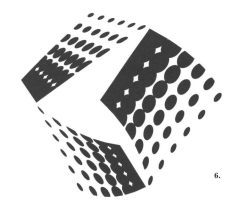

3.

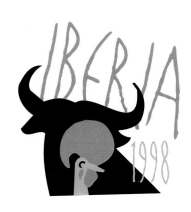

4.

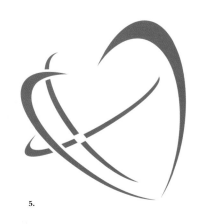

5.

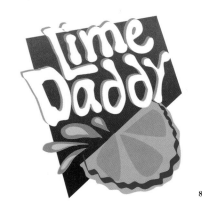

6.

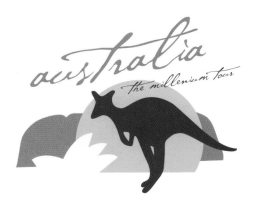

7.

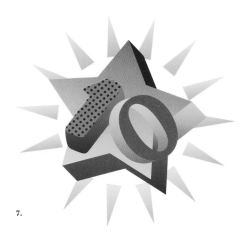

8.

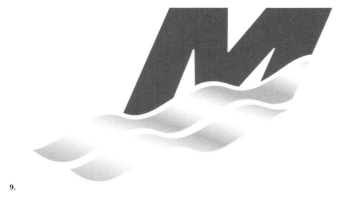

9.

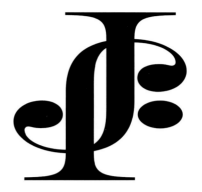

10.

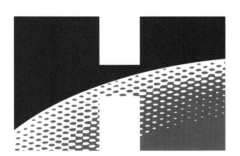

11.

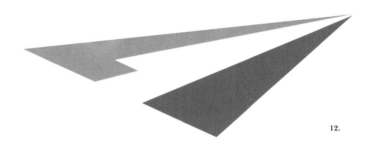

12.

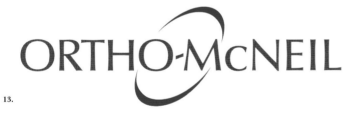

13.

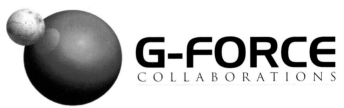

14.

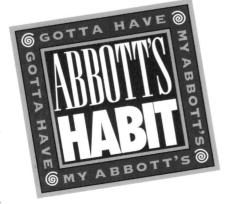

15.

1 - 13		
Design Firm	**Congdon & Company LLC**	
14 - 15		
Design Firm	**McElveney & Palozzi Design Group**	

1. Client — Council of Faiths of Southwestern Connecticut
   Designer — Arthur Congdon

2. Client — New Canaan Connecticut Community Foundation
   Designer — Arthur Congdon

3. Client — New Canaan (Connecticut) High School Madrigal Ensemble
   Designer — Arthur Congdon

4. Client — New Canaan (Connecticut) High School Madrigal Ensemble
   Designer — Arthur Congdon

5. Client — Biosense Webster, Johnson & Johnson Co.
   Designer — Arthur Congdon

6. Client — Novasource
   Designer — Arthur Congdon

7. Client — BMG
   Designer — Arthur Congdon

8. Client — Delaware Valley Distributing
   Designer — Arthur Congdon

9. Client — Mercury Marine
   Designer — Arthur Congdon

10. Client — Jeniam Foundation
    Designer — Athur Congdon

11. Client — Hypernex
    Designer — Arthur Congdon

12. Client — Corp Air
    Designer — Arthur Congdon

13. Client — Ortho-McNeil
    Designer — Arthur Congdon

14. Client — G-Force Collaborations
    Designers — William McElveney, Matt Nowicki, & Dillon Constable

15. Client — Abbott's Frozen Custard
    Designers — Bill McElveney & Lisa Parenti

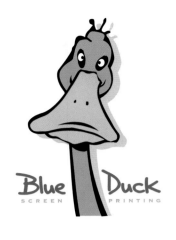

1.

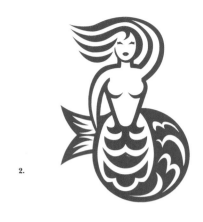

2.

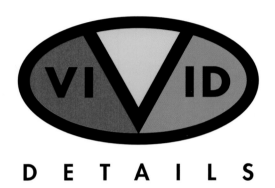

3.

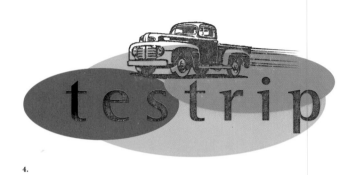

4.

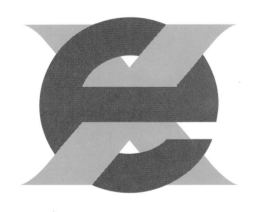

5.

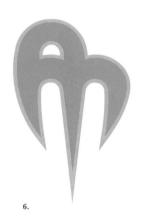

6.

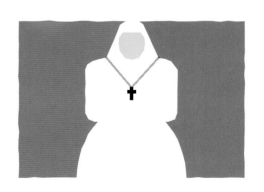

7.

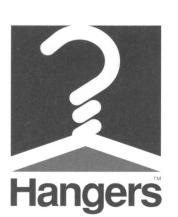

8.

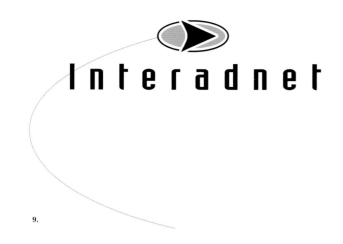

Interadnet

9.

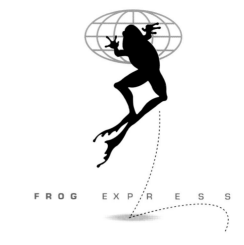

10.

FROG EXPRESS

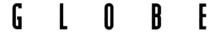

GLOBE

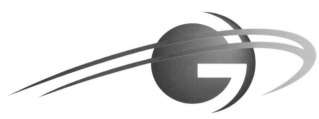

11.

T **P**

12.

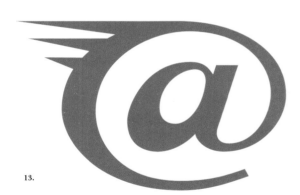

13.

ST. PATRICK
PARTNERSHIP CENTER

14.

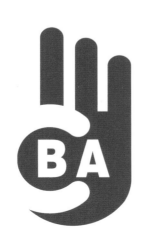

15.

(all)

Design Firm	**Bartels & Company, Inc.**	

1. Client
   Designers
   Blue Duck Screen Printing
   David Bartels
   & Ron Rodemacher

2. Client
   Designers
   Blue Deep, Ltd.
   David Bartels, Mary Flock,
   & Chris Schott

3. Client
   UI

4. Client
   Designers
   Testrip
   David Bartels
   & Ron Rodemacher

5. Client
   Designers
   Executive Expression
   Ron Rodemacher
   & David Bartels

6. Client
   Designers
   American Manicure
   Ron Rodemacher, David Bartels,
   & Don Strander

7. Client
   Designer
   Sacred Heart Villa
   Bob Thomas

8. Client
   Designers
   Micell Technologies, Inc.
   Ron Rodemacher
   & David Bartels

9. Client
   Designers
   Interadnet
   Chris Schott & David Bartels

10. Client
    Designers
    Frog Express
    David Bartels &
    Ron Rodemacher

11. Client
    Designers
    The Sandcastle
    Ron Rodemacher &
    David Bartels

12. Client
    Designers
    Top Graphics
    Ron Rodemacher &
    David Bartels

13. Client
    Designers
    Generalife Insurance Company
    David Bartels &
    Ron Rodemacher

14. Client
    Designers
    St. Patrick Partnership Center
    Ron Rodemacher &
    David Bartels

15. Client
    Designer
    Ceci Bartels Associates
    Ron Rodemacher

1.

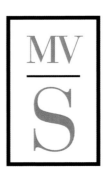

LAWYERS FOR THE ARTS   2.

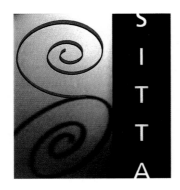

3.

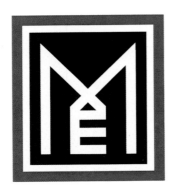

4.

WiNK

5.

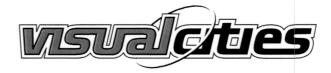

6.

A E R I E

networks

7.

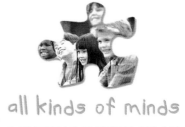

all kinds of minds

A NON-PROFIT INSTITUTE FOR THE
UNDERSTANDING OF DIFFERENCES IN LEARNING   8.

76

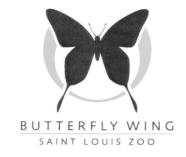

BUTTERFLY WING
SAINT LOUIS ZOO

9.

10.

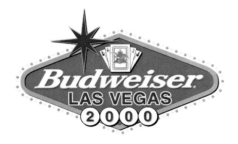

11.

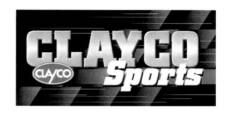

12.

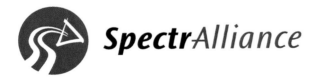

SpectrAlliance

13.

Therapoint™

14.

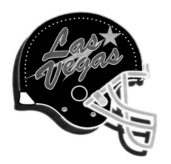

15.

ⓜ Market Central™

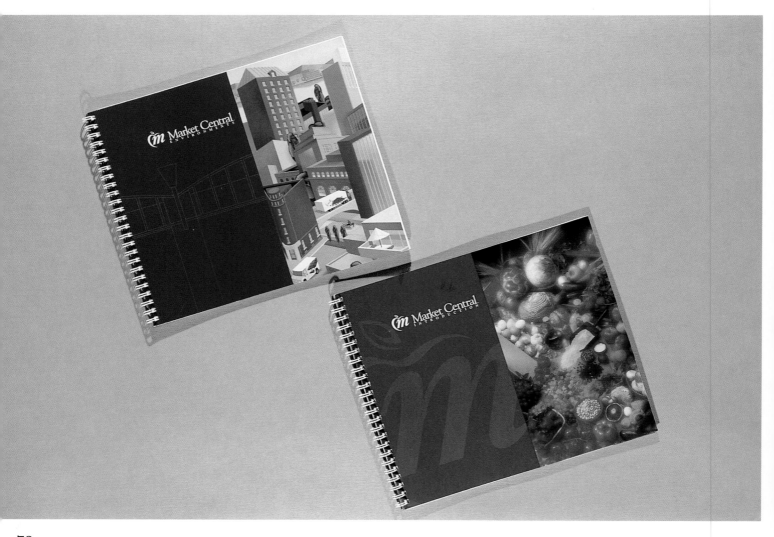

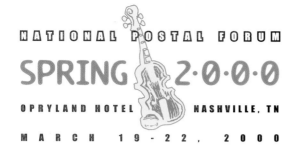

1.

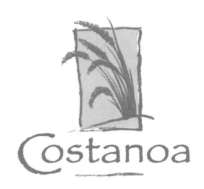

2.

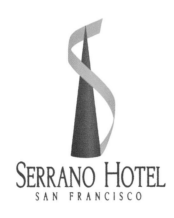

3.

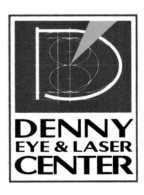

4.

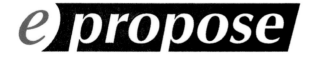

Hawthorne Lane

5.

DENNY
EYE & LASER
CENTER

6.

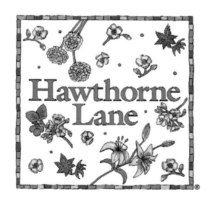

7.

(opposite)
Design Firm Bailey Design Group, Inc.

Client   Compass Group of America

3 -4
Design Firm McGaughy Design
5 -9
Design Firm Hunt Weber Clark
             Associates, Inc.

1. Client   National Postal Forum
   Designer   Malcolm McGaughy

2. Client   McGaughy Design
   Designer   Malcolm McGaughy

3. Client   Kimpton Hotel
              & Restaurant Group
   Designers Jim Deeken
              & Nancy Hunt-Weber

4. Client   Joie deVivre Hospitality
   Designers Nancy Hunt-Weber
              & Christine Chung

5. Client   Hawthorne Lane
   Designers Nancy Hunt-Weber & Jason Bell

6. Client   Denny Eye + Laser Center
   Designers Christine Chung
              & Nancy Hunt-Weber

7. Client   epropose
   Designers Jason Bell & Nancy Hunt-Weber

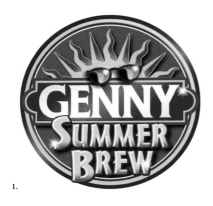

1.

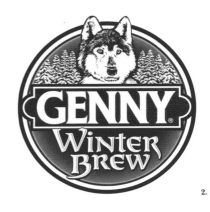

2.

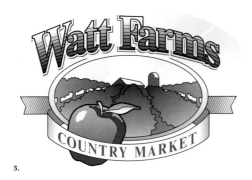

3.

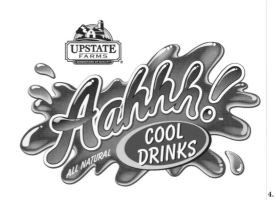

4.

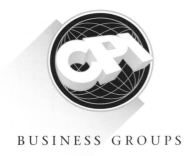

BUSINESS GROUPS

5.

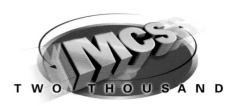

6.

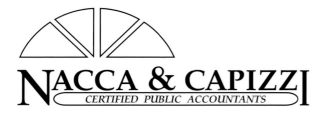

7.

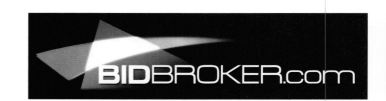

8.

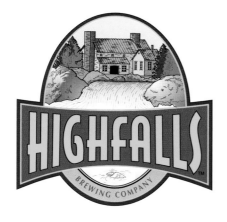

9.

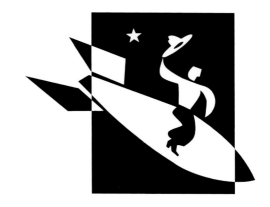

10.

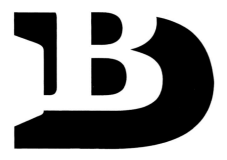

11.

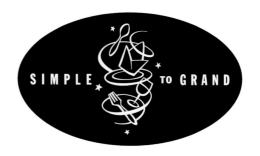

12.

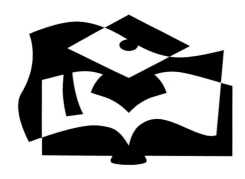

13.

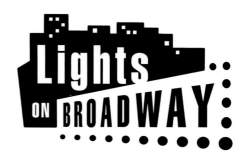

14.

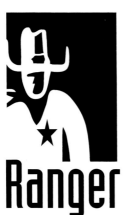

15.

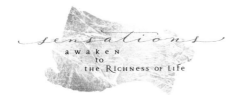

LifeSongs
Giving Voice To The Spirit Within

1.

Fresh Air

2.

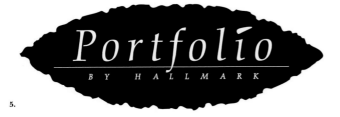

sensations
awaken
to
the Richness of Life

scent

how often we associate the warmth
of a place or event with the memory
of a scent. scent is nostalgia's best
friend. the impression of smell lingers
in us longer and evokes reflection
more than any other sense.

3.

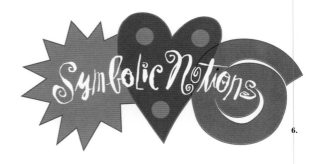

Gardens
and
MEMORIES

4.

Portfolio
BY HALLMARK

5.

Symbolic Notions

6.

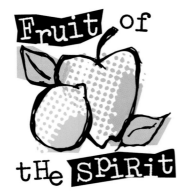

Fruit of
the SPIRIT

7.

1 - 7		
Design Firm	**Hallmark Cards, Inc.**	
1. Client	Hallmark Cards	
Designer	Peg Carlson-Hoffman	
2. Client	Hallmark Cards	
Designer	Peg Carlson-Hoffman	
3. Client	Hallmark Cards	
Designer	Sean Branagan	
4. Client	Hallmark Cards	
Designer	Barb Mizik	

5. Client	Hallmark Cards
Designer	John Marak
6. Client	Hallmark Cards
Designer	Erica Becker
7. Client	Hallmark Cards
Designer	Jake Mikolic
(opposite)	
Design Firm	**Bailey Design Group, Inc.**
Client	Cultivations
Designers	Tisha Armour, David Fiedler,
	& Christian Williamson

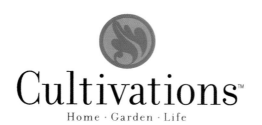

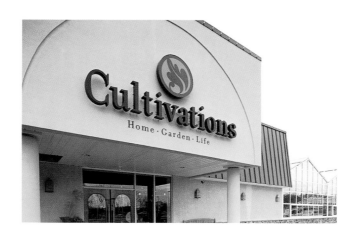

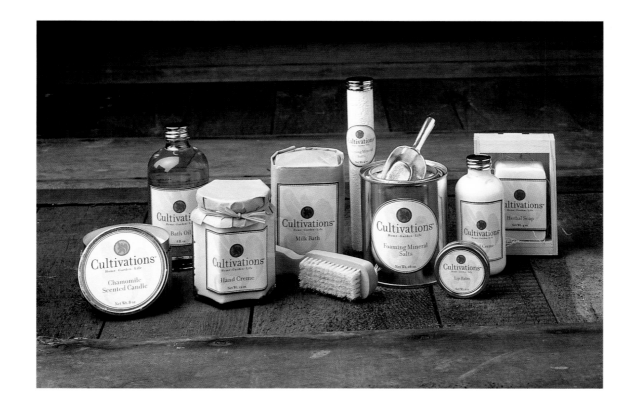

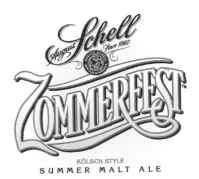

ALL MALT
VIENNA STYLE LAGER

1.

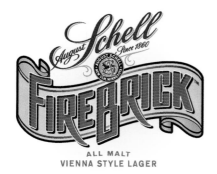

KÖLSCH STYLE
SUMMER MALT ALE

2.

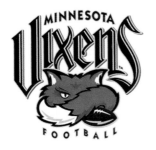

3.

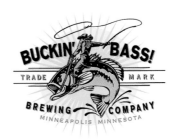

4.

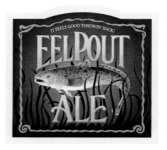

5.

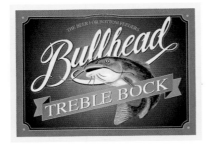

6.

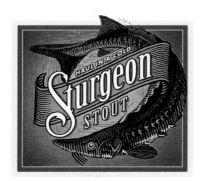

7.

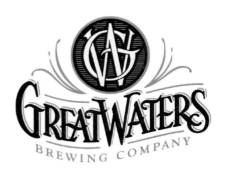

8.

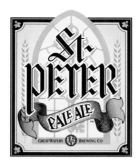

9.

St. PETER PALE ALE
GREAT WATERS BREWING CO

HARRIET BISHOP'S IPA
GREAT WATERS BREWING CO

10.

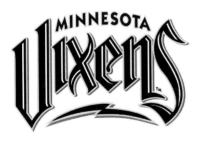

MINNESOTA Vixens FOOTBALL

11.

12.

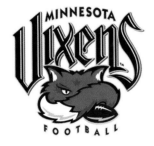

MINNESOTA Vixens

13.

LAKE MICHIGAN MINX FOOTBALL

14.

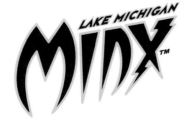

LAKE MICHIGAN MINX

15.

(all)
Design Firm **Compass Design**

1 - 3
  Client   August Schell Brewing Co.
  Designers   Mitchell Lindgren, Tom Arthur,
              & Rich McGowen

4 - 7
  Client   Buckin' Bass Brewing Co.
  Designers   Mitchell Lindgren, Tom Arthur,
              & Rich McGowen

8 - 10
  Client   Great Waters Brewing Co.
  Designers   Mitchell Lindgren, Tom Arthur,
              & Rich McGowen

11 - 15
  Client   World Wide Sports
  Designers   Mitchell Lindgren, Tom Arthur,
              & Rich McGowen

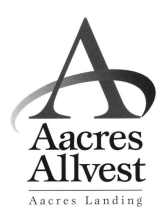

Aacres
Allvest

Aacres Landing

1.

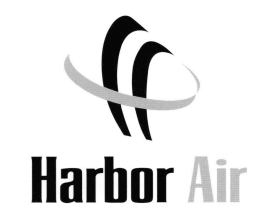

Harbor Air

2.

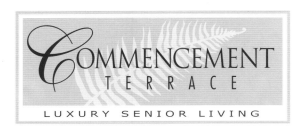

COMMENCEMENT
TERRACE

LUXURY SENIOR LIVING

3.

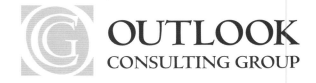

OUTLOOK
CONSULTING GROUP

4.

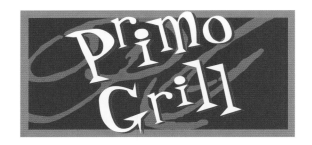

Primo
Grill

5.

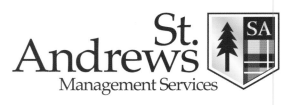

St.
Andrews
Management Services

6.

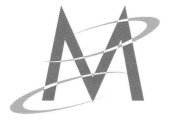

MILLENNIUM
RESTAURANT
CONSULTANTS

7.

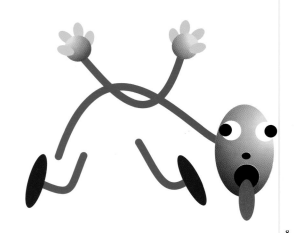

8.

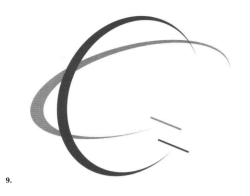

9.

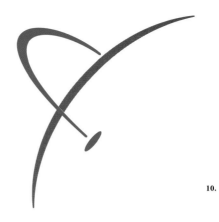

10.

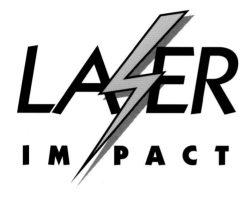

11.

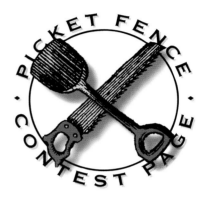

12.

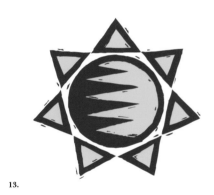

13.

14.

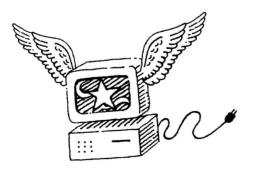

15.

1 - 6		
Design Firm	**L.J. Sands & Associates**	
7 - 10		
Design Firm	**Bruce Yelaska Design**	
11 - 15		
Design Firm	**Wet Paper Bag Graphic Design**	

1.	Client	Aacres Allvest
	Designer	Mary Pugliese
2.	Client	Harbor Air
	Designer	Courtenay Watson
3.	Client	Commencement Terrace
	Designer	Mary Pugliese
4.	Client	Outlook
	Designer	Mary Pugliese
5.	Client	Primo Grill
	Designer	Mary Pugliese
6.	Client	St. Andrews
	Designer	Mary Pugliese
7.	Client	Millennium Restaurant Consultants
	Designer	Bruce Yelaska

8.	Client	Messenger Cards
	Designer	Bruce Yelaska
9.	Client	The Gauntlett Group
	Designer	Bruce Yelaska
10.	Client	Simmons, Ungar, Helbush, Steinberg & Bright
	Designer	Bruce Yelaska
11.	Client	Laser Impact
	Designer	Lewis Glaser
12.	Client	Geocities Inc.
	Designer	Lewis Glaser
13.	Client	TCU Student Development Services
	Designer	Lewis Glaser
14.	Client	J & D Productions
	Designer	Lewis Glaser
15.	Client	Texas Christian University Graphic Design Program
	Designer	Lewis Glaser

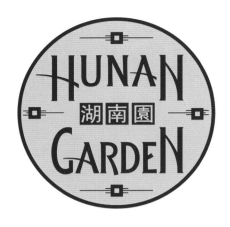

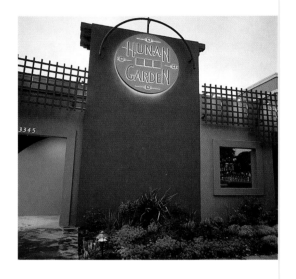

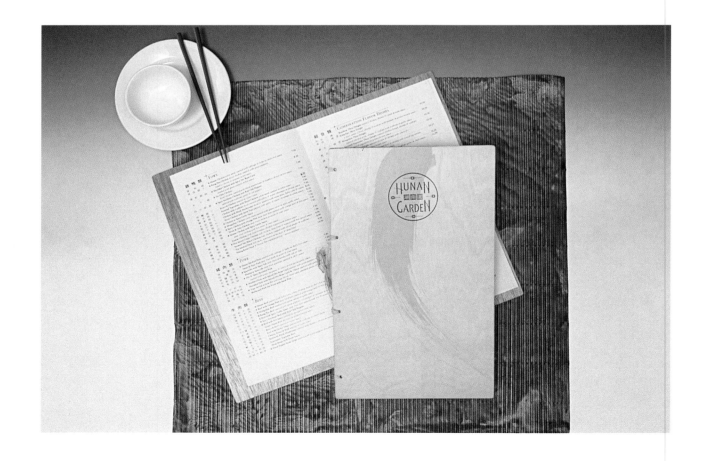

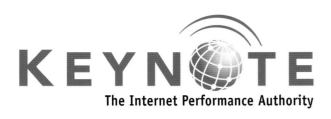

1.

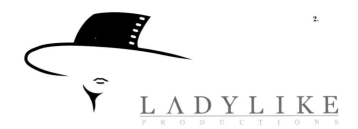

2.

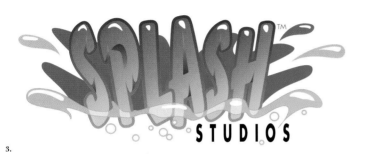

3.

4.

5.

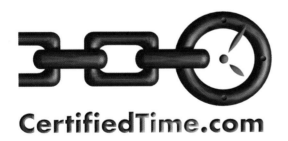

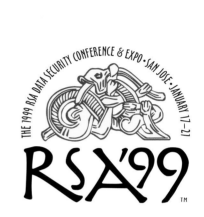

6.

7.

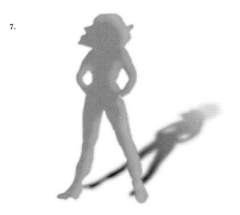

überbabe™ media, inc.

(opposite)
Design Firm Bruce Yelaska Design

Client   Hunan Garden
Designer   Bruce Yelaska

1 - 7
Design Firm Coda Creative, Inc.

1. Client   Keynote Systems
    Designers Paola Coda &
               Kurt Stammberger

2. Client   Ladylike Productions
    Designers Pavida Hoparsatsuk &
               Kurt Stammberger

3. Client   Splash Studios
    Designers Mark Deamer & Paola Coda

4. Client   RSA Data
               Security Conference 1999
    Designers Paola Coda &
               Kurt Stammberger

5. Client   Certified Time
    Designers Paola Coda &
               Kurt Stammberger

6. Client   RSA Data Security
    Designers Paola Coda &
               Kurt Stammberger

7. Client   überbabe media, inc.
    Designers Lisa Voldeng & Ashley Phelps

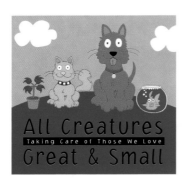

1.

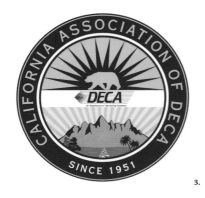

2.

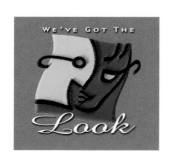

3.

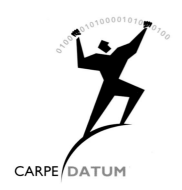

4.

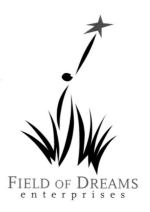

5.

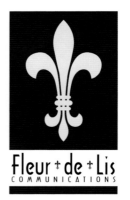

6.

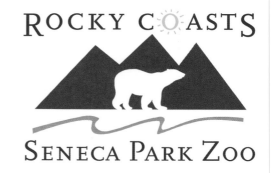

7.

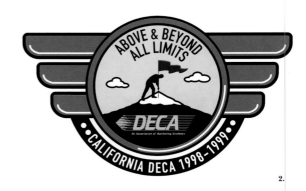

8.

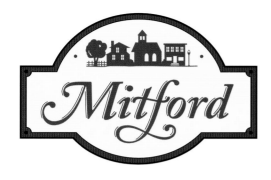

9.

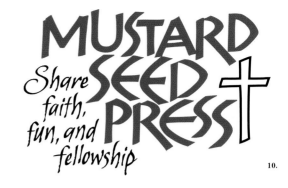

10.

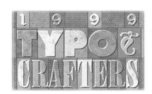

11.

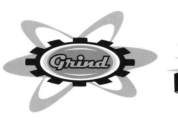

From the life & letters of Anna Kannenberg

12.

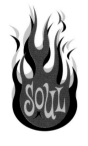

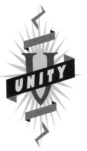

Goody Goody Gumdrops

14.

13.

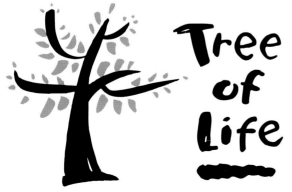

15.

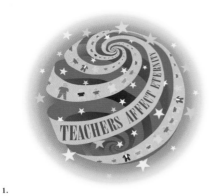

1.

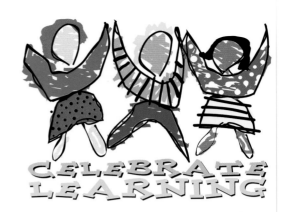

2.

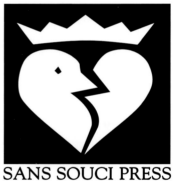

DREAM
WIZARDS

3.

PAPILIO

4.

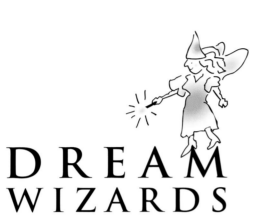

5.

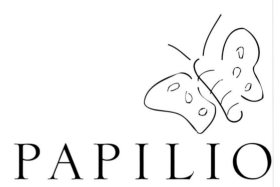

SANS SOUCI PRESS

6.

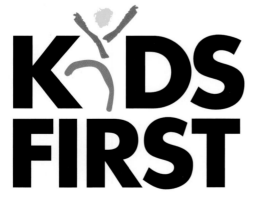

7.

1 - 7
Design Firm Designsmith

1. Client   Teachers Affect Eternity/
                 The Education People
    Designer   Richard Smith

2. Client   Celebrate Learning/
                 The Education People
    Designer   Richard Smith

3. Client   Dream Wizards
    Designer   Richard Smith

4. Client   Papilio
    Designer   Richard Smith

5. Client   The Future Begins/
                 The Education People
    Designer   Richard Smith

6. Client   Sans Souci Press
    Designer   Richard Smith

7. Client   Kids First/
                 The Education People
    Designer   Richard Smith

(opposite)
Design Firm Bailey Design Group, Inc.

    Client   Compass Group of America
    Designer   Steve Perry

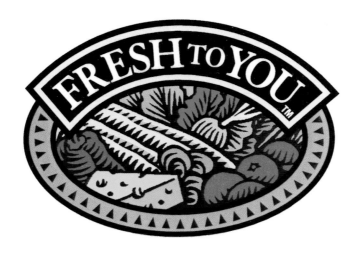

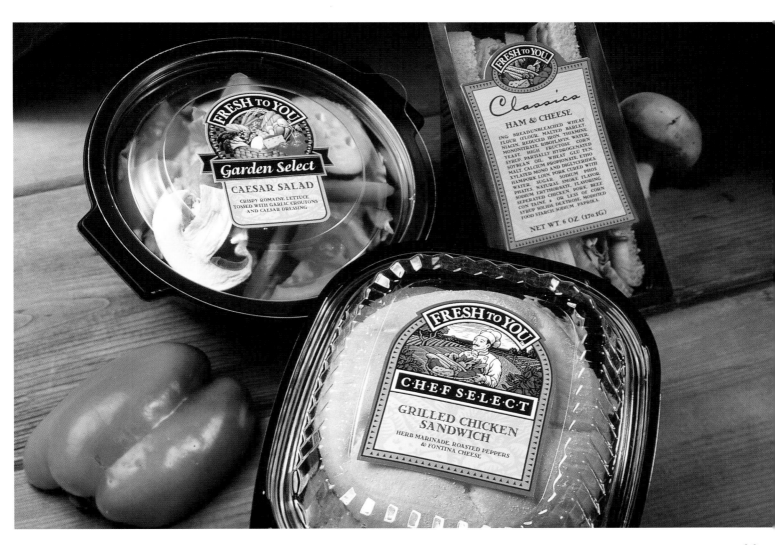

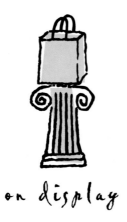

on display

1.

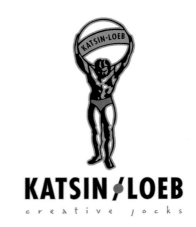

KATSIN/LOEB
creative jocks

2.

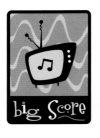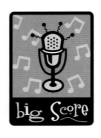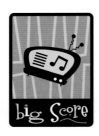

3.

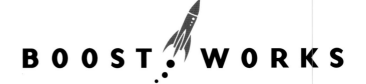

BOOST.WORKS

4.

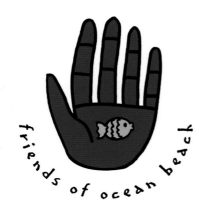

friends of ocean beach

5.

6.

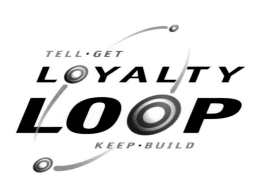

TELL·GET
LOYALTY
LOOP
KEEP·BUILD

7.

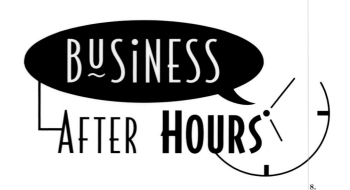

BUSINESS
AFTER HOURS

8.

94

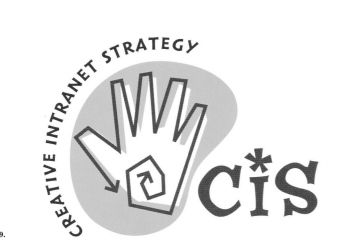

9.

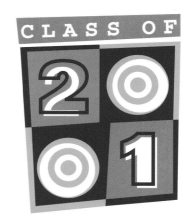

10.

CARDS FOR TODAY'S FAMILIES & LIFESTYLES

11.

SPECIALTY DESIGN STUDIO

12.

13.

studioB

14.

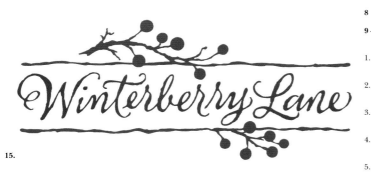

15.

1 - 2		
	Design Firm	**Rubber Design**
3 - 5		
	Design Firm	**Duncan/Channon**
6 - 7		
	Design Firm	**Griffith Phillips Creative**
8		
	Design Firm	**double entendre**
9 - 15		
	Design Firm	**Hallmark Cards, Inc.**

1.	Client	Stoneridge Shopping Center
	Designer	Jacquie VanKeuren
2.	Client	Katsin-Loeb Advertising
	Designer	Jacquie VanKeuren
3.	Client	Big Score
	Designer	Jacquie VanKeuren
4.	Client	Boostworks
	Designer	Jacquie VanKeuren
5.	Client	California Coastal Commission
	Designer	Jacquie VanKeuren
6.	Client	Craig Varjabedian Photography
	Designer	Alan Benest

7.	Client	GPCInteractive - Loyalty Loop Program
	Designer	Brian Niemann
8.	Client	Greater Seattle Chamber of Commerce
	Designers	Daniel P. Smith & Richard A. Smith
9.	Client	Hallmark Cards
	Designer	Jake Mikolic
10.	Client	Specialty Design
	Designer	Jake Mikolic
11.	Client	Hallmark Cards
	Designer	Sean Branagan
12.	Client	Specialty Design
	Designer	Barb Mizik
13.	Client	Specialty Design
	Designer	Jake Mikolic
14.	Client	Specialty Design
	Designer	Jake Mikolic
15.	Client	Specialty Design
	Designer	Lee Stork

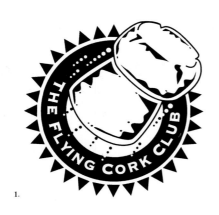

1.

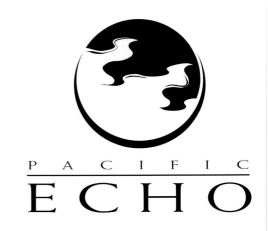

PACIFIC
ECHO

2.

Committed to Excellence

3.

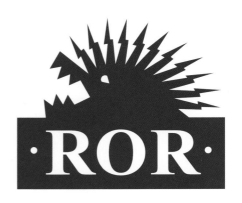

·ROR·

4.

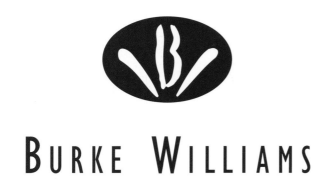

BURKE WILLIAMS

5.

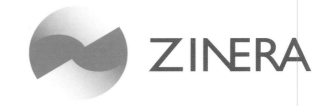

ZINERA

6.

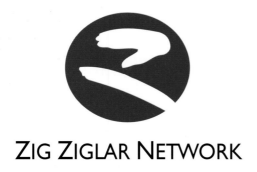

ZIG ZIGLAR NETWORK

7.

THE
METROPOLITAN
OPERA

8.

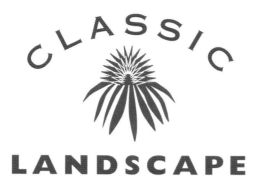

9.

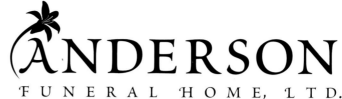

FUNERAL HOME, LTD.

10.

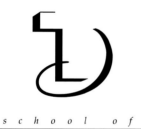 SASAir, Inc.

11.

D E S I G N

12.

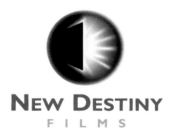

NEW DESTINY
F I L M S

14.

school of
THEATRE & DANCE

13.

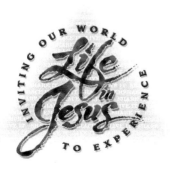

15.

1 - 3		7. Client	Zig Ziglar Network
Design Firm **Designsmith**		Designers	Mamory Shimokochi
4 - 7			& Anne Reeves
Design Firm **Shimokochi/Reeves**		8. Client	The Metropolitan Opera
8		Designers	David Sterling, Mark Randall,
Design Firm **World Studio**			Jeroen Jas, Stefan Hengst, Klaus
9 - 13			Kempenaars & Michael Samuels
Design Firm **B² Design**		9. Client	Classic Landscape
14 - 15		Designer	Carol M. Benthal-Bingley
Design Firm **Dotzler Creative Arts**		10. Client	Anderson Funeral Home

1. Client   The Flying Cork Club/
      Pacific Echo Cellars
  Designer Richard Smith

2. Client   Pacific Echo
  Designer Richard Smith

3. Client   Committed to Excellence/
      The Education People
  Designer Richard Smith

4. Client   ROR
  Designers Mamoru Shimokochi, Anne
      Reeves, & Eugene Bustillos

5. Client   Burke Williams
  Designers Mamoru Shimokochi
      & Anne Reeves

6. Client   Zig Ziglar Network
  Designers Mamoru Shimokochi
      & Anne Reeves

10. Client   Anderson Funeral Home
    Designers Julie Wojak & Carol
      Benthal-Bingley

11. Client   SASAir, Inc.
    Designer Carol M. Benthal-Bingley

12. Client   B² Design
    Designer Carol Benthal-Bingley

13. Client   Northern Illinois University
      School of Theatre and Dance
    Designer Carol Benthal-Bingley

14. Client   New Destiny Films

15. Client   Trinity Church

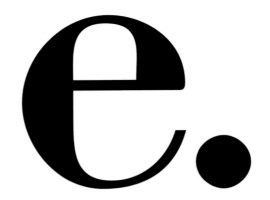

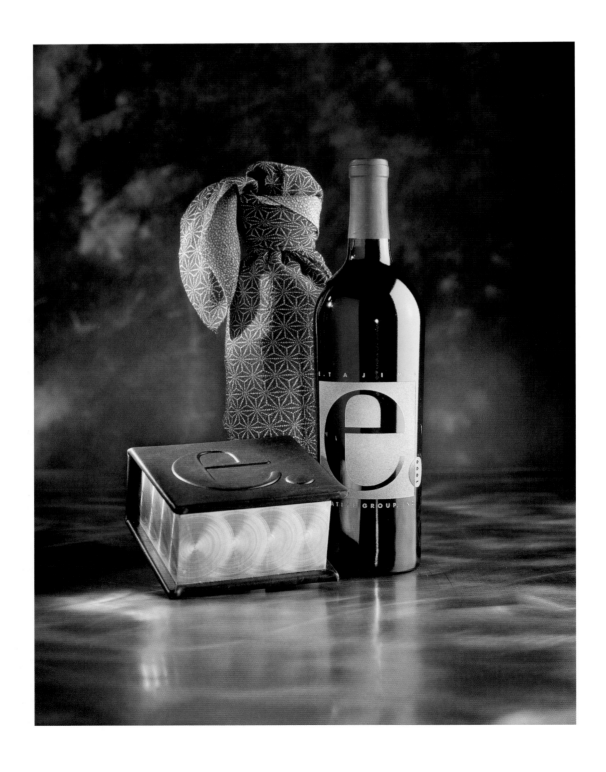

1.

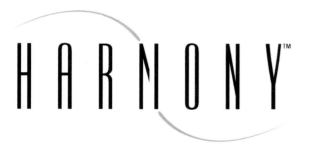

DIVI RESTAURANT

2.

CONSTRUCTION SUCCESS
CLAYCO
15
·YEARS·

3.

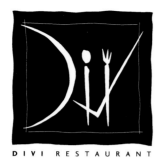

insectarium
Saint Louis Zoo

4.

RETAIL RESULTS
314 434 7237

5.

HARMONY™

6.

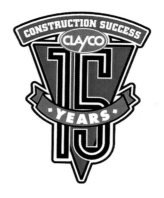   LABARGE CLAYCO WIRELESS, LLC

7.

STEEL STUD · MANUFACTURERS ASSOCIATION
SSMA℠

(opposite)
Design Firm E. Tajima Creative Group, Inc.

Client   E. Tajima Creative Group, Inc.
Designers   Roz Roos Designs for the
              E. Tajima Creative Group, Inc.

1 - 8
Design Firm CUBE Advertising & Design
9
Design Firm J G M Design

1. Client   Divi Restaurant
    Designer   David Chiow

2. Client   Clayco Construction Company
    Designers David Chiow & Kevin Hough

3. Client   Saint Louis Zoo
    Designer   David Chiow

4. Client   Retail Results
    Designer   David Chiow

5. Client   Crown Therapeutics, Inc.
    Designer   David Chiow

6. Client   LaBarge Clayco Wireless, LLC
    Designers Steve Wienke & David Chiow

7. Client   Steel Stud Manufacturers
               Association
    Designer   Joan Gilbert Madsen

1.

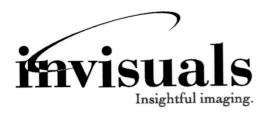

2.

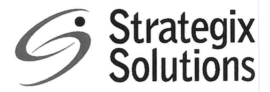

3.

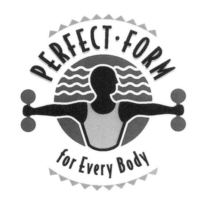

4.

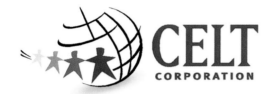

5.

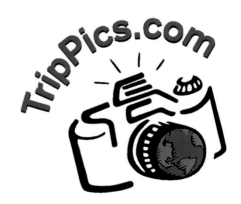

6.

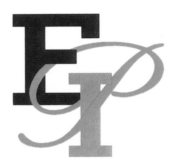

7.

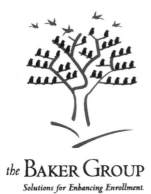

8.

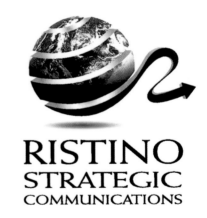

9.

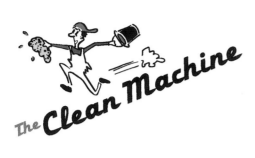

10.

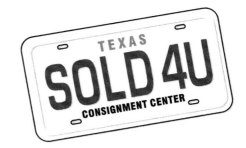

11.

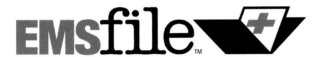

12.

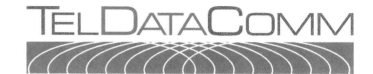

14.

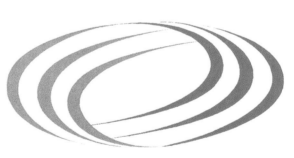

13.

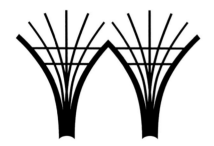

15.

1 - 9
Design Firm Hess Design Inc.
10 - 15
Design Firm Michael Lee Advertising
& Design, Inc.

1. Client   Invisuals
    Designer   Karyn Goba

2. Client   Strategix Solutions
    Designer   Karyn Goba

3. Client   CELT Corp.
    Designer   Kim Daly

4. Client   Equity Industrial Partners
    Designer   Kim Daly

5. Client   Perfect Form
    Designer   Kim Daly

6. Client   Ristino Strategic
                 Communications
    Designer   Jim Harrington

7. Client   the Baker Group
    Designers   Kim Daly & Karyn Goba

8. Client   Trippics.Com
    Designers   Kim Daly & Melissa Meinhold

9. Client   The Clean Machine
    Designers   Hannah Gilmore
                 & Heather Knopf

10. Client   SOLD4U
    Designer   Michael Lee

11. Client   EMSfile
    Designer   Michael Lee

12. Client   TelDataComm
    Designer   Michael Lee

13. Client   Wester Landscape Management
    Designer   Michael Lee

14. Client   Efficient Systems
    Designer   Michael Lee

15. Client   On Stage Hair Design
    Designer   Michael Lee

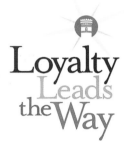

1.

ELE MEN TAL

2.

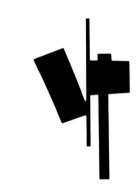

3.

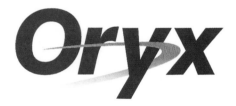

Loyalty Leads the Way

4.

Presbytery of Philadelphia

5.

Oryx

6.

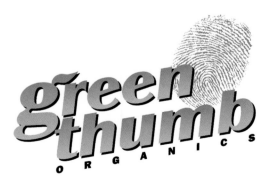

green thumb ORGANICS

7.

1 - 3
Design Firm   EAI
4 - 6
Design Firm   Art 270, Inc.
7
Design Firm   Schlatter Design

1. Client   The Coca-Cola Company
    Designer   Todd Simmons

2. Client   Elemental Interactive Design
                  & Development
    Designer   Matt Rollins

3. Client   Human Arts Gallery
    Designer   Matt Rollins

4. Client   Beaver College
    Designer   John Opet

5. Client   Presbytery of Philadelphia
    Designers   Carl Mill, Sean Flanagan,
                  & Holly Kempf

6. Client   LHS Priority Call
    Designer   Holly Kempf

7. Client   Green Thumb Organics, Inc.
    Designer   Richard Schlatter

(opposite)
Design Firm   Bailey Design Group, Inc.

    Client   Marriott Corporation
    Designer   David Fiedler

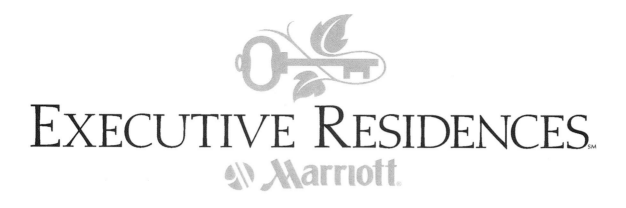

EXECUTIVE RESIDENCES℠

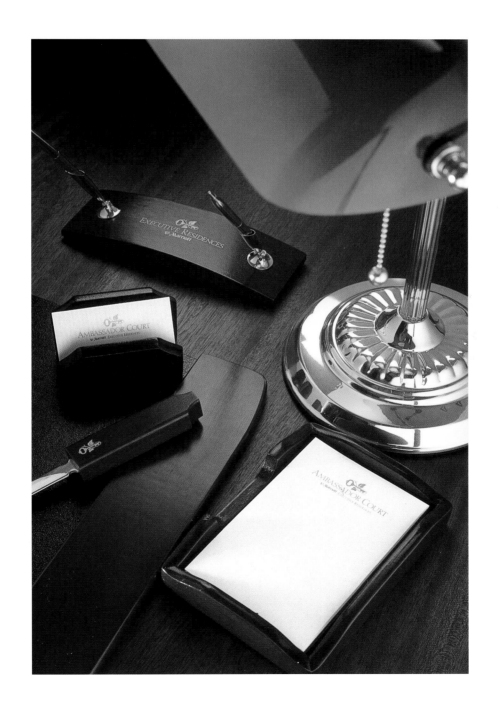

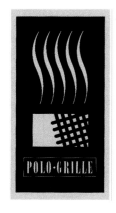

1.

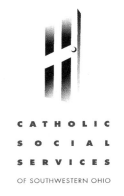

DESIGNING WOMEN

2.

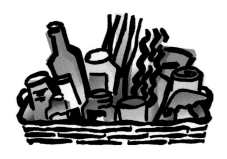

RESOURCE

3.

CATHOLIC
SOCIAL
SERVICES
OF SOUTHWESTERN OHIO

4.

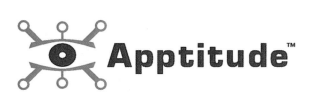

POLO·GRILLE

5.

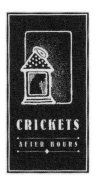

CRICKETS
AFTER HOURS

6.

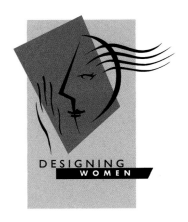

Apptitude™

7.

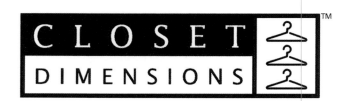

CLOSET DIMENSIONS ™

8.

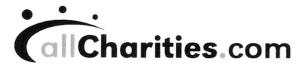

9.

10.

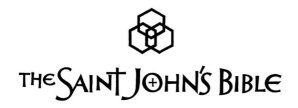

11.

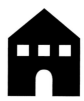

MICHAEL GRAVES
DESIGN™

12.

THEATER ZERO

13.

ORGANIC COTTON

14.

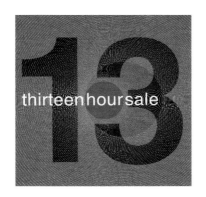

15.

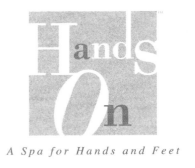

1.

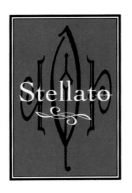

2.

A Spa for Hands and Feet

cyber*gourmet.*

3.

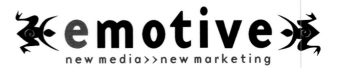

new media>>new marketing

4.

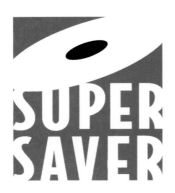

gmo

connect. commune. converge.

5.

maha

yoga

6.

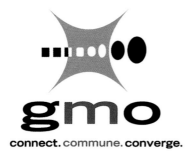

7.

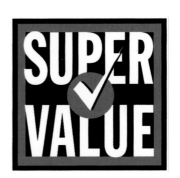

8.

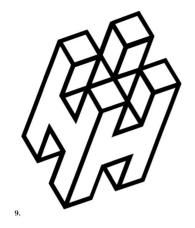

9.

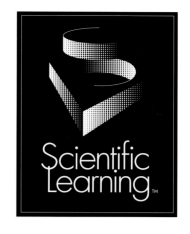

10.

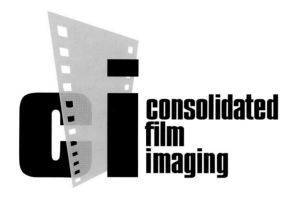

consolidated
film
imaging

11.

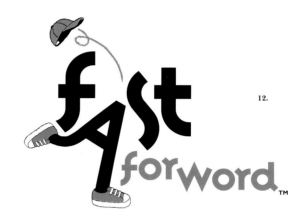

12.

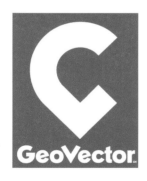

GeoVector.

13.

14.

SYMPLECTIC
ENGINEERING CORPORATION

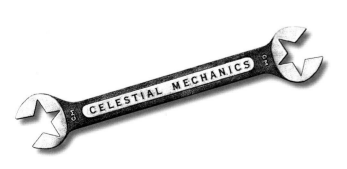

15.

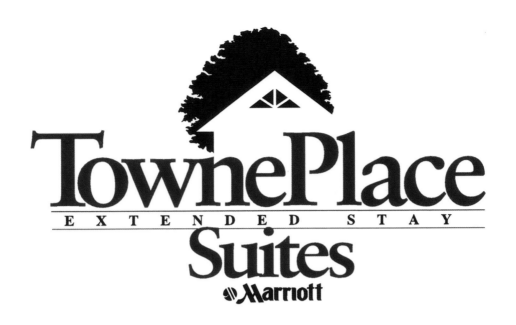

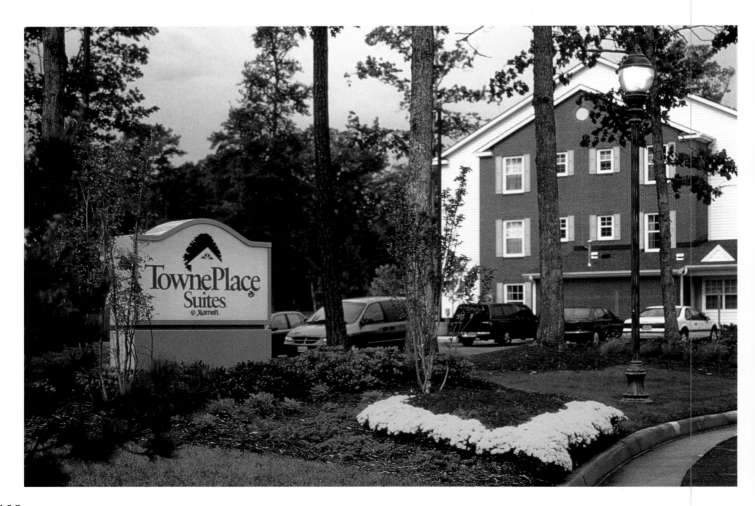

1.

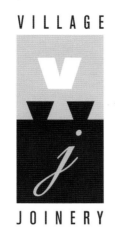

VILLAGE

JOINERY

2.

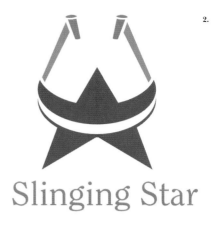

Slinging Star

3.

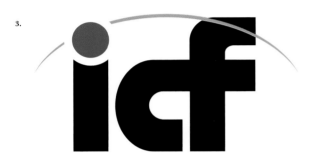

4.

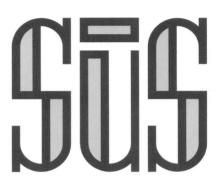

5.

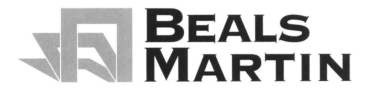

BEALS MARTIN

6.

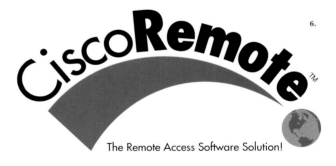

7.

kindercotton.com

(opposite)
Design Firm Bailey Design Group, Inc.

Client   Marriott Corporation
Designer   Gary LaCroix

1 - 7
Design Firm Stratford Design Associates

1. Client   Village Joinery
   Designer   Silvia Stephenson

2. Client   Slinging Star
   Designer   Tim Gerould

3. Client   ICF
   Designer   Silvia Stephenson

4. Client   SUS
   Designer   Tim Gerould

5. Client   Beals Martin
   Designers Gerald Stratford, Sr.
              & Tim Gerould

6. Client   Cisco
   Designers Gerald Stratford, Sr.
              & Rebecca Lambing

7. Client   Kindercotton
   Designer   Silvia Stephenson

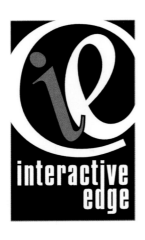

1.

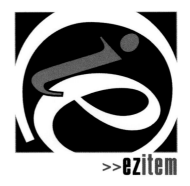

2.

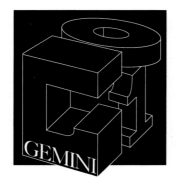

3.

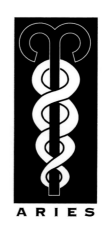

4.

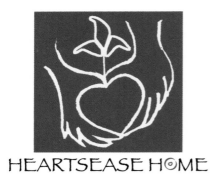

5.

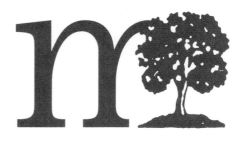

6.

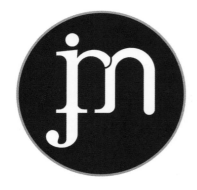

7.

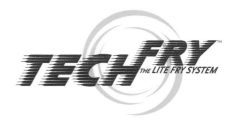

8.

9.

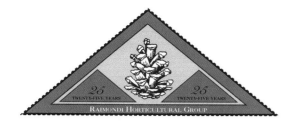

10.

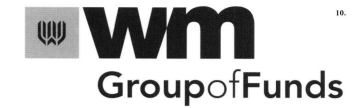

11.

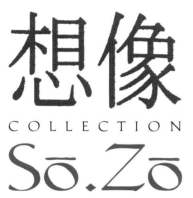

12.

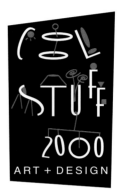

13.

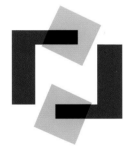

nSite Software, Inc.

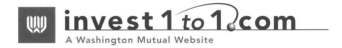

14.

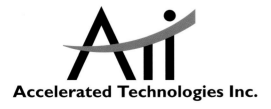

15.

1 - 5, 7 - 9			8.	Client	Techfoods USA
Design Firm	**John R. Mongelli & Assoc. Inc.**			Designer	Dara Mongelli
6					
Design Firm	**Nightlight Design**		9.	Client	Raimondi Horticultural Group
10 - 14				Designer	Dara Mongelli
Design Firm	**E. Tajima Creative Group, Inc.**				
15			10.	Client	Washington Mutual
Design Firm	**Guy Design**				Group of Funds
				Designer	Janice Wong
1, 2					
Client	Interactive Edge		11.	Client	SÒ-ZÒ - Collection SÒ-ZÒ
Designers	John Mongelli & Dara Mongelli			Designer	George Hoehn
3, 4					
Client	Paramount Capital		12.	Client	San Jose Museum of Art
	Financial Investment			Designer	Daniel Tiburcio
Designer	Dara Mongelli				
			13.	Client	nSite Software Inc.—Paul Tabet
5.	Client	Heartsease Home, Inc.		Designer	Janice Wong
	Designer	Dara Mongelli			
			14.	Client	Washington Mutual Bank
6.	Client	Morgan Management		Designer	Rich Nelson
	Designers	Lisa Haim & Dara Mongelli			
			15.	Client	ATI
7.	Client	John R. Mongelli & Assoc., Inc.		Designer	Debbie Guy
	Designer	Dara Mongelli			

1.

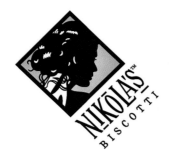

2.

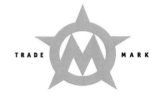

3.

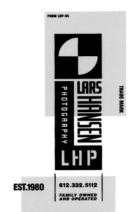

4.

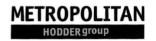

5.

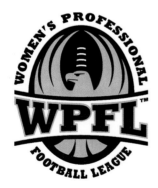

6.

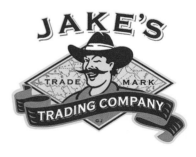

7.

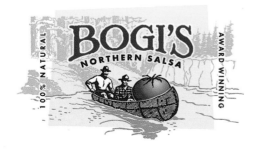

1 - 7

Design Firm Compass Design

1. Client   Nikola's Biscotti
    Designers   Mitchell Lindgren, Tom Arthur,
                  & Rich McGowen

2. Client   Juntunen Media Group
    Designers   Mitchell Lindgren, Tom Arthur,
                  & Rich McGowen

3. Client   Lars Hansen Photography
    Designers   Mitchell Lindgren, Tom Arthur,
                  & Rich McGowen

4. Client   Metropolitan Hodder Group
    Designers   Mitchell Lindgren, Tom Arthur,
                  & Rich McGowen

5. Client   World Wide Sports
    Designers   Mitchell Lindgren, Tom Arthur,
                  & Rich McGowen

6. Client   International Foods, Inc.
    Designers   Mitchell Lindgren, Tom Arthur,
                  & Rich McGowen

7. Client   Red Wing Foods
    Designers   Mitchell Lindgren, Tom Arthur,
                  & Rich McGowen

(opposite)

Design Firm Dixon & Parcels Associates, Inc.

    Client   The Bachman Company

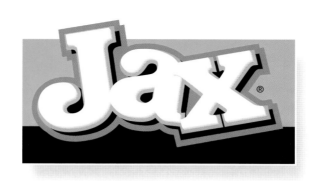

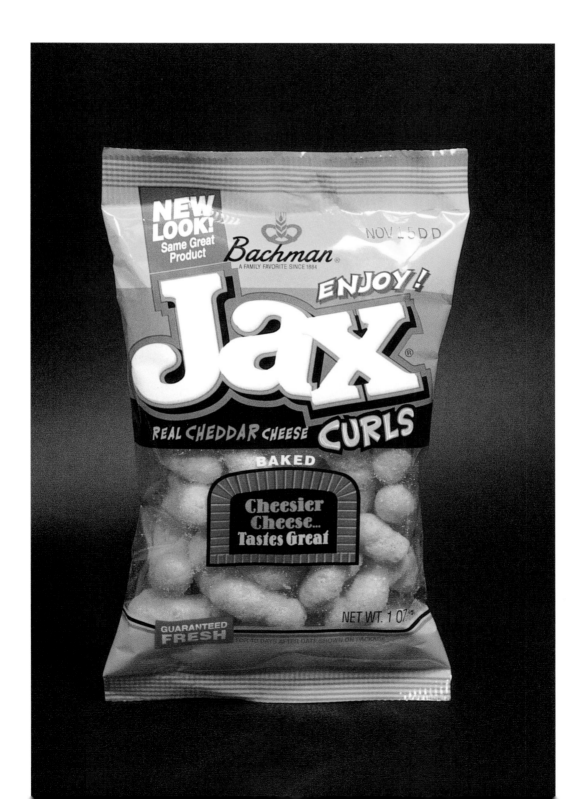

1.

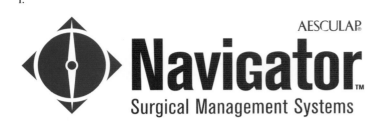

AESCULAP®
Navigator™
Surgical Management Systems

2.

GLENBOROUGH

3.

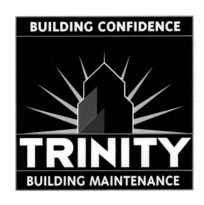

BUILDING CONFIDENCE

TRINITY

BUILDING MAINTENANCE

4.

6.

5.

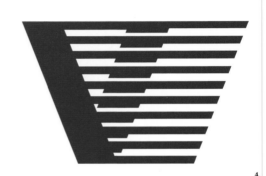

COMPUTER SYSTEMS DIVISION

NEC solutions

powerware

8.

7.

Mercer

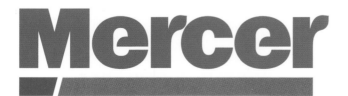

114

Crawford & Associates
INTERNATIONAL

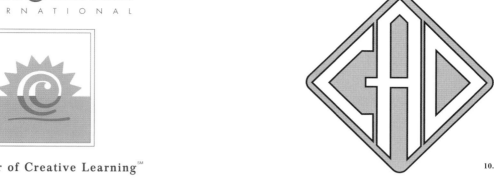

The Power of Creative Learning^{SM}

9.

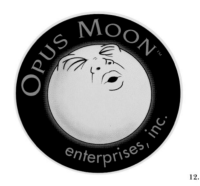

10.

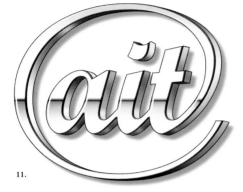

11.

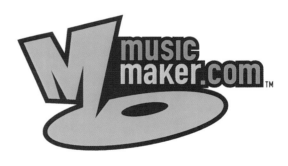

12.

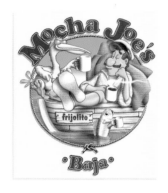

13.

music maker.com ™

14.

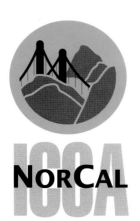

NorCal

15.

1 - 7			7. Client	Mercer
Design Firm	Stratford Design Associates		Designer	Tim Gerould
8 - 13				
Design Firm	Electric Illustration + Design		8. Client	Electric Illustration & Design
14			Designer	Jeff Flower
Design Firm	Doublespace			
15			9. Client	Crawford & Associates, Int'l
Design Firm	Square Peg Graphics		Designers	Jeff Flower & Karen Allison
1. Client	Aesculap		10. Client	Cindy Diamond Attorney @ Law
Designer	Tim Gerould		Designer	Jeff Flower
2. Client	Glenborough		11. Client	Advanced Integrated Training
Designer	Tim Gerould		Designer	Jeff Flower
3. Client	Trinity Building Maintenance		12. Client	Opus Moon Enterprises
Designer	John F. Morgan		Designers	Jeff Flower & Jim Brown
4. Client	Valley Communications		13. Client	Mocha Joe's
Designer	Tim Gerould		Designer	Jeff Flower
5. Client	NEC		15. Client	Independent Computer
Designer	Tim Gerould			Consultants Assoc. Northern
				California Chapter
6. Client	Powerware Solutions		Designer	Jack Jackson
Designer	Tim Gerould			

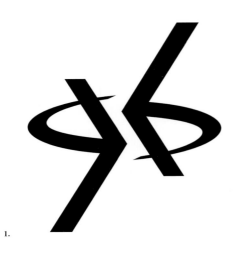

1.

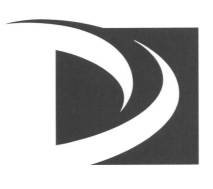

2.

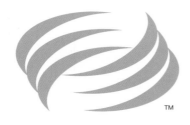

health **quarters**

your source for sexuality education and medical care

3.

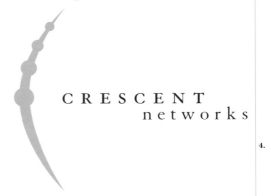

CRESCENT
networks

4.

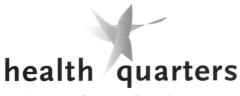

XyEnterprise™

5.

ĸallix

6.

E✕PAND
networks

7.

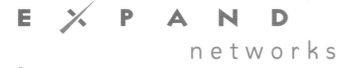

LEAGUESCHOOL

8.

116

9.

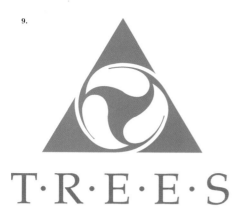

T·R·E·E·S

10.

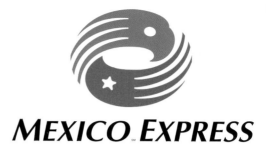

MEXICO EXPRESS

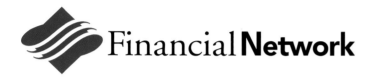

Financial **Network**

12.

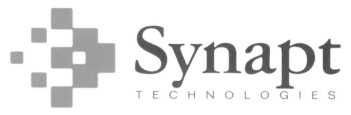

Synapt
T E C H N O L O G I E S

11.

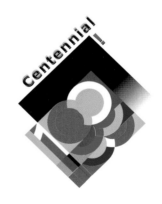

CEATECH USA

14.

13.

15.

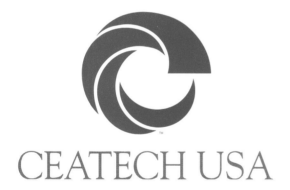

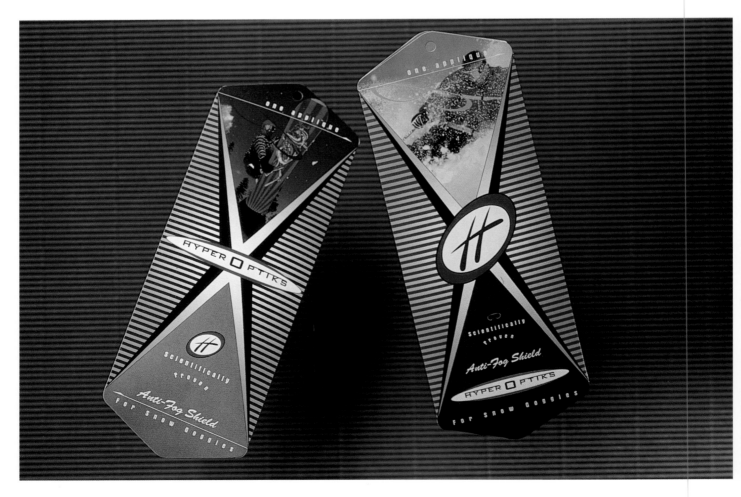

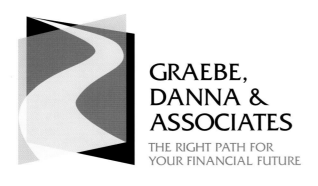

GRAEBE,
DANNA &
ASSOCIATES

THE RIGHT PATH FOR
YOUR FINANCIAL FUTURE

1.

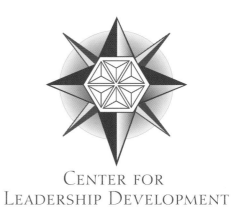

CENTER FOR
LEADERSHIP DEVELOPMENT

2.

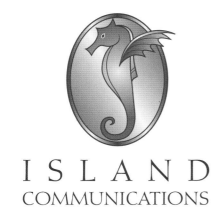

ISLAND
COMMUNICATIONS

3.

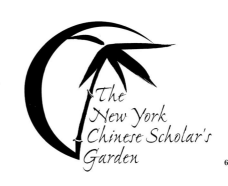

SUCCESS
EXPRESS
A BRIDGE TO THE FUTURE

4.

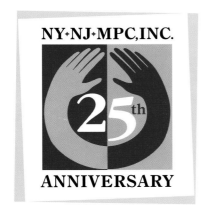

5.

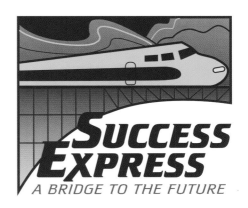

6.

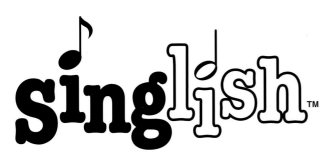

7.

(opposite)
Design Firm Onyx Design Inc.

Client   Modern World Ventures Inc.
Designer   Paul Morales

1 - 6
Design Firm Island Communications
7
Design Firm Philbrook & Associates

1. Client   Graebe, Danna & Associates
    Designer   Linda E. Danaher

2. Client   Center for Leadership
               Development at Bristol-Myers
               Squibb Company
    Designer   Linda E. Danaher

3. Client   Island Communications
    Designer   Linda E. Danaher

4. Client   Success Express at Bristol-Myers
               Squibb Company
    Designer   Linda E. Danaher

4. Client   NY, NJ Minority
               Purchasing Council, Inc.
    Designer   Linda E. Danaher

6. Client   New York Chinese
               Scholar's Garden
    Designer   Linda E. Danaher

7. Client   Singlish Enterprises, Inc.
    Designer   Bill Philbrook

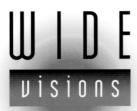

PANA-VU FRAMES

1.

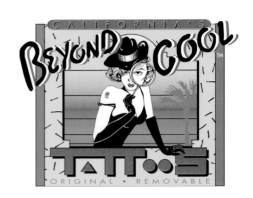

2.

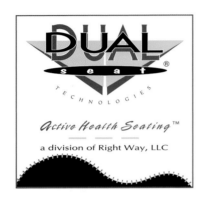

3.

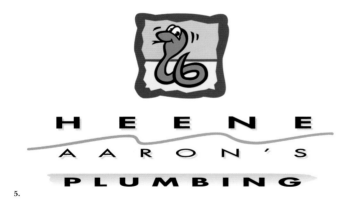

4.

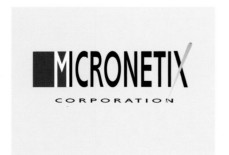

5.

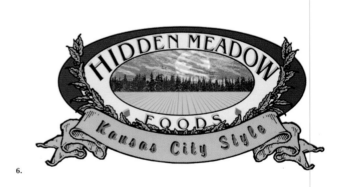

6.

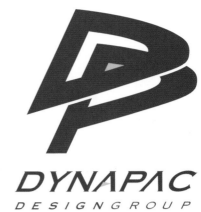

7.

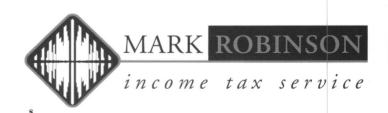

8.

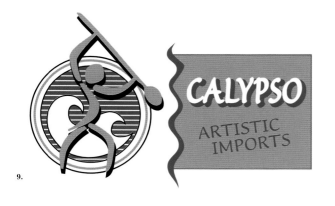

9.

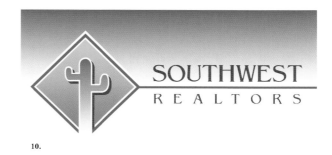

10.

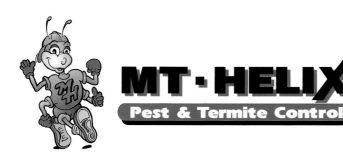

11.

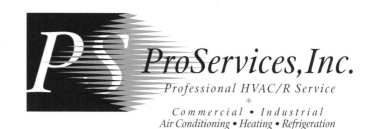

12.

13.

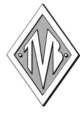

14.

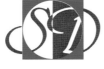

15.

(all)

Design Firm DYNAPAC Design Group

1.	Client	Advance Plastics
	Designers	Lee A. Aellig & Elsa Valdez
2.	Client	DYNAPAC Design Group
	Designers	Lee A. Aellig, Marland Chow, & Angus R. Colson
3.	Client	Dual Seat Technologies
	Designer	Lee A. Aellig
4.	Client	Beyond Cool Tattoos
	Designer	Lee A. Aellig
5.	Client	Heene Aaron's Plumbing
	Designer	Lee Aellig
6.	Client	Hidden Meadow Foods
	Designer	Lee A. Aellig
7.	Client	Micronetix Corporation
	Designer	Lee A. Aellig

8.	Client	Mark Robinson Income Tax Service
	Designer	Lee A. Aellig
9.	Client	Calypso Artistic Imports
	Designers	Lee A. Aellig & Robert Alexander
10.	Client	Southwest Realtors
	Designer	Lee A. Aellig
11.	Client	Mt. Helix Pest & Termite Control
	Designer	Lee A. Aellig
12.	Client	ProServices, Inc.
	Designer	Lee A. Aellig
13.	Client	PhoneChip.com
	Designer	Lee A. Aellig
14.	Client	The Voice Broadcasting
	Designer	Lee A. Aellig
15.	Client	San Diego Real Estate Associates
	Designer	Lee A. Aellig

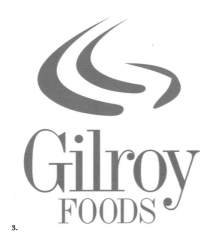

1.

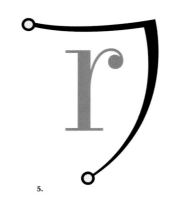

2.

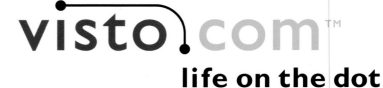

3.

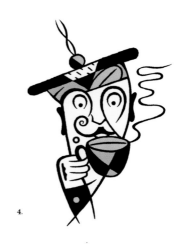

4.

5.

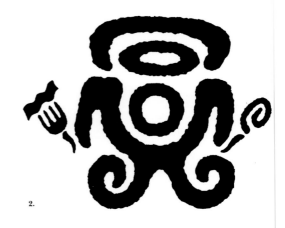

visto.com™

life on the dot

6.

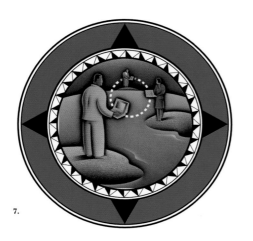

7.

1 - 6
Design Firm Onyx Design Inc.

7
Design Firm Primo Angeli Inc.

1. Client   Larkspur Hospitality Hotels
    Designers   Paul Morales & Dean Alvarez

2. Client   La Raza Centro legal
    Designer   Paul Morales

3. Client   Gilroy Foods/Con Agra
    Designers   Paul Morales & Dean Alvarez

4. Client   Caffe Marseille
    Designer   Paul Morales

5. Client   Riscorian Enterprise
    Designers   Dean Alvarez & Paul Morales

6. Client   Visto Corporation
    Designers   Dean Alvarez, Paul Morales,
                       & Wendy McPhee

7. Client   Informix/Software
    Designers   Paul Morales & Jeff Keogel

(opposite)
Design Firm Dynapac Design Group

    Client   C & H International
    Designers   Lee A. Aellig & Paula Hong

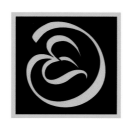

EUROPEAN
AVANTÁGE ™

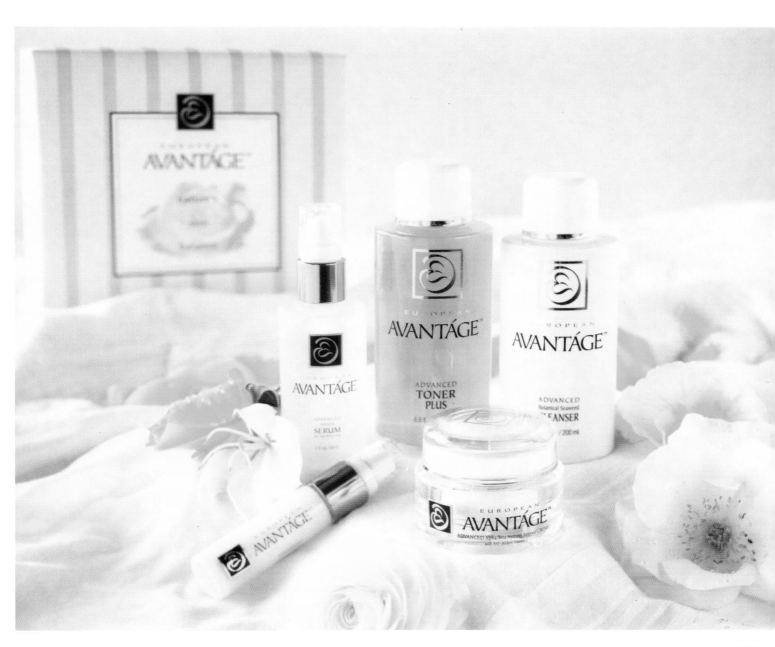

1.

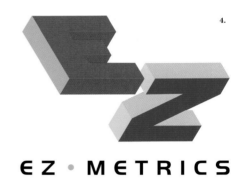

2.

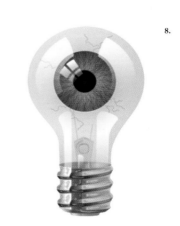

3.

4.

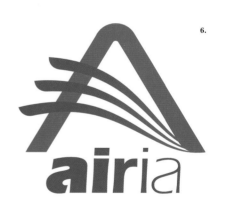

EZ · METRICS

5.

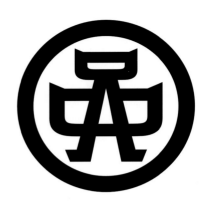

6.

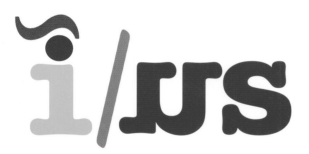

7.

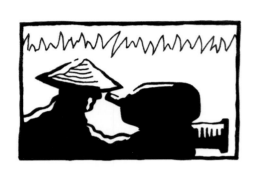

8.

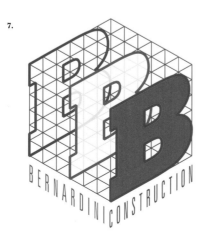

124

9.

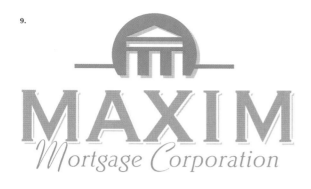

10.

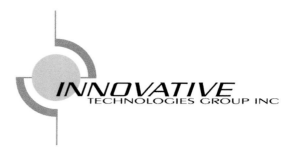

11.

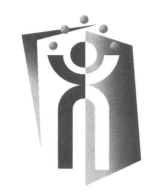

12.

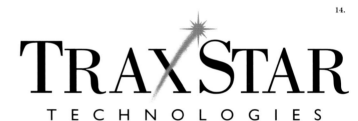

13.

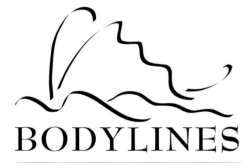

14.

TRAX STAR

TECHNOLOGIES

15.

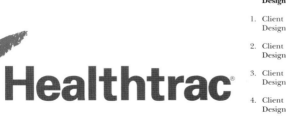

125

1.

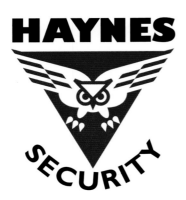

HAYNES

SECURITY

2.

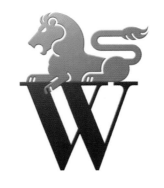

3.

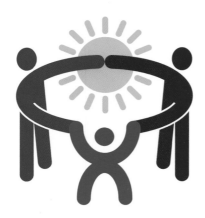

4.

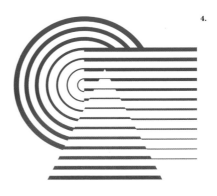

6.

H1

HamiltonInk

5.

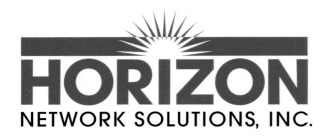

HORIZON

NETWORK SOLUTIONS, INC.

7.

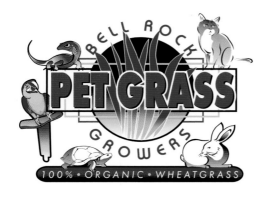

BELL ROCK

PET GRASS

GROWERS

100% • ORGANIC • WHEATGRASS

8.

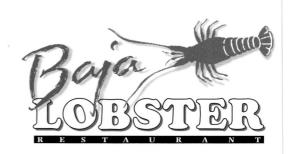

Baja

LOBSTER

R E S T A U R A N T

9.

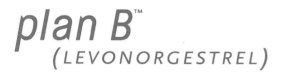

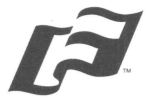

10.

F I S H E R

TACOMA **POWER**
TACOMA PUBLIC UTILITIES

TACOMA **WATER**
TACOMA PUBLIC UTILITIES

TACOMA **RAIL**
TACOMA PUBLIC UTILITIES

11.

12.

plan B™
(LEVONORGESTREL)

13.

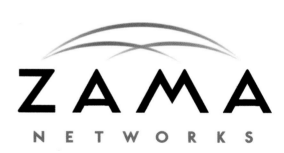

Z A M A
N E T W O R K S

14.

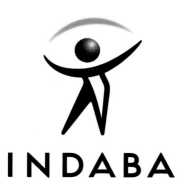

INDABA

15.

1 - 6				
Design Firm	**De Martino Design**		8. Client	Baja Lobster Restaurant
7 - 8			Designer	Lee A. Aellig
Design Firm	**DYNAPAC Design Group**			
9 - 15			9. Client	Inn at the Market
Design Firm	**The Leonhardt Group**		Designer	Janee Kreinheder
1. Client	Haynes Security		10. Client	Fisher Companies, Inc.
Designer	Erick De Martino		Designer	Steve Watson
2. Client	Whitehall Capital Association		11. Client	Tacoma Public Utilities
Designer	Erick De Martino		Designers	Ben Graham, John Cannell,
				& Greg Morgan
3. Client	Family Connections			
Designer	Erick De Martino		12. Client	N2H2
			Designer	Thad Boss
4. Client	T.J. Willard & Assoc.			
Designer	Erick De Martino		13. Client	Elgin DDB
			Designer	Jon King
5. Client	Horizon Network Solutions			
Designer	Erick De Martino		14. Client	ZAMA
			Designer	Janee Kreinheder
6. Client	Hamilton Ink			
Designer	Erick De Martino		15. Client	INDABA
			Designer	Janee Kreinheder
7. Client	Bell Rock Growers			
Designer	Lee A. Aellig			

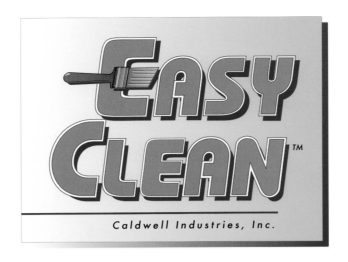

Caldwell Industries, Inc.

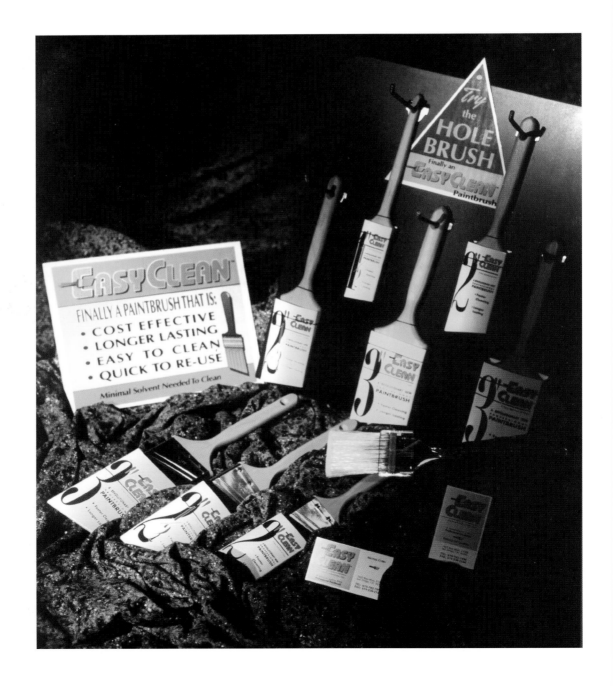

1.

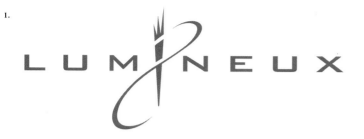

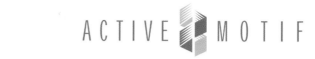

2.

3.

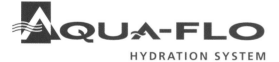

4.

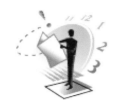
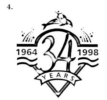

5.

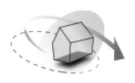
AQUA-FLO
HYDRATION SYSTEM

6.

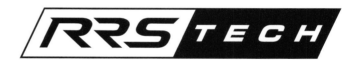

7.

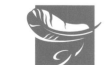

(opposite)
Design Firm DYNAPAC Design Group

Client   Caldwell Industries, Inc.
Designer   Lee A. Aellig

1 - 7
Design Firm Laura Coe Design Assoc.

1. Client   Lumineux
    Designers   Laura Coe Wright
                & Leanne Leveillee

2. Client   Active Motif
    Designers   Ryoichi Yotsumoto
                & Laura Coe Wright

3. Client   Dataquick
    Designer   Ryoichi Yotsumoto

4. Client   Sea World of California
    Designers   Leanne Leveillee
                & Ryoichi Yotsumoto

5. Client   Taylor Made Golf Co.
    Designer   Ryoichi Yotsumoto

6. Client   Road Runner Sports
    Designer   Darryl Glass

7. Client   Road Runner Sports
    Designer   Ryoichi Yotsumoto

1.

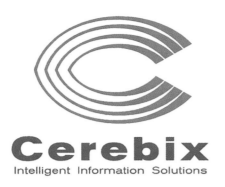

Cerebix
Intelligent Information Solutions

2.

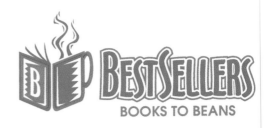

BESTSELLERS
BOOKS TO BEANS

3.

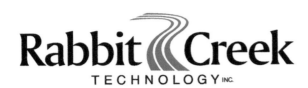

4.

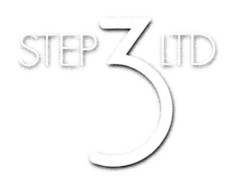

A Catered Experience

5.

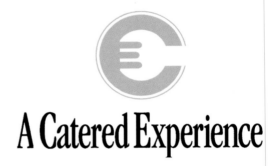

6.

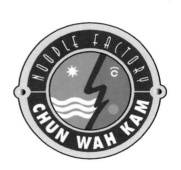

7.

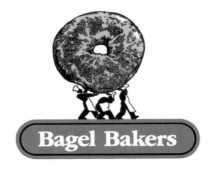

8.

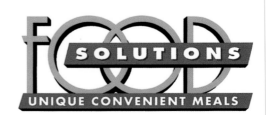

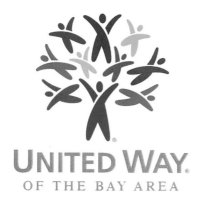

9.

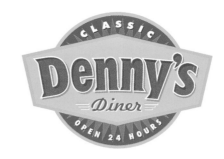

10.

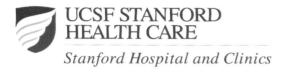

11.

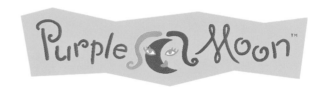

12.

E^xponent™

13.

Cheskin Research

14.

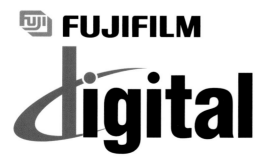

15.

1 - 3		8. Client	Food Solutions
Design Firm	Jansen Design	Designer	Nick Kaars
4 - 8			
Design Firm	Nick Kaars Associates Inc.	9. Client	The United Way of the Bay Area
9 - 14		Designers	Mark Bergman
Design Firm	SBG Enterprise		& Richard Patterson
15			
Design Firm	Irwin Levine & Assoc.	10. Client	Flagstow Corp./Advantica Restaurant Group
		Designers	Mark Bergman & Tom Kane
1. Client	Cerebix		
Designer	Glenn Jansen	11. Client	UCSF Stanford
		Designers	Mark Bergman
2. Client	BestSellers		& Richard Patterson
Designer	Glenn Jansen		
		12. Client	Interval
3. Client	Rabbit Creek	Designers	Mark Bergman
Designer	Glenn Jansen		& Jessie McAnulty
4. Client	A Catered Experience	13. Client	Exponent
Designer	Nick Kaars	Designers	Mark Bergman & Amy Hershman
5. Client	Step 3	14. Client	Cheskin Research
Designer	Nick Kaars	Designers	Mark Bergman & Jessie McAnulty
6. Client	Chun Wah Kam Noodle Factory		
Designers	Darryl Soon & Nick Kaars	15. Client	Fuji Photo Film
		Designer	Brad Levine
7. Client	Bagel Bakers		
Designers	Oliver Kinney & Nick Kaars		

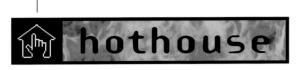

hothouse

digital

1.

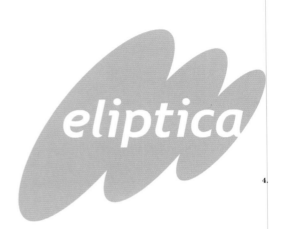

2.

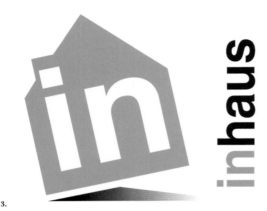

inhaus

3.

eliptica

4.

SOLARIAN

KARMA

5.

6.

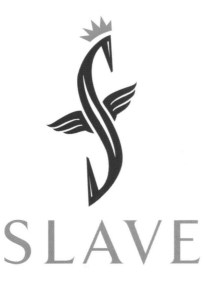

SLAVE

7.

1 - 7
Design Firm be.

1. Client   Hot House
    Designers   Eric Read & Enrique Gaston

2. Client   Light Rain
    Designers   Coralie Russo & Eric Read

3. Client   In Haus
    Designer   Eric Read

4. Client   Eliptica
    Designer   Yubuke Asaka

5. Client   Armstrong Solarian
    Designer   Will Burke

6. Client   Karma
    Designer   Eric Read

7. Client   Slave
    Designer   Eric Read

(opposite)
Design Firm DYNAPAC Design Group

    Client   ClassMate, Inc.
    Designer   Lee A. Aellig

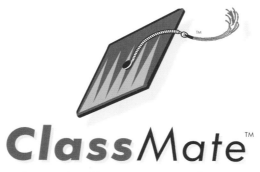

ClassMate™

Curricular Management Software

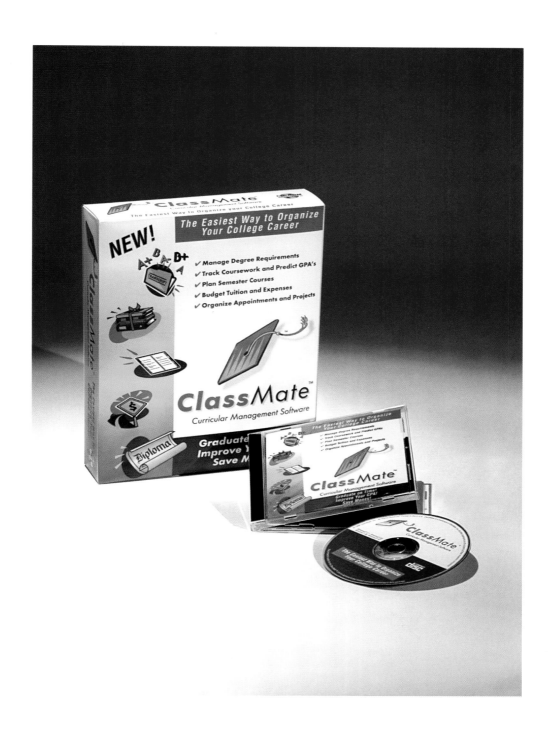

1.

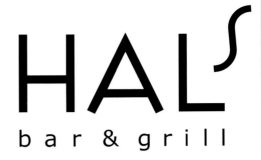

AT&T

2.

HAL's
bar & grill

3.

NOMADIX

4.

m**e**dschool.com

5.

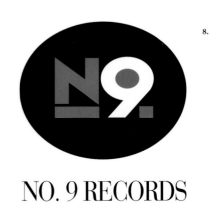

BEVERLY HILLS
FARMERS MARKET

6.

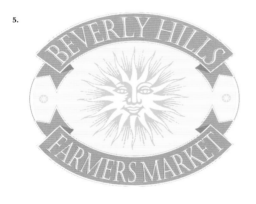

HealthVest.com

7.

NetZero™

8.

N9.

NO. 9 RECORDS

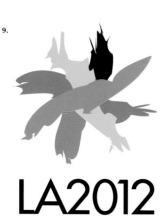

9.

LA2012

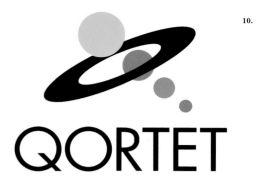

10.

QORTET

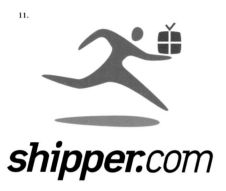

11.

shipper.com

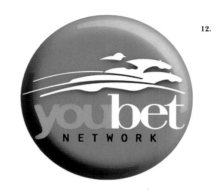

12.

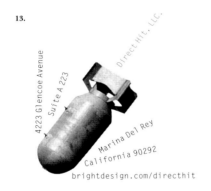

13.

Direct Hit, LLC.
4223 Glencoe Avenue
Suite A 223
Marina Del Rey
California 90292
brightdesign.com/directhit

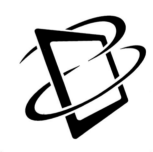

14.

Streamaster

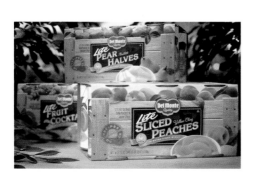

15.

1 - 13
Design Firm Bright Strategic Design
14
Design Firm McNulty & Co.
15
Design Firm SBG Enterprises

1. Client   AT&T Corporation
    Designers   Keith Bright & Chad White

2. Client   Hal's Bar & Grill
    Designer   Keith Bright

3. Client   Nomadix
    Designers   Keith Bright & Weina Dinata

4. Client   Medschool.com
    Designers   Keith Bright & Stephanie Tsao

5. Client   Beverly Hills Farmers Market
    Designers   Keith Bright & Weina Dinata

6. Client   HealthVest.com
    Designers   Keith Bright & Weina Dinata

7. Client   Netzero Inc.
    Designers   Keith Bright & Stephanie Tsao

8. Client   No. 9 Records
    Designer   Keith Bright

9. Client   Los Angeles
                   Olympic Committee
    Designer   Keith Bright

10. Client   Qorus.com
    Designers   Keith Bright & Denis Parkhurst

11. Client   Shipper.com
    Designers   Keith Bright & Denis Parkhurst

12. Client   You Bet Racing Network
    Designers   Keith Bright, Matthew Bright,
                   & Richard Vasquez

13. Client   Direct Hit
    Designer   Keith Bright

14. Client   Motorola Streamaster
    Designers   Brian Jacobson & Dan McNulty

15. Client   Del Monte Foods
    Designer   Mark Bergman

1.

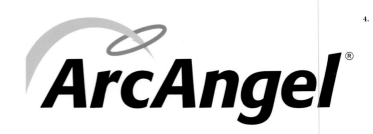

FIRSTENERGY
MILLENNIUM OF LIGHT
CLEVELAND 2000

2.

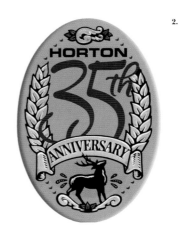

HORTON

35th

ANNIVERSARY

3.

Realty One | **Welcome Home**

Advantage
Program

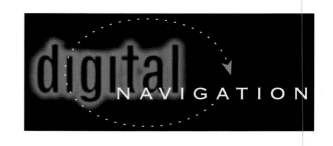

4.

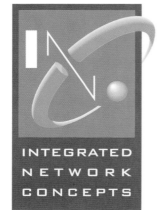

ArcAngel®

5.

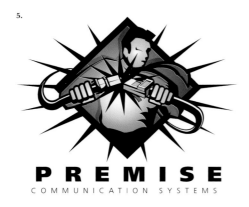

P R E M I S E
COMMUNICATION SYSTEMS

6.

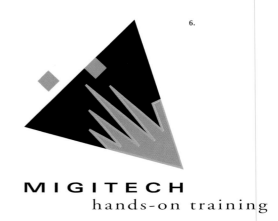

M I G I T E C H
hands-on training

7.

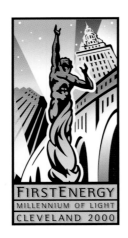

INTEGRATED
NETWORK
CONCEPTS

8.

digital
NAVIGATION

9.

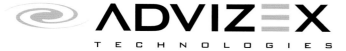

SKILLCRAFT™

10.

11.

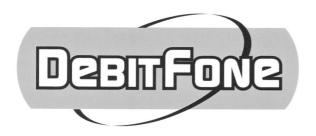

12.

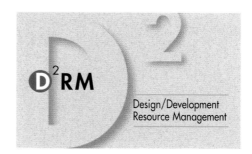

13.

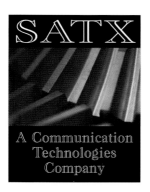

14.

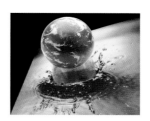

FURUTANI
USA · INC.

15.

LOUD

1 - 9				
Design Firm	**Stein and Company Communications**			
10 - 15				
Design Firm	**LOUDesign**			

1.	Client	First Energy	9.	Client	Advizex
	Designers	Susan Lesko, John Ferguson, & Jerome Yates		Designers	Susan Lesko, Diane Roberto, & Josh Stein
2.	Client	Horton Manufacturing	10.	Client	Suntech
	Designers	Susan Lesko, Jerome Yates, & Brian Sooy		Designers	Craig Loud, David Armstrong, Brennan Ishida, & Hui-suk Han
3.	Client	Realty One	11.	Client	DebitFone
	Designers	Susan Lesko & John Ferguson		Designers	Brennan Ishida, Craig Loud, Hui-suk Han, & David Armstrong
4.	Client	Arc Angel	12.	Client	D²RM
	Designer	John Ferguson		Designers	Hui-suk Han, Craig Loud, David Armstrong, & Brennan Ishida
5.	Client	Premise Communications Systems	13.	Client	SATX
	Designers	Susan Lesko & Randall Herrera		Designers	David Armstrong, Craig Loud, Hui-suk Han, & Brennan Ishida
6.	Client	Modern International Graphics	14.	Client	Furutani
	Designer	Susan Lesko		Designers	Brennan Ishida, Craig Loud, David Armstrong, & Hui-suk Han
7.	Client	Integrated Network Concepts	15.	Client	LOUDesign
	Designer	Susan Lesko		Designers	Craig Loud, David Armstrong, Brian Dalton, Brennan Ishida, & Hui-suk Han
8.	Client	Digital Navigation			
	Designer	Susan Lesko			

WOODSIDE
biomedical

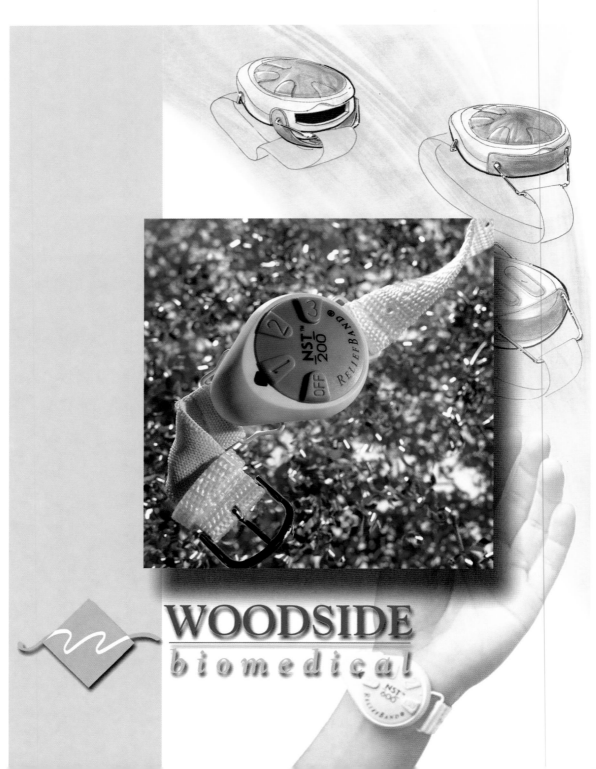

1.

TorreyView

Fine Furnishings and Design

2.

CLASSIC INTERIORS

3.

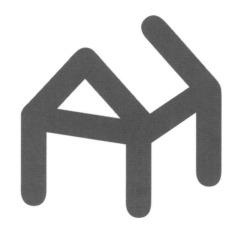

4.

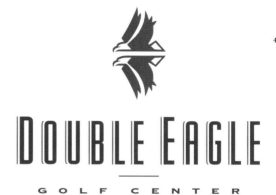

DOUBLE EAGLE

G O L F   C E N T E R

5.

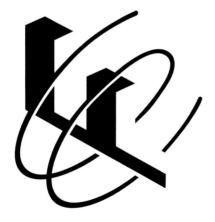

6.

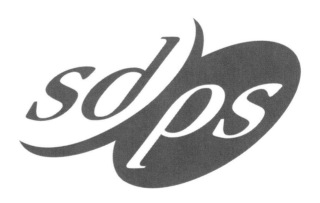

7.

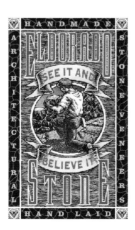

(opposite)
Design Firm **DYNAPAC Design Group**

Client   Woodside Biomedical, Inc.
Designer   Lee A. Aellig

1 - 7
Design Firm **Conover**

1. Client   Torrey View
    Designer   David Conover

2. Client   Classic Interiors
    Designers   Amy Williams & David Conover

3. Client   Addison Homes
    Designer   David Conover

4. Client   Double Eagle
    Designer   David Conover

5. Client   Fraseworks
    Designer   David Conover

6. Client   Sejersen Digital
                     Processing Services
    Designer   Carlos Avina

7. Client   El Dorado Stone
    Designers   David Conover, Carlos Avina,
                     & Amy Williams

1.

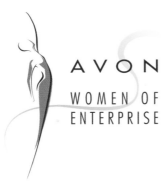

AVON
WOMEN OF
ENTERPRISE

AVON the company for women

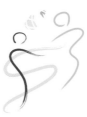

AVON
worldwide fund for
women's health

AVON the company for women

2.

3.

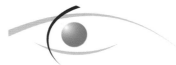

@AVON

AVON
the company for women

4.

5.

AVON

Women
inSight
Data base

6.

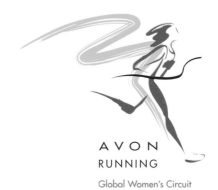

AVON
RUNNING

Global Women's Circuit

AVON the company for women

7.

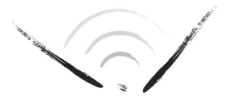

AVON
PRODUCTS
FOUNDATION

AVON the company for women

8.

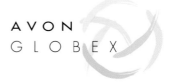

AVON
GLOBEX

GLOBAL EXCHANGE

AVON the company for women

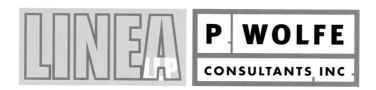

9.

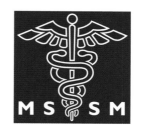

10.

MOUNT SINAI
SCHOOL OF
MEDICINE

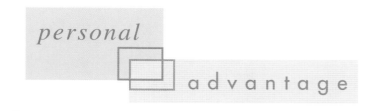

11.

the acme **idea** company LLC

12.

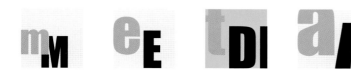

CCG metaMEDIA inc

13.

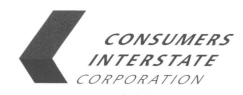

Revolutionizing
The Buying Process™

14.

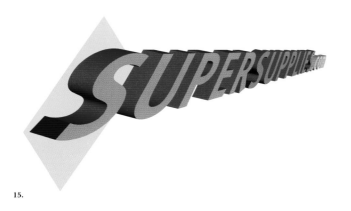

15.

(all)

Design Firm O & J Design, Inc.

1 - 8   Client   Avon Products, Inc.
Designers   Andrzej Olejniczak
& Heishin Ra

9. Client   P. Wolfe Consultants, Inc.
Designer   Andrzej Olejniczak

10. Client   Mount Sinai School of Medicine
Designers   Barbara Olejniczak
& Heishin Ra

11. Client   Avon Products, Inc.
Designers   Andrzej Olejniczak
& Heishin Ra

12. Client   The Acme Idea Company
Designers   Barbara Olejniczak
& Heishin Ra

13. Client   CCG MetaMedia, Inc.
Designers   Andrzej Olejniczak
& Christina Mueller

14. Client   Consumers Interstate
Corporation
Designers   Andrzej Olejniczak
& Lia Camara-Mariscal

15. Client   Consumer Interstate
Corporation
Designers   Andrzej Olejniczak
& Lia Camara-Mariscal

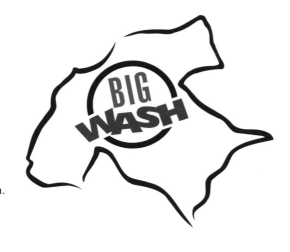

1.

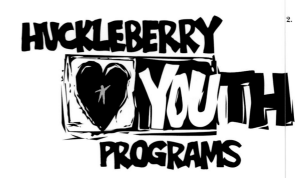

2.

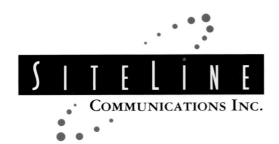

3.

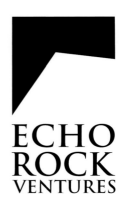

4.

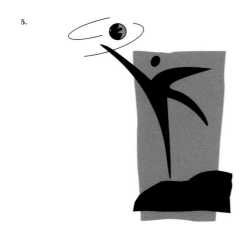

5.

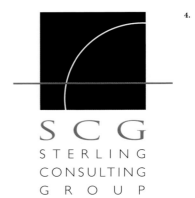

6.

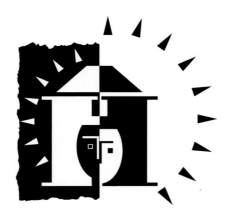

7.

1 - 7

Design Firm Clark Creative Group

1. Client   Big Wash
    Designers   Annemarie Clark & Craig Stout

2. Client   HuckleberryYouth Programs
    Designers   Annemarie Clark &
                Ozzie Patton

3. Client   Siteline Communications Inc.
    Designers   Annemarie Clark & Craig Stout

4. Client   Sterling Consulting Group
    Designers   Annemarie Clark
                & Thurlow Washam

5. Client   J. Eiting & Co.
    Designers   Annemarie Clark
                & Carol Piechocki

6. Client   Echo Rock Ventures
    Designers   Annemarie Clark
                & Thurlow Washam

7. Client   Hope Housing
    Designers   Annemarie Clark
                & Hiroko Chastain

(opposite)
Design Firm DYNAPAC Design Group

    Client   Experience Coffee
    Designer   Lee A. Aellig

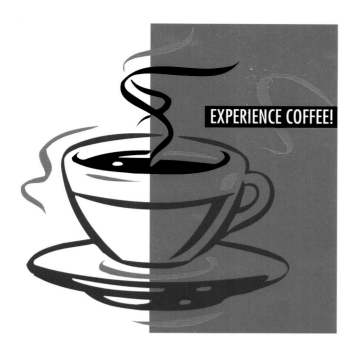

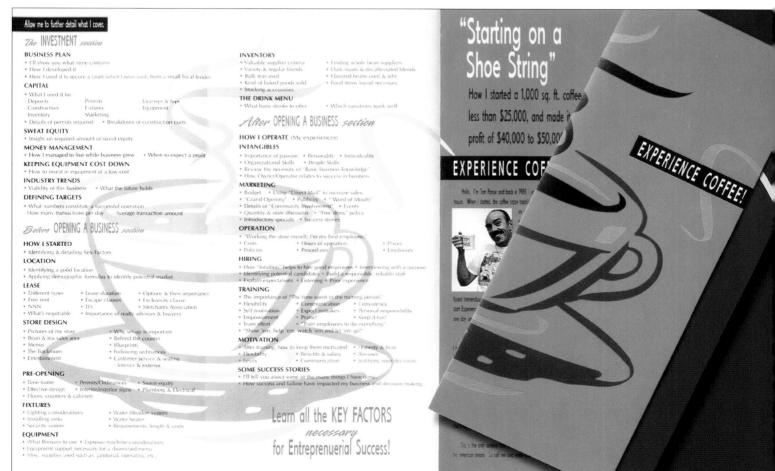

1.

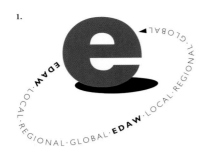

2.

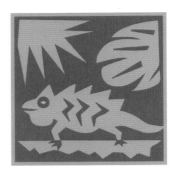

3.

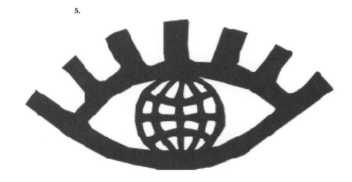

4.

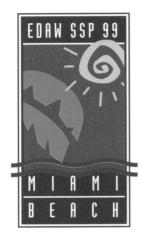

5.

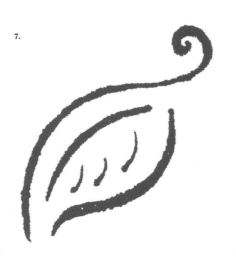

6.

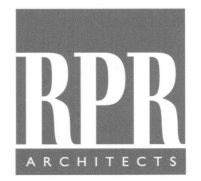

7.

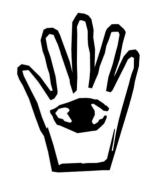

8.

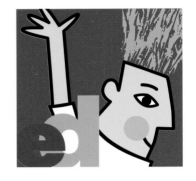

144

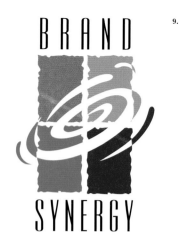

9.

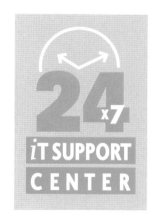

10.

11.

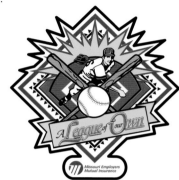

12.

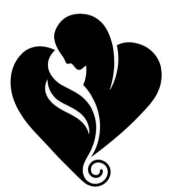

13.

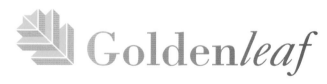

14.

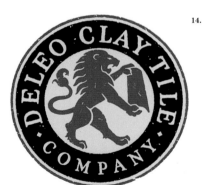

15.

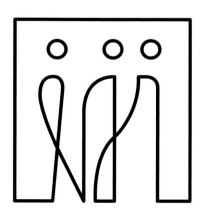

1 - 8					
Design Firm	**EDAW, Inc.**		7. Client		Kate Stickley
9 - 11					Landscape Architect
Design Firm	**Ervin Marketing**			Designer	Marty McGraw
	Creative Communications		8. Client		RPR Architects
12 - 13				Designer	Marty McGraw
Design Firm	**Julie Johnson Design**		9. Client		Brand Synergy
14				Designer	Erica Schwan
Design Firm	**Mires Design**				
15			10. Client		Visteon Information Technology/
Design Firm	**Doppelgänger, Inc.**	.			Ford Motor Company
				Designer	Erica Schwan
1. Client	EDAW Corporate Logo				
Designer	Marty McGraw		11. Client		Missouri Employers
					Mutual Insurance
2. Client	EDAW Principals Meeting 1998			Designer	Jean Corea
Designer	Marty McGraw				
			12. Client		Mclean County Prenatal Clinic
3. Client	EDAW Summer			Designer	Julie Johnson
	Student Program				
Designer	Marty McGraw		13. Client		Goldenleaf
				Designer	Julie Johnson
4. Client	EDAW Intranet				
Designer	Marty McGraw		14. Client		Deleo Clay Tile Company
				Designer	José Serrano, Miguel Perez,
5. Client	EDAW Human Resources Eye				& Dan Thoner
Designer	Marty McGraw				
			15. Client		Amana Corporation
6. Client	EDAW Human Resources Hand			Designer	Otto Steininger
Designer	Marty McGraw				

145

1.

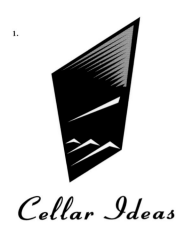

Cellar Ideas

2.

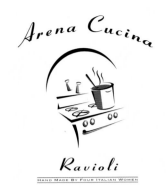

Arena Cucina

Ravioli

HAND MADE BY FOUR ITALIAN WOMEN

3.

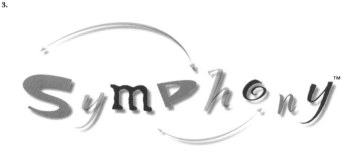

Symphony™

4.

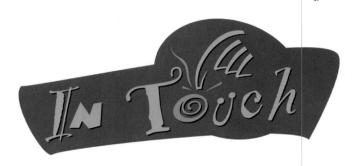

In Touch

5.

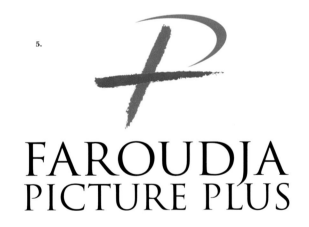

FAROUDJA
PICTURE PLUS

6.

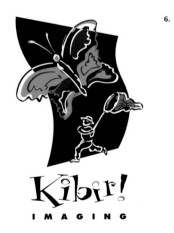

Kibir!
IMAGING

7.

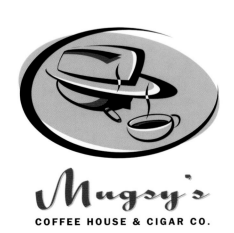

Mugsy's
COFFEE HOUSE & CIGAR CO.

8.

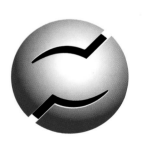

Silicon*Exchange*

9.

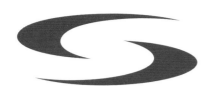

Synplicity®

10.

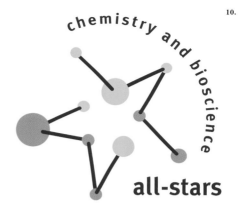

11.

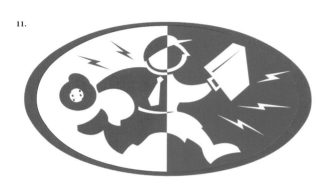

12.

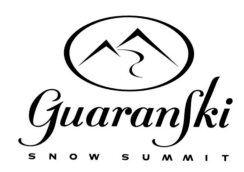

13.

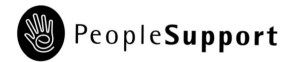

14.

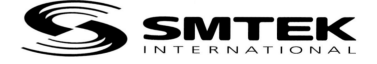

15.

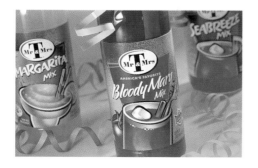

1 - 11
Design Firm Cellar Ideas
12 - 14
Design Firm McNulty & Co.
15
Design Firm SBG Enterprise

1. Client   Cellar Ideas
    Designer   Don Barnes

2. Client   Arena Cucina
    Designer   Don Barnes

3. Client   Proxim Symphony
    Designer   Don Barnes

4. Client   Applied Materials: In Touch
    Designer   Don Barnes

5. Client   Faroudja Picture Plus
    Designer   Don Barnes

6. Client   Kibir!
    Designer   Don Barnes

7. Client   Mugsy's
    Designer   Don Barnes

8. Client   SGI: Silicon Exchange
    Designer   Don Barnes

9. Client   Synplicity
    Designer   Don Barnes

10. Client   SGI: CBS all-stars
    Designer   Don Barnes

11. Client   SGI: Son 2 work
    Designer   Don Barnes

12. Client   Snow Summit
    Designer   Dan McNulty

13. Client   People Support
    Designers   Brian Jacobson & Dan McNulty

14. Client   SMTEK International
    Designers   Eugene Bustillos & Dan McNulty

15. Client   Cadbury Beverages, Inc.
    Designers   Mark Bergman & Jessie McAnulty

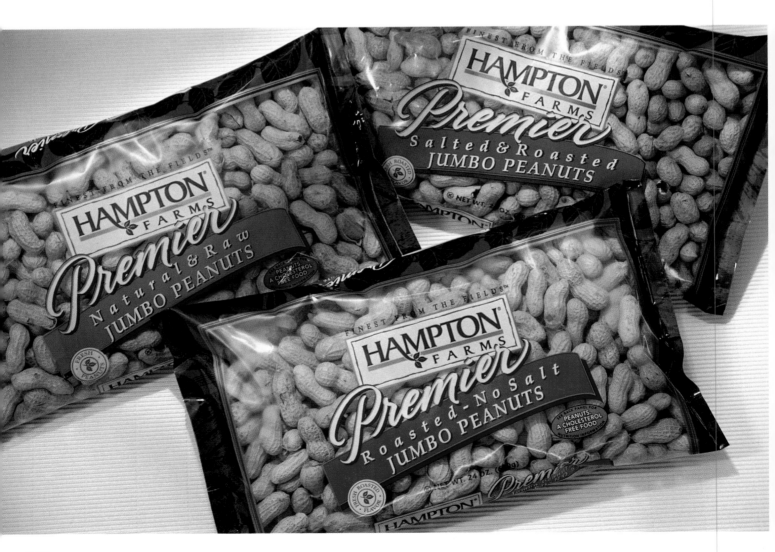

1.

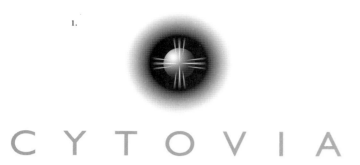

CYTOVIA

2.

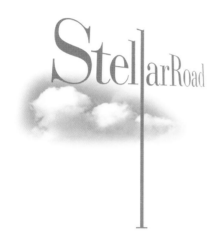

3.

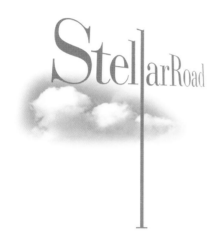

4.

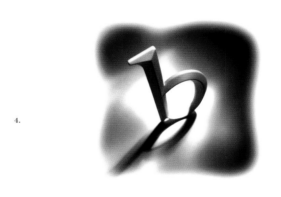

6.

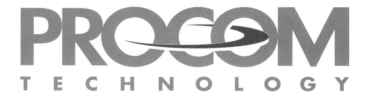

5.

7.

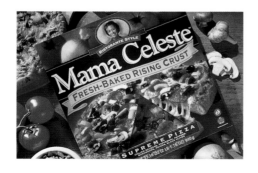

(opposite)
Design Firm Kollberg/Johnson

Client   Hampton Farms
Designer   Eileen Strauss

1 - 6
Design Firm Stoyan Design
7
Design Firm SBG Enterprise

1. Client   Cytovia
    Designer   Michael Stinson

2. Client   Virtrue
    Designer   Michael Stinson

3. Client   Stellar Road
    Designer   Michael Stinson

4. Client   Bell Photography
    Designer   Michael Stinson

5. Client   Global Technology
                Distribution Council
    Designer   Michael Stinson

6. Client   Procom Technology
    Designer   Michael Stinson

7. Client   Van de Kamp's
    Designers   Mark Bergman & Phillip Ting

1.

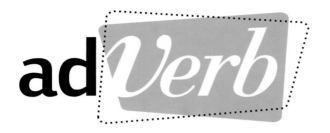

2.

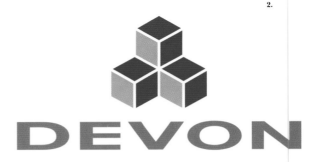

3.

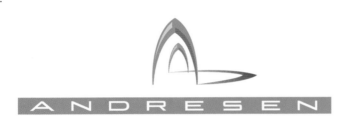

4.

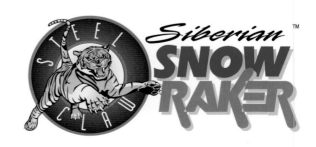

5.

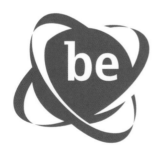

6.

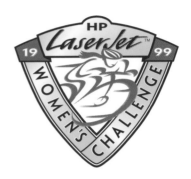

7.

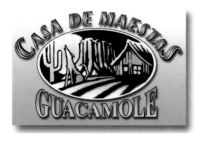

8.

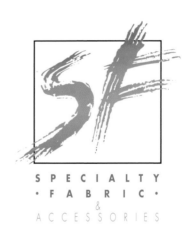

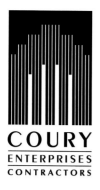

COURY
ENTERPRISES
CONTRACTORS

9.

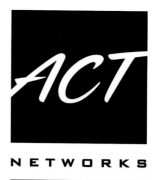

N E T W O R K S

10.

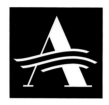

Alberstone Enterprises

11.

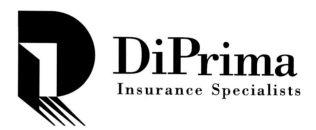

DiPrima
Insurance Specialists

12.

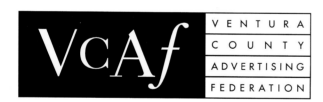

| V E N T U R A |
| C O U N T Y |
| A D V E R T I S I N G |
| F E D E R A T I O N |

13.

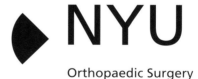

Orthopaedic Surgery

14.

NEW YORK UNIVERSITY

School of Continuing and
Professional Studies

15.

1 - 5
Design Firm be.
6 - 8
Design Firm DYNAPAC Design Group
9 - 13
Design Firm McNulty & Co.
14 - 15
Design Firm O & J Design, Inc.

1. Client   AdVerb
    Designer   Eric Read

2. Client   Devon
    Designers   Enrique Gaston & Eric Read

3. Client   Andresen
    Designer   Eric Read

4. Client   HP LaserJet Women's Challenge
    Designers   Will Burke & Yusuke Asaka

5. Client   be.
    Designers   Will Burke, Eric Read
                & Coralie Russo

6. Client   Specialty Fabric & Accessories
    Designer   Lee A. Aellig

7. Client   Casa De Maestas
    Designers   Lee A. Aellig & Jeff Maestas

8. Client   Innotech, LLC
    Designer   Lee A. Aellig

9. Client   Coury Enterprises
    Designers   Kristen Borg & Dan McNulty

10. Client   ACT Networks
    Designers   Mark Luscombe & Dan McNulty

11. Client   Alberstone Enterprises
    Designers   Mark Luscombe & Dan McNulty

12. Client   Di Prima Insurance
    Designers   Eugene Bustillos & Dan McNulty

13. Client   Ventura County
                Advertising Federation
    Designer   Dan McNulty

14. Client   New York University,
                Hospital for Joint Diseases
    Designers   Barbara Olejniczak & Heishin Ra

15. Client   New York University, School of
                Continuing & Professional Studies
    Designers   Andrzej Olejniczak, Christina
                Mueller & Leslie Nayman

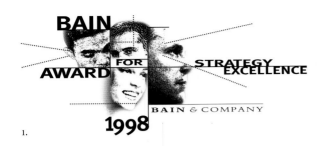

1.

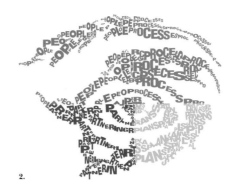

2.

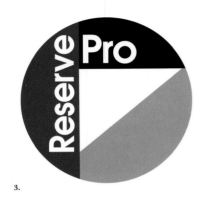

3.

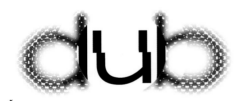

4.

6.

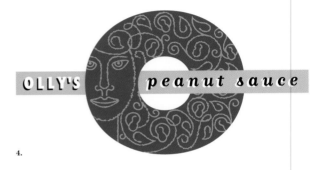

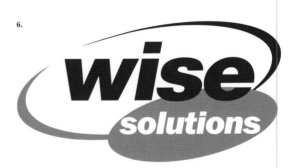

5.

7.

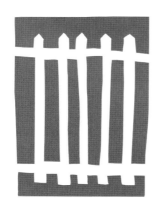

8.

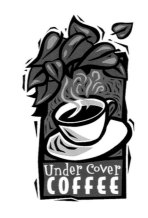

9.

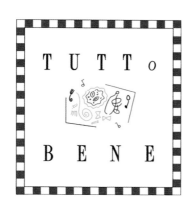

10.

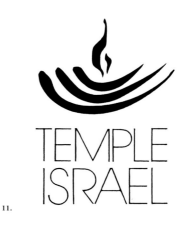

11.

12.

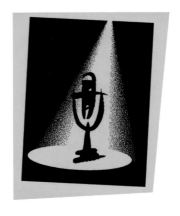

13.

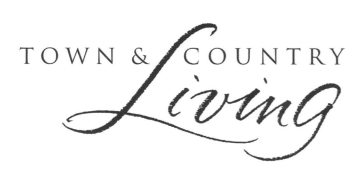

14.

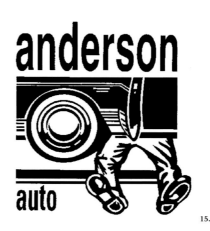

15.

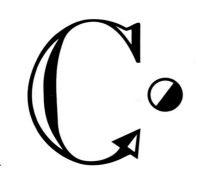

1.

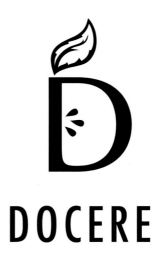

DOCERE

2.

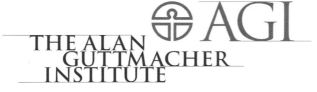

THE ALAN
GUTTMACHER
INSTITUTE

NEW YORK &
WASHINGTON

3.

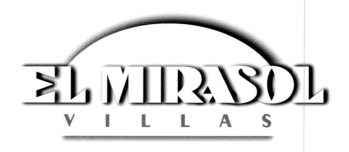

4.

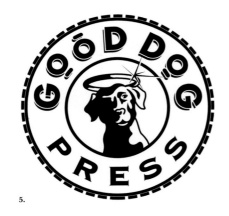

5.

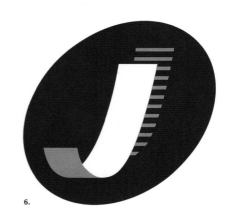

6.

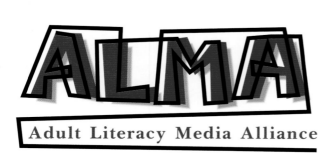

Adult Literacy Media Alliance

7.

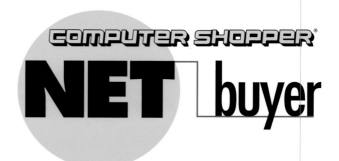

8.

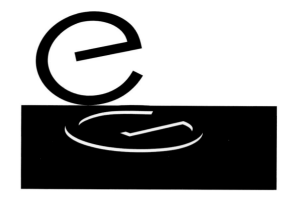

9.

10.

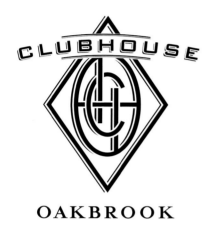

CLUBHOUSE

OAKBROOK

11.

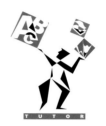

TUTOR

PUBLISHER   AUTHOR

12.

DENTAL CARE

13.

mayhem

14.

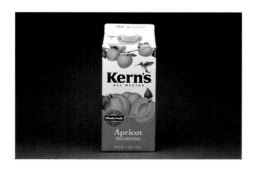

15.

1 - 11
Design Firm Edward Walter Design, Inc.
12 - 14
Design Firm Clark Creative Group
15
Design Firm SBG Enterprise

1. Client   Counterpoint
                    Capital Management
    Designer   Per Evander

2. Client   Docere Studios
    Designer   Edward Walter

3. Client   The Alan Guttmacher Institute
    Designer   Martin Brynell

4. Client   El Mirasol Villas
    Designer   Martin Brynell

5. Client   Good Dog Press
    Designer   Edward Walter

6. Client   Jamestowm Packing + Display
    Designer   Manfred Junkert

7. Client   Alma
    Designer   Yuly Monsanto

8. Client   Computer Shopper Net Buyer
    Designer   Martin Brynell

9. Client   Prescient Energy Corp.
    Designer   Manfred Junkert

10. Client   Goller Productions Ink
    Designers   Edward Walter & Yuly Monsanto

11. Client   The Clubhouse
    Designer   Edward Walter

12. Client   Oracle Corporation
    Designers   Annemarie Clark
                    & Thurlow Washam

13. Client   Dr. Baglio D.D.S.
    Designers   Annemarie Clark & Kelly Clark

14. Client   Mayhem Productions
    Designer   Annemarie Clark

15. Client   Nestle, USA
    Designers   Mark Bergman & Laura Cramer

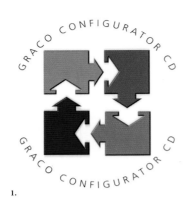

1.

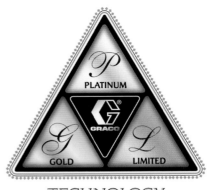

2.

TECHNOLOGY
DISTRIBUTOR PROGRAM

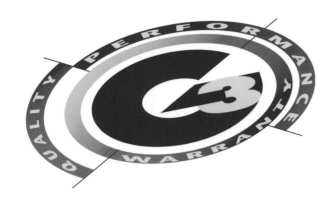

3.

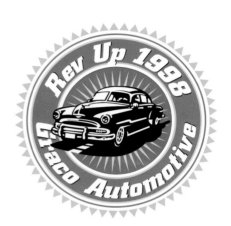

4.

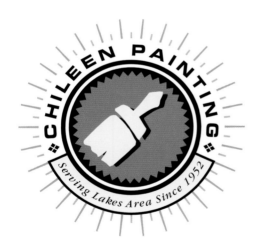

5.

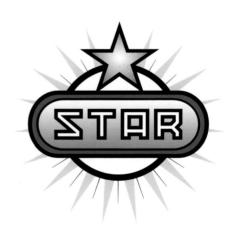

6.

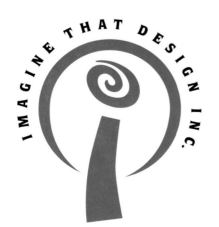

7.

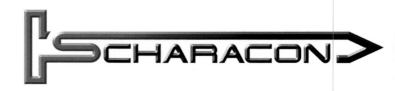

8.

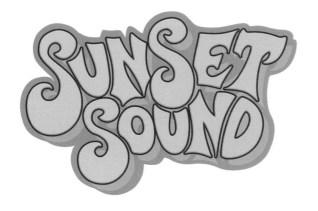

9.

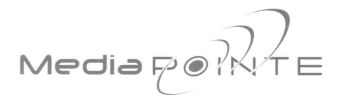

10.

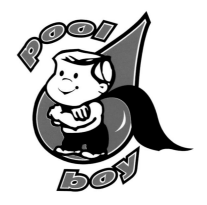

11.

12.

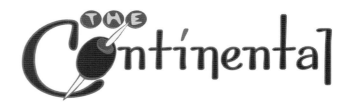

13.

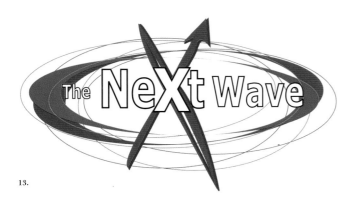

14.

The
Fitness Choice

15.

1 - 4
Design Firm Graco Advertising
5 - 8
Design Firm Imagine That Design
9 - 15
Design Firm [i]e design

1, 2
Client   Graco Industrial Division
Designer   Gary Schmidt

3. Client   Contractor Equip Division,
                Graco Inc
    Designer   Gary Schmidt

4. Client   Graco Automotive Division
    Designer   Gary Schmidt

5. Client   Chileen Painting
    Designer   Terry Austin

6. Client   Star Cleaning
    Designer   Terry Austin

7. Client   Imagine That Design
    Designer   Gary Schmidt

8. Client   Scharacon General Contractors
    Designer   Terry Austin

9. Client   Sunset Sound
    Designers   Marcie Carson, Mirjam Selmi,
                & David Gilmour

10. Client   MediaPointe
    Designers   Cya Nelson & Marcie Carson

11. Client   The Continental
    Designer   Cya Nelson

12. Client   The Continental Olive Restaurant
    Designer   David Gilmour

13. Designer   David Gilmour

14. Client   Pool Boy
    Designer   Marcie Carson

15. Client   Fitness Choice
    Designers   Marcie Carson & David Gilmour

157

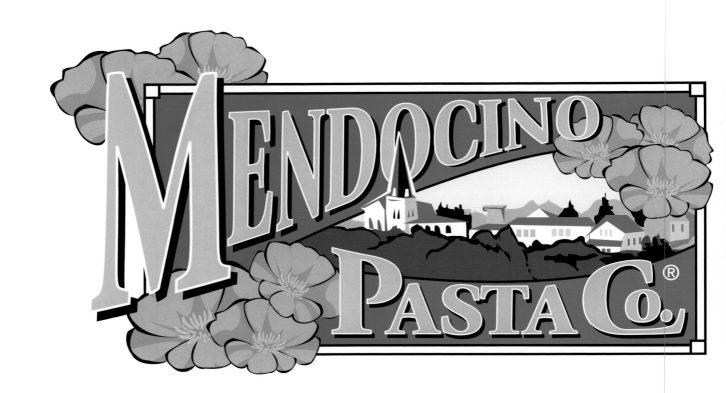

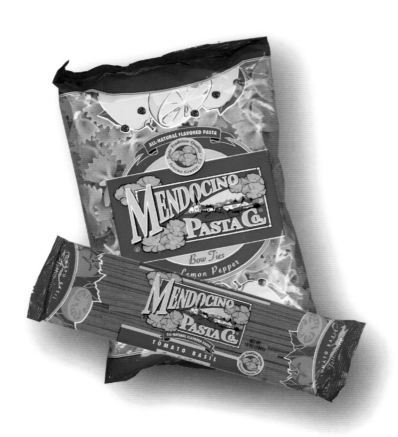

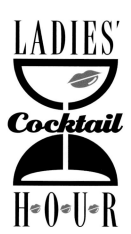

1.

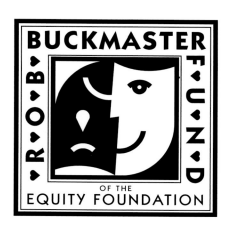

2.

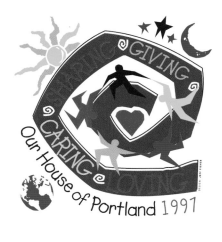

3.

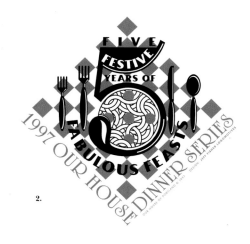

4.

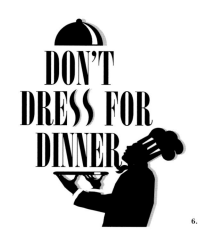

5.

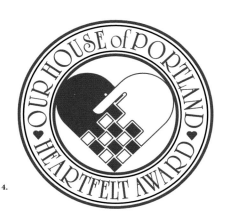

6.

7.

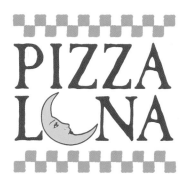

(opposite)
Design Firm JC Design

Client   Mendocino Pasta Inc.
Designer   James Cardell

1 - 7
Design Firm Jeff Fisher LogoMotives

1. Client   Rob Buckmaster Fund
    Designer   Jeff Fisher

2. Client   Our House of Portland
    Designer   Jeff Fisher

3 - 4
    Client   Our House of Portland
    Designer   Jeff Fisher

5. Client   Ladies' Cocktail Hour
    Designer   Jeff Fisher

6. Client   triangle productions!
    Designer   Jeff Fisher

7. Client   Pizza Luna
    Designer   Jeff Fisher

1.

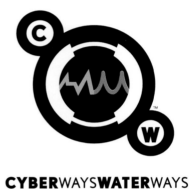

2.

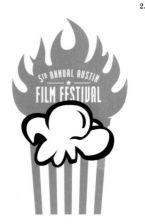

3.

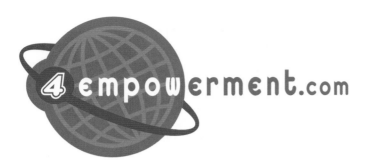

4.

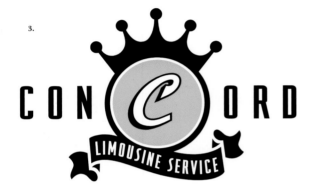

5.

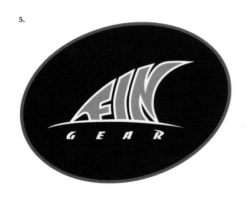

6.

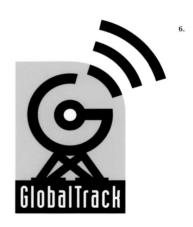

7.

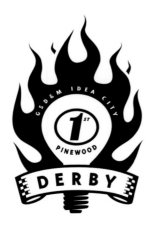

8.

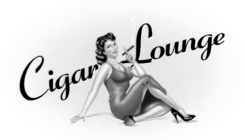

9.

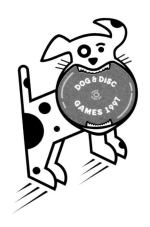

10.

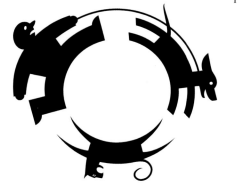

11.

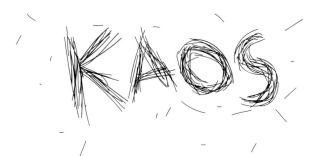

12.

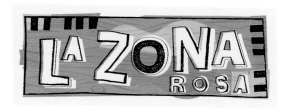

13.

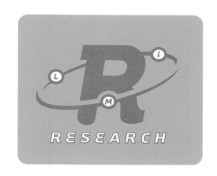

14.

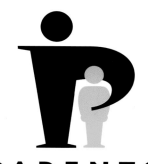

PARENTS
ANONYMOUS

15.

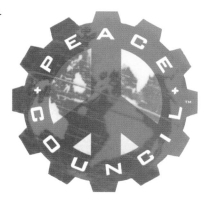

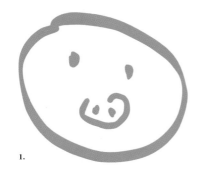

1.

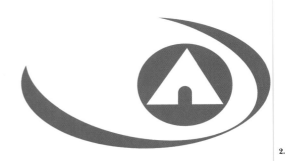

2.

3.

4.

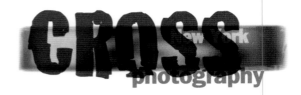

5.

6.

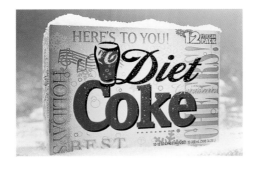

7.

1, 4
Design Firm Product 101
2, 3
Design Firm Rowan & Martin Design
5, 6
Design Firm Ayse Celem
7
Design Firm SBG Enterprises

1. Client   Happy Capitalist Productions
    Designer   Ayse Celem

2. Client   Airwalk-WalMart
    Designer   Ayse Celem

3. Client   Sportzine
    Designer   Ayse Celem

4. Client   Dave Cross Photography
    Designer   Ayse Celem

5. Client   Atwood Day Sail
    Designer   Ayse Celem

6. Client   Ayse Celem Design
    Designer   Ayse Celem

7. Client   The Coca-Cola Company
    Designers   Mark Bergman, Margaret Lee,
                  & Laura Cramer

(opposite)
    Design Firm Cathey Associates, Inc.

    Client   Jwana Juice
    Designer   Isabel Campos

162

Jwana Juice

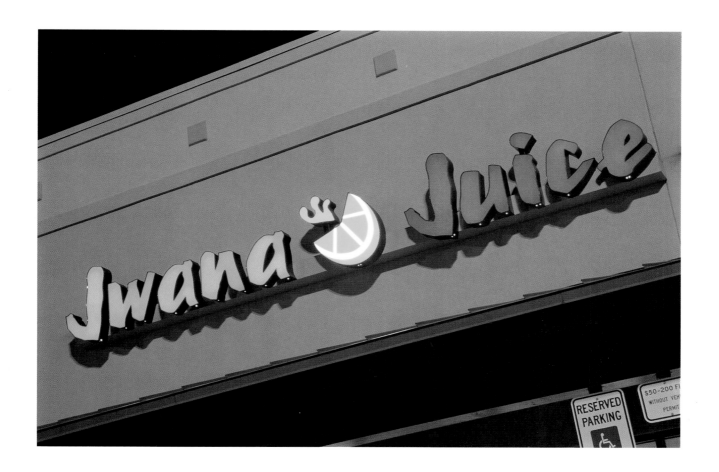

1.

belyea.

VANDER HOUWEN PUBLIC RELATIONS

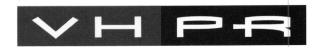

2.

3.

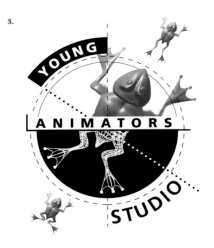

4.

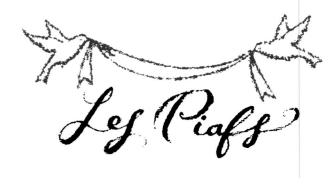

5.

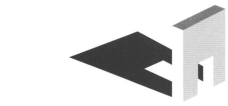

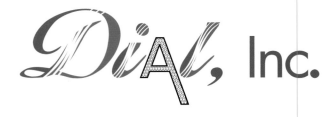

6.

7.

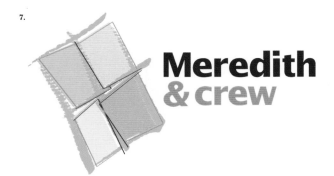

8.

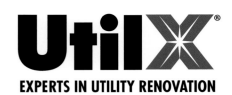

164

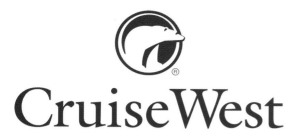

CruiseWest

9.

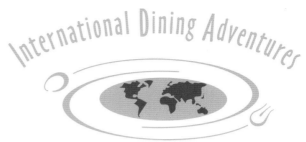

10.

12.

11.

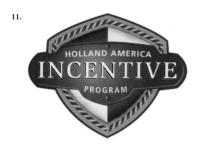

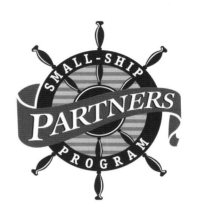

14.

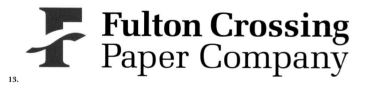

Fulton Crossing
Paper Company

MAISON
DE
FRANCE

13.

15.

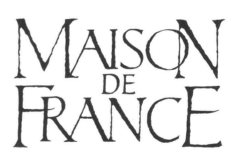

GeoTrust SM

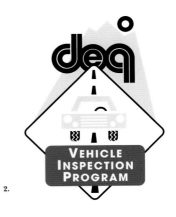

Kay Johnson's Sing Out Productions

1.

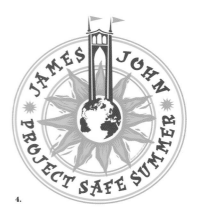

Vehicle Inspection Program

2.

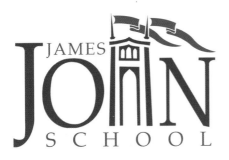

JAMES JOHN SCHOOL

3.

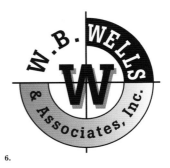

JAMES JOHN PROJECT SAFE SUMMER

4.

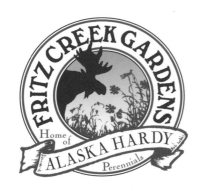

FRITZ CREEK GARDENS Home of **ALASKA HARDY** Perennials

5.

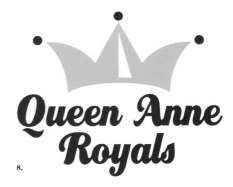

W.B. WELLS & Associates, Inc.

6.

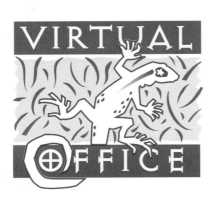

VIRTUAL OFFICE

7.

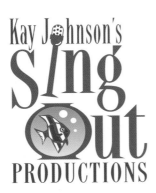

Queen Anne Royals

8.

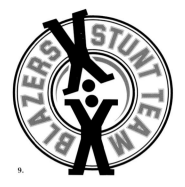

9.

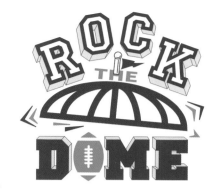

10.

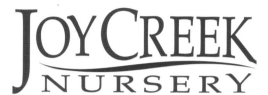

11.

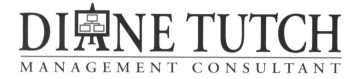

12.

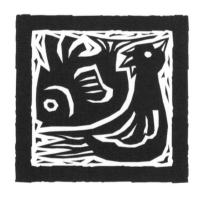

13.

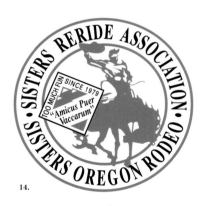

14.

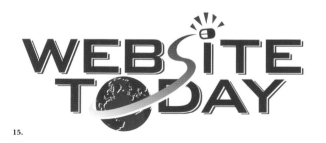

15.

(all)

Design Firm **Jeff Fisher LogoMotives**

1. Client — Kay Johnson's Sing Out Productions
   Designer — Jeff Fisher

2. Client — Oregon Dept. of Environmental Quality
   Designers — Jeff Fisher & Marcia Danab

3, 4
   Client — James John School
   Designer — Jeff Fisher

5. Client — Frit Creek Gardens
   Designer — Jeff Fisher

6. Client — W.B. Wells & Associates
   Designers — Jeff Fisher & Esther Lorance

7. Client — Virtual Office
   Designer — Jeff Fisher

8. Client — Queen Anne Royals
   Designer — Jeff Fisher

9. Client — Portland Trail Blazers
   Designers — Jeff Fisher & Sara Perrin

10. Client — Seattle Seahawks
    Designers — Jeff Fisher & Sara Perrin

11. Client — Joy Creek Nursery
    Designer — Jeff Fisher

12. Client — Diane Tutch
    Designer — Jeff Fisher

13. Client — Kristin & Tim Kelly
    Designer — Jeff Fisher

14. Client — Sisters Reride Association
    Designer — Jeff Fisher

15. Client — Website Today
    Designer — Jeff Fisher

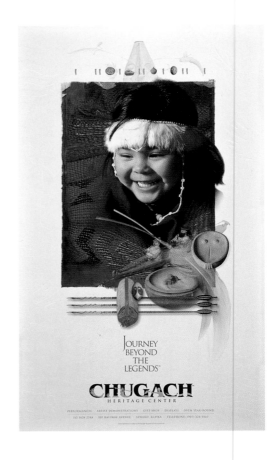

CHUGACH℠
HERITAGE CENTER

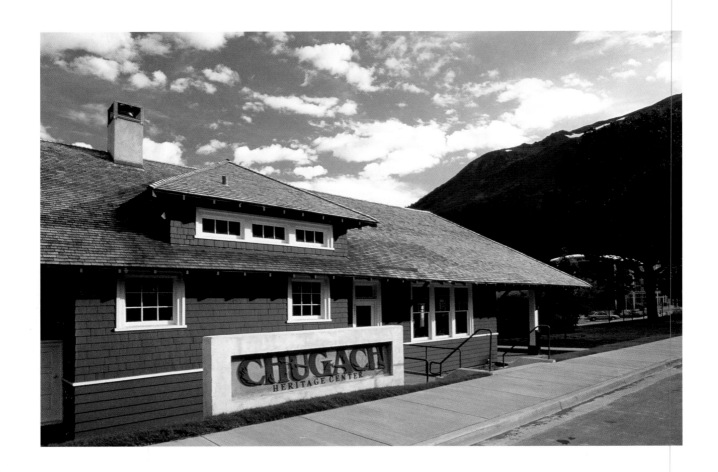

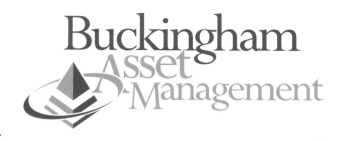

1.

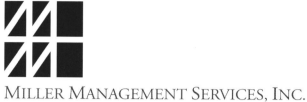

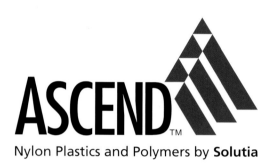

3.

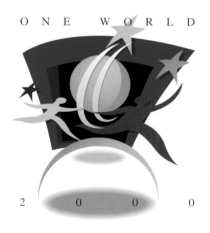

4.

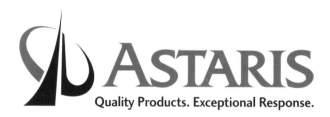

6.

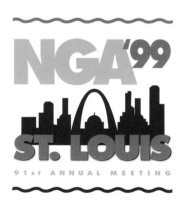

7.

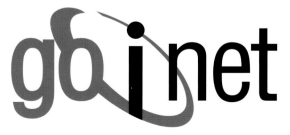

www.goinet.com

(opposite)
Design Firm Walsh & Associates, Inc.

Client   Chugach Heritage
              Center/Alaska
Designer   Miriam Lisco

1 - 7
Design Firm Stan Gellman
**   Graphic Design Inc.**

1. Client   Buckingham Asset Management
    Designers   Chris Reifschneider
                & Barry Tilson

2. Client   Miller Management
    Designers   Barry Tilson & Erin Goter

3. Client   Solutia
    Designers   Barry Tilson & Jill Lampen

4. Client   Astaris
    Designers   Mike Donovan & Barry Tilson

5. Client   1999 National
                Governor's Association
    Designers   Mike Donovan & Barry Tilson

6. Client   Promotional Consultants/
                The Peernet Group
    Designers   Barry Tilson & Mike Donovan

7. Client   Goinet
    Designers   Erin Goter & Barry Tilson

1.

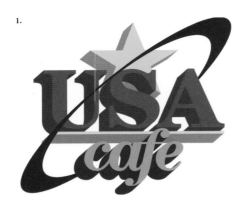

2.

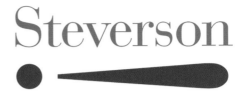

3.

SECOND
BAPTIST
CHURCH

4.

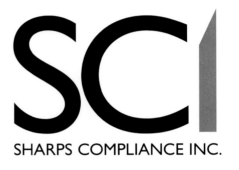

SHARPS COMPLIANCE INC.

5.

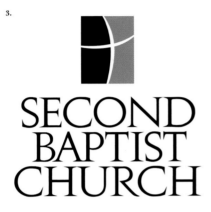

Med Synergies

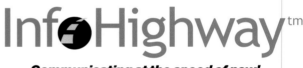

Communicating at the speed of now!

6.

7.

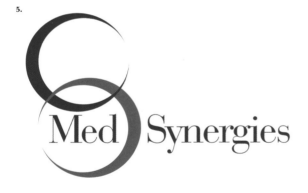

Integrated
Electrical
Services

8.

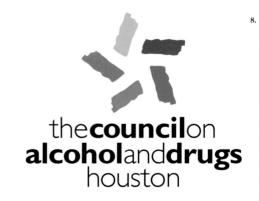

the council on
alcohol and drugs
houston

170

9.

Cornerstone Solutions

10.

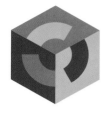

centegra™

11.

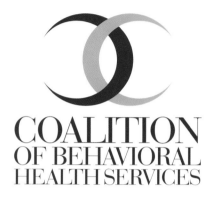

COALITION
OF BEHAVIORAL
HEALTH SERVICES

12.

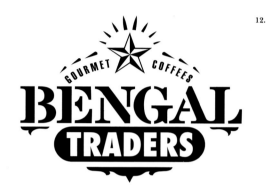

13.

ASSOCIATED COUNSEL of AMERICA℠

14.

Oiltanking

15.

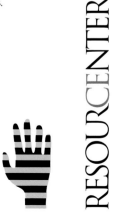

RESOURCENTER

(all)
		Design Firm	Loucks & Johnson

1.	Client	USA Cafe
	Designers	Tim Johnson & Jay Loucks

2.	Client	Steverson Staffing Services
	Designers	Tim Johnson & Jay Loucks

3.	Client	Second Baptist Church
	Designers	Tim Johnson & Jay Loucks

4.	Client	Sharps Compliance
	Designers	Tim Johnson & Jay Loucks

5.	Client	MedSynergies
	Designers	Tim Johnson & Jay Loucks

6.	Client	InfoHighway
	Designers	Tim Johnson & Jay Loucks

7.	Client	Integrated Electrical Services
	Designers	Tim Johnson & Jay Loucks

8.	Client	The Council on Alcohol and Drugs
	Designers	Tim Johnson & Jay Loucks

9.	Client	Cornerstone Solutions
	Designers	Tim Johnson & Jay Loucks

10.	Client	Centegra
	Designers	Tim Johnson & Jay Loucks

11.	Client	Coalition of Behavioral Health Services
	Designers	Tim Johnson & Jay Loucks

12.	Client	Exxon
	Designers	Tim Johnson & Jay Loucks

13.	Client	Associated Counsel of America
	Designers	Tim Johnson & Jay Loucks

14.	Client	Oiltanking
	Designers	Tim Johnson & Jay Loucks

15.	Client	Resource Center
	Designers	Tim Johnson & Jay Loucks

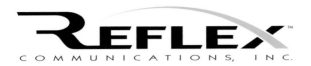

1.

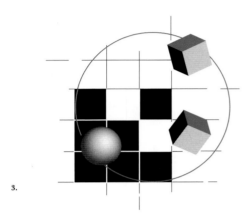

Seattle Children's *home*

2.

3.

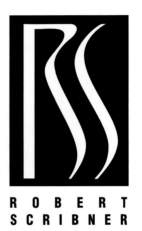

ROBERT
SCRIBNER

4.

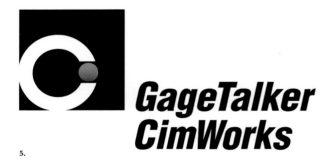

GageTalker
CimWorks

5.

SAKSON & TAYLOR

6.

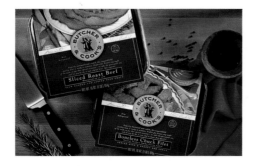

7.

1 - 6
Design Firm Walsh & Associates

7
Design Firm SBG Enterprise

1. Client   Reflex Communications
   Designers   Mark Ely & Miriam Lisco

2. Client   Seattle Children's Home
   Designer   Miriam Lisco

3. Client   Parker Le Pla,
               Brand Development
   Designer   Miriam Lisco

4. Client   Robert Scribner Salon
   Designers   Miriam Lisco & Glen Yoshiyama

5. Client   GageTalker CimWorks
   Designer   Miriam Lisco

6. Client   Sakson & Taylor
   Designer   Miriam Lisco

7. Client   Excel Corp.
   Designer   Mark Bergman

(opposite)
Design Firm Walsh & Associates, Inc.

Client   PC Fixx
Designer   Miriam Lisco

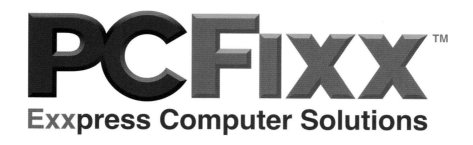

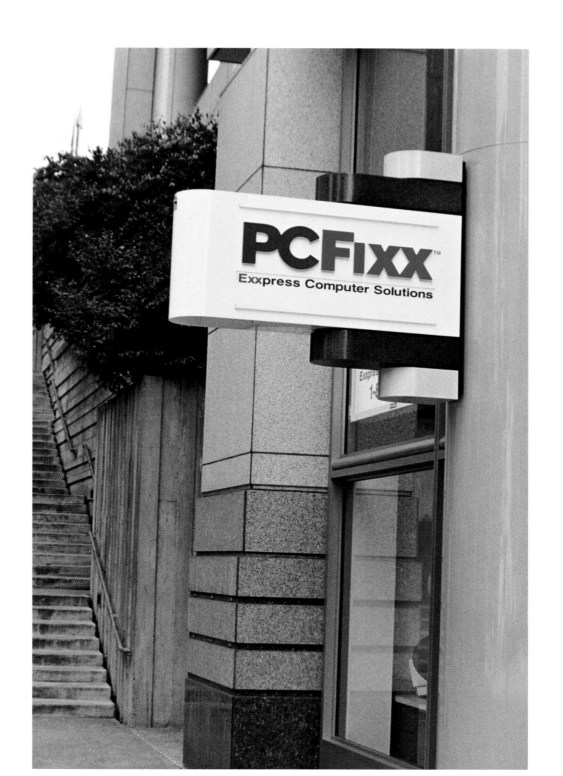

1.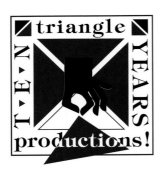

2.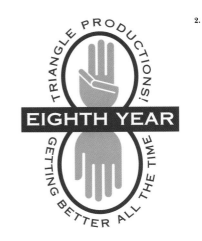

3.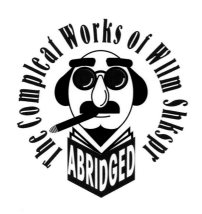

4.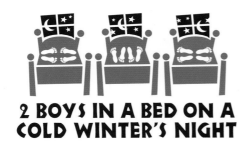

5.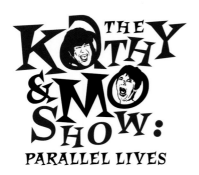

6.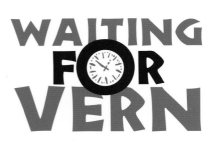

7.

8.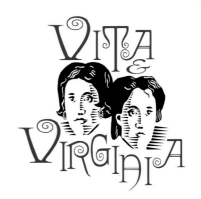

9.

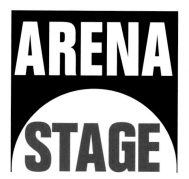

10.

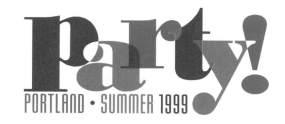

11.

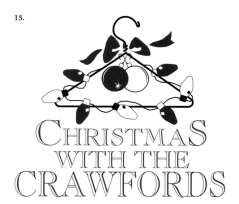

12.

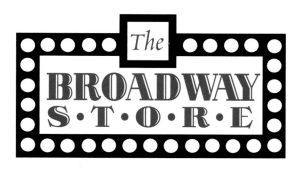

13.

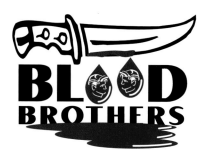

14.

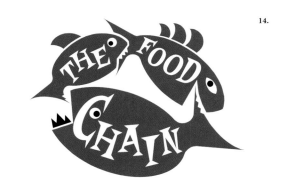

15.

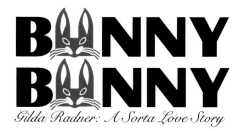

(all)
Design Firm Jeff FisherLogoMotives

1 - 15
   Client   triangle productions!
   Designer   Jeff Fisher

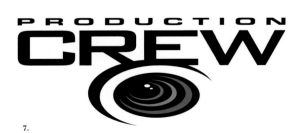

1.

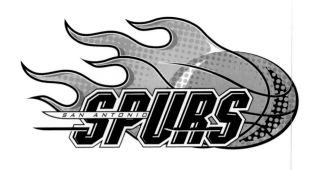

2.

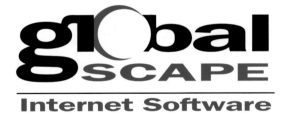

3.

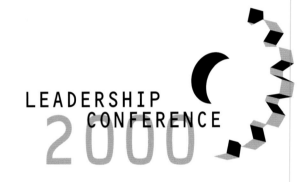

4.

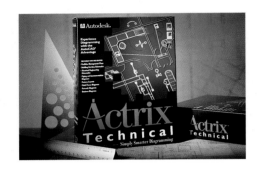

5.

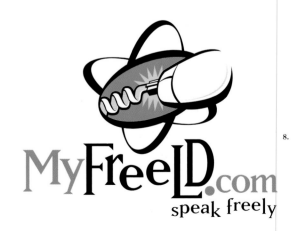

6.

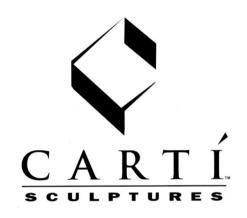

7.

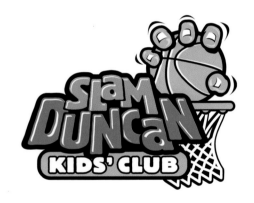

8.

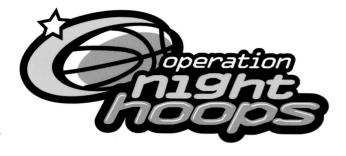

9.

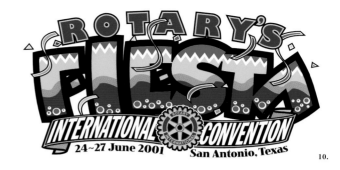

10.

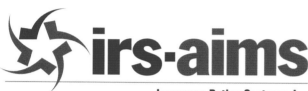

11.

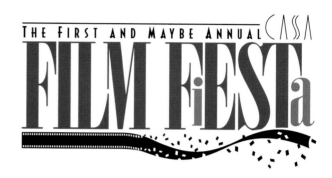

12.

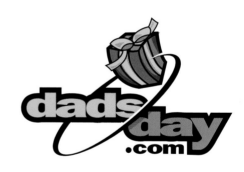

13.

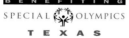

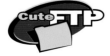

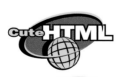

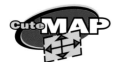

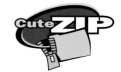

14.

15.

1
Design Firm **SBG Enterprises**
2 - 15
Design Firm **Creative Link Studio, Inc.**

1. Client   Autodesk
   Designers Mark Bergman, Richard
              Patterson & Iratxe Mumford

2. Client   San Antonio Spurs/
             Harley Silent Auction
   Designers Mark Broderick, Kyle Derr,
              & Kevin La Rue

3. Client   Carti Paper Sculptures
   Designers Kyle Derr, Kevin La Rue,
              & Mark Broderick

4. Client   Racquetball & Fitness Clubs
   Designers Kyle Derr, Kevin La Rue,
              & Mark Broderick

5. Client   Global Scape
   Designers Kyle Derr, Mark Broderick,
              & Kevin La Rue

6. Client   Kids Sports Network
   Designers Kyle Derr, Mark Broderick, &
              Kevin La Rue

7. Client   Production Crew
   Designers Kyle Derr, Kevin La Rue,
              & Mark Broderick

8. Client   My Free LD.com
   Designers Kyle Derr, Kevin La Rue
              & Mark Broderick

9. Client   Kids Sports Network
   Designers Kyle Derr, Mark Broderick,
              & Kevin LaRue

10. Client   Rotary International
    Designers Mark Broderick, Kyle Derr,
              & Kevin LaRue

11. Client   IRS-AIMS
    Designers Kevin LaRue, Mark Broderick,
              & Kyle Derr

12. Client   Communications Arts Society
             of San Antonio
    Designers Mark Broderick, Kevin LaRue,
              & Kyle Derr

13. Client   Special Olympics Texas
    Designers Kyle Derr, Kevin LaRue,
              & Mark Broderick

14. Client   Dads Day.com
    Designers Kyle Derr, Kevin LaRue,
              & Mark Broderick

15. Client   Global Scape Products
    Designers Kyle Derr, Kevin LaRue,
              & Mark Broderick

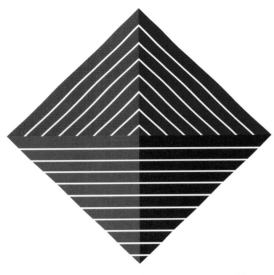

Advanced Network Technologies, Inc.

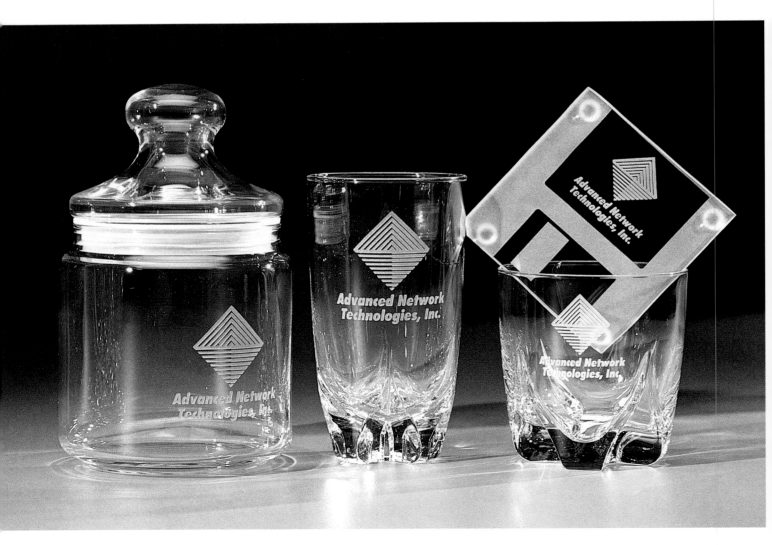

1.

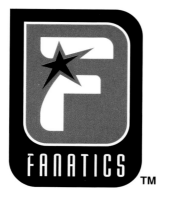

2.

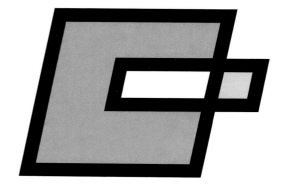

3.

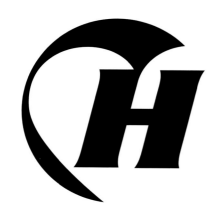

4.

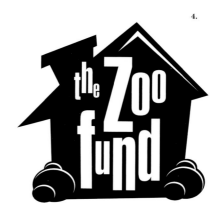

5.

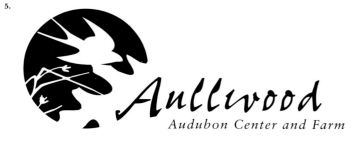

6.

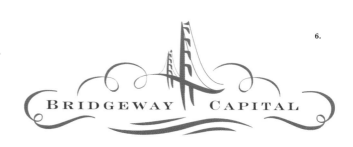

7.

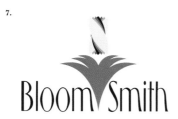

(opposite)
Design Firm Cathey Associates, Inc.

Client   Advanced Network
               Technologies, Inc.
Designer   Gordon Cathey

1 - 5
Design Firm Visual Marketing
**   Associates, Inc.**
6
Design Firm Lori Powell Design Exploration
7
Design Firm Cathey Associates, Inc.

1. Client   Telestar Interactive Corporation
    Designer   Tom Davie

2. Client   CYND Snowboard Apparel
    Designer   Jason Selke

3. Client   Heartland Airlines
    Designer   Lynn Sampson

4. Client   Columbus Zoo
    Designer   Tom Davie

5. Client   Aullwood Audubon Center
               and Farm
    Designer   Michael Butts

6. Client   Bridgeway Capital
    Designer   Lori Powell

7. Client   BloomSmith
    Designer   Matt Westapher

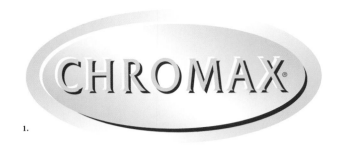

1.

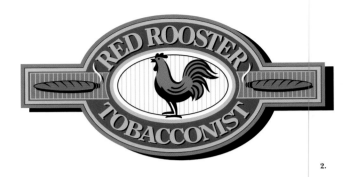

2.

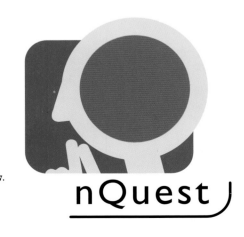

3.

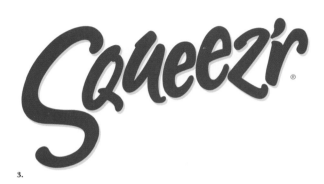

4.

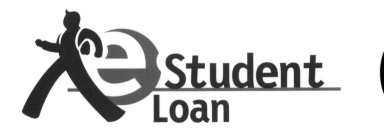

5.

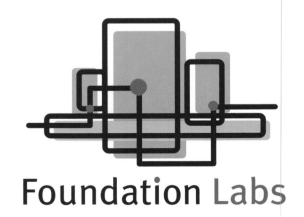

6.

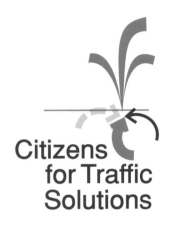

7.

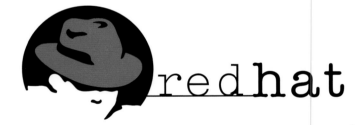

8.

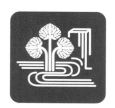

R E G I O N

9.

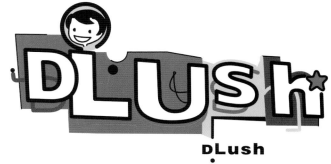

DLush

10.

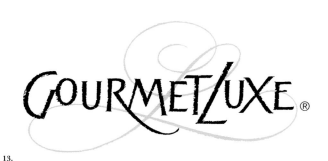

Potomac Marine

11.

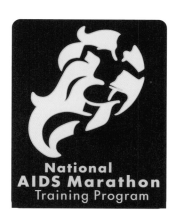

National
AIDS Marathon
Training Program

12.

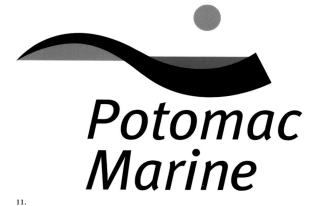

GOURMETLUXE ®

13.

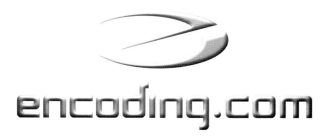

encoding.com

14.

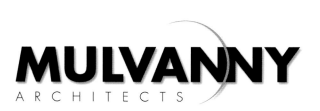

MULVANNY
ARCHITECTS

15.

1 - 3
Design Firm Kollberg/Johnson
4 - 12
Design Firm Blank
13 - 15
Design Firm Walsh & Associates, Inc.

1. Client   Ambi Inc.
   Designers   Kollberg/Johnson

2. Client   Red Rooster Tobacconist
   Designer   Gary Kollberg

3. Client   Brooklyn Bottling
   Designer   Eileen Strauss

4. Client   end gridlock.com
   Designers   Robert Kent Wilson
                 & Susan Burch Ahlers

5. Client   e student loan
   Designers   Robert Kent Wilson
                 & Suzanne Ultman

6. Client   Red Hat Software
   Designers   Robert Kent Wilson, Suzanne
                 Ultman & Adam Cohn

7. Client   Natural Question Technology
   Designer   Robert Kent Wilson

8. Client   Foundation Labs
   Designer   Robert Kent Wilson

9. Client   Responsible Economic Growth
                 In Our Nation
   Designer   Robert Kent Wilson

10. Client   Dlush
    Designers   Robert Kent Wilson
                 & Suzanne Ultman

11. Client   Potomac Marine
    Designer   Robert Kent Wilson

12. Client   Walk the Talk Productions
    Designers   Robert Kent Wilson, Suzanne
                 Ultman & Adam Cohn

13. Client   GourmetLuxe
    Designer   Miriam Lisco

14. Client   Encoding.com
    Designers   Mark Ely & Miriam Lisco

15. Client   Mulvanny Architects
    Designers   Lyn Blanchard &Miriam Lisco

1.

perrydesign

2.

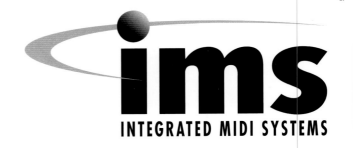

The Aurora Group
Manufacturers' Representatives

3.

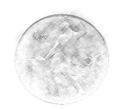

LiRA Enterprises

4.

ims
INTEGRATED MIDI SYSTEMS

5.

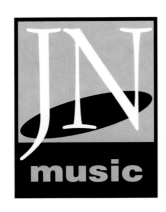

JN music

6.

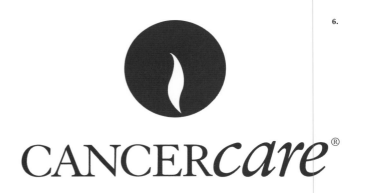

CANCER*care*®

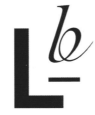

Lieber Brewster Design, Inc.

7.

1 - 5
Design Firm   Perry Design
6 -7
Design Firm   Lieber Brewster Design, Inc.

1. Client   Perry Design
   Designer   Kim Perry

2. Client   The Aurora Group
   Designer   Kim Perry

3. Client   Lira Enterprises
   Designers   Kim Perry & Kenneth DiPaola

4. Client   Integrated Midi Systems
   Designer   Kim Perry

5. Client   JN Music
   Designer   Kim Perry

6. Client   Cancer Care
   Designers   Elisa Carson & Anna Lieber

7. Client   Lieber Brewster Design, Inc.
   Designer   Anna Lieber

(opposite)
Design Firm   Zunda Design Group

   Client   Newman's Own Inc.
   Designers   Jon Voss & Charles Zunda

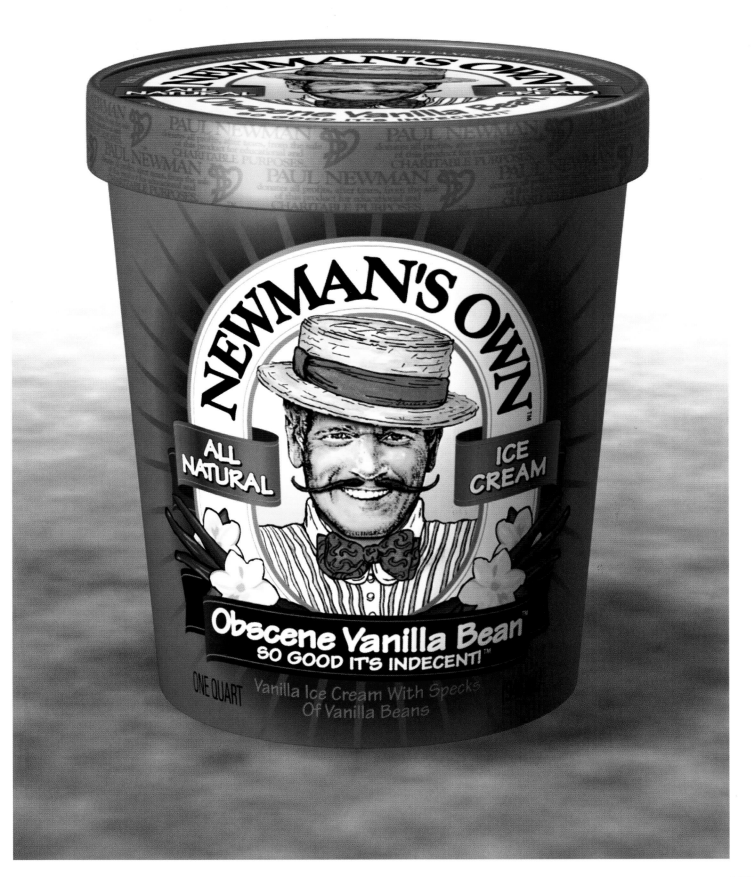

1.

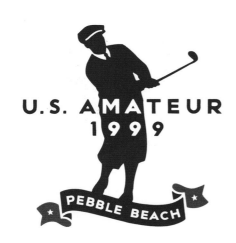

U.S. AMATEUR
1999
PEBBLE BEACH

2.

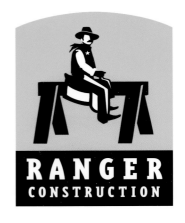

RANGER
CONSTRUCTION

3.

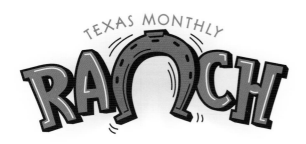

TEXAS MONTHLY
RANCH

4.

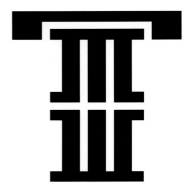

5.

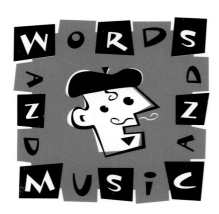

WORDS ADD MUSIC

6.

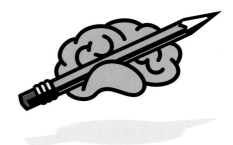

WRITE BRAIN
WORKS

7.

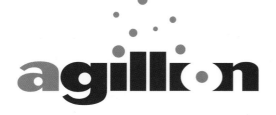

agillion

8.

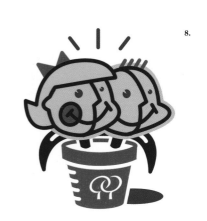

184

9.

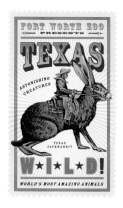

10.

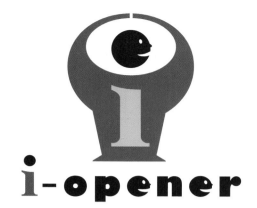

11.

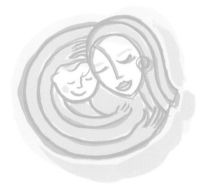

12.

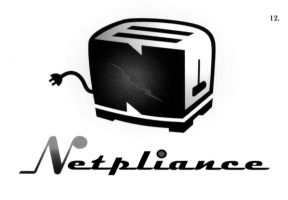

13.

SHRED DOC®

14.

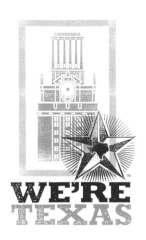

15.

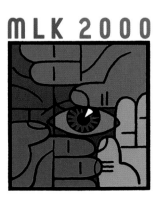

GIRLS' NIGHT OUT

1.

FAMILY VALUE MATINEES AT THEATER! THEATRE! ON BELMONT

2.

THE HOME OF STARK RAVING THEATRE THEATER! THEATRE! & TRIANGLE PRODUCTIONS! ON BELMONT

3.

RUTHERFORD INVESTMENT MANAGEMENT

4.

OREGON ADULT SOCCER ASSOCIATION

5.

OREGON ADULT SOCCER ASSOCIATION

6.

PALM SPRINGS PACRAO '98

7.

PACRAO 1999 PORTLAND OREGON

8.

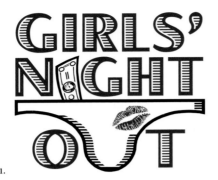

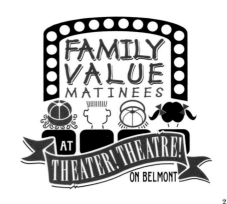

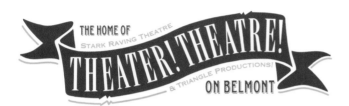

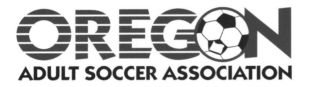

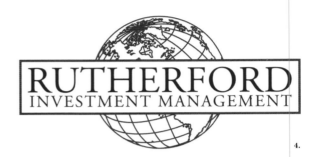

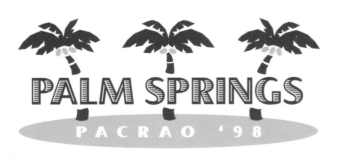

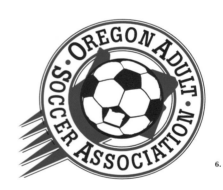

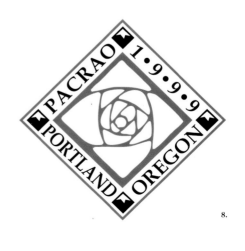

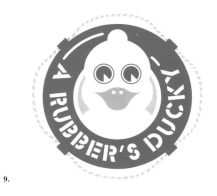

9.

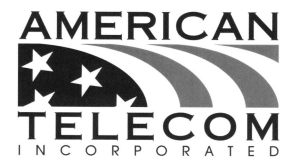

10.

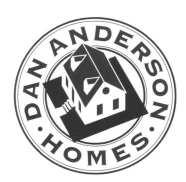

11.

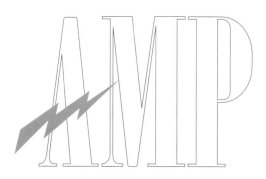

12.

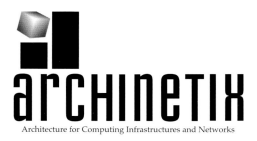

Architecture for Computing Infrastructures and Networks

13.

14.

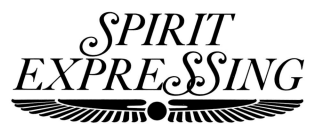

15.

(all)

Design Firm Jeff Fisher LogoMotives

1. Client   triangle productions!
    Designer   Jeff Fisher

2, 3
    Client   triangle productions!/
                Stark Raving Theatre
    Designer   Jeff Fisher

4. Client   Shleifer Marketing
                Communications (Rutherford
                Investment Management)
    Designer   Jeff Fisher

5. Client   Oregon Adult
                Soccer Association
    Designer   Jeff Fisher

6. Client   Oregon Adult
                Soccer Association
    Designer   Jeff Fisher

7. Client   Pacific Association of College
                Registrars and Admissions
                Officers
    Designer   Jeff Fisher

8. Client   Pacific Association of
                College Registrars and
                Admissions Officers
    Designer   Jeff Fisher

9. Client   A Rubber's Ducky
    Designer   Jeff Fisher

10. Client   Shleifer Marketing
                Communications
                (American Telecom)
    Designer   Jeff Fisher

11. Client   Dan Anderson Homes
    Designer   Jeff Fisher

12. Client   AMP/Anne-Marie Petrie
    Designer   Jeff Fisher

13. Client   Archinetix
    Designer   Jeff Fisher

14. Client   Smith Freed Heald & Chock
    Designer   Jeff Fisher

15. Client   Spirit Expressing
    Designer   Jeff Fisher

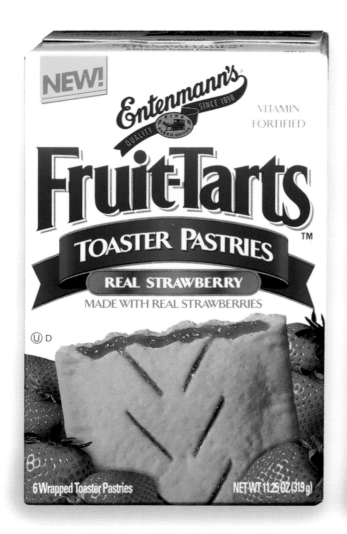

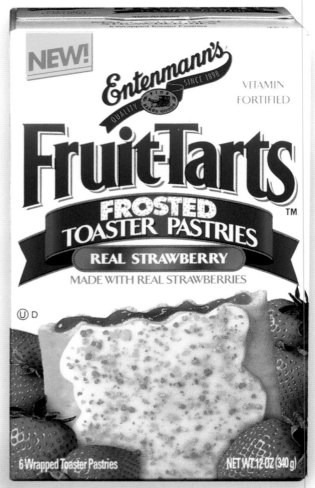

188

1.

H E I D I G I L M O R E

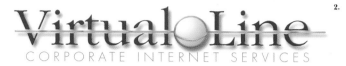

2.

3.
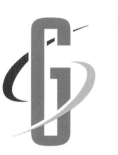

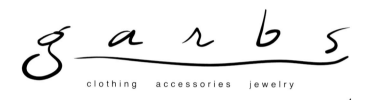

4.

6.
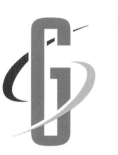

5.

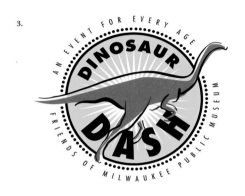

GRAPHICSOURCE
PRODUCTION/FULFILLMEN!

7.

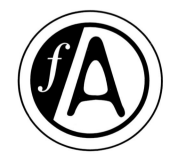

F R A M I N G A M Y

(opposite)
Design Firm Zunda Design Group

Client   Bestfoods Baking
Designer   Charles Zunda

1, 3 - 7
Design Firm Becker Design
2
Design Firm Cathey Associates, Inc.

1. Client   Heidi Gilmore
    Designer   Neil Becker

2. Client   Virtual Line
    Designer   Gordon Cathey

3. Client   Friends of the Milwaukee
               Public Museum
    Designer   Neil Becker

4. Client   Garbs
    Designer   Neil Becker

5. Client   Its Something Blue.com
    Designer   Neil Becker

6. Client   Graphicsource
    Designer   Neil Becker

7. Client   Framing Amy
    Designer   Neil Becker

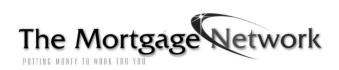

The Mortgage Network

PUTTING MONEY TO WORK FOR YOU

1.

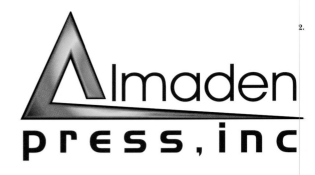
2.

3.

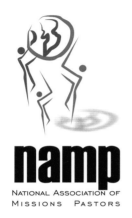

namp

NATIONAL ASSOCIATION OF
MISSIONS PASTORS

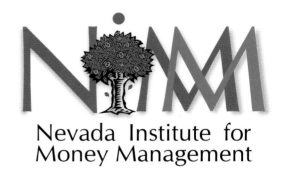

Nevada Institute for
Money Management
4.

5.

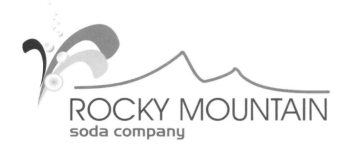

ROCKY MOUNTAIN
soda company

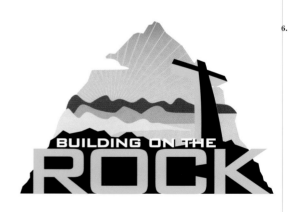
6.

7.

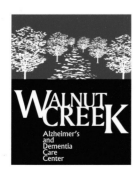
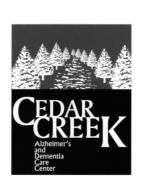

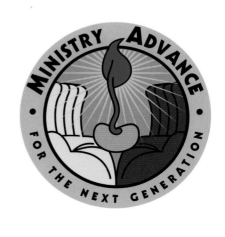
8.

9.

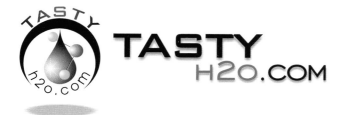

10.

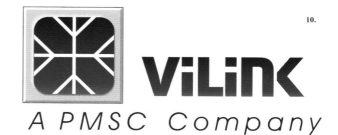

11.

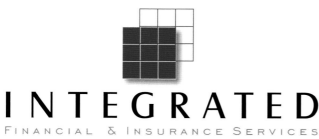

12.

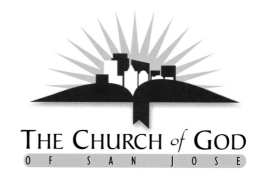

13.

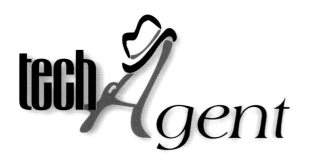

14.

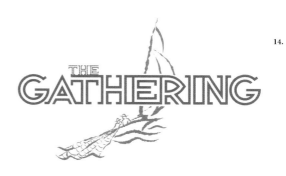

15.

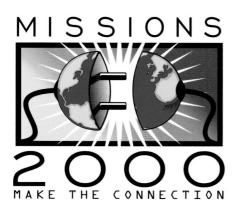

(all)

Design Firm Imagine Graphics

1. Client	The Mortgage Network	8. Client	First Baptist Church of Los Altos
Designer	Steve Guy	Designer	Kyle Maxwell
2. Client	Almaden Press		
Designer	Steve Guy	9. Client	TastyH$_2$O.com
		Designer	Steve Guy
3. Client	Nat'l Assoc. of Missions Pastors		
Designer	Steve Guy	10. Client	ViLink
		Designer	Steve Guy
4. Client	Nevada Institute for Money Management		
		11. Client	Integrated Financial
Designer	Steve Guy	Designers	Steve Guy & Kyle Maxwell
5. Client	Rocky Mountain Soda Company	12. Client	Church of God of San Jose
Designer	Steve Guy	Designer	Kyle Maxwell
6. Client	South Valley Christian Church	13. Client	Tech-Agent, Inc.
Designer	Kyle Maxwell	Designer	Steve Guy
7. Client	The Creeks Alzheimer's & Dementia Care Ctrs.	14 - 15	
		Client	South Valley Christian Church
Designer	Kyle Maxwell	Designer	Kyle Maxwell

SwigBurris

1.

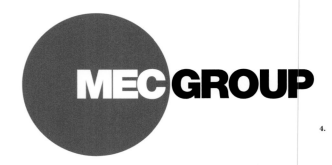

2.

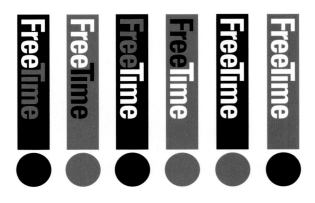

3.

4.

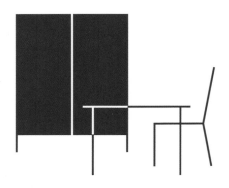

5.

6.

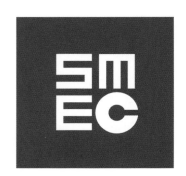

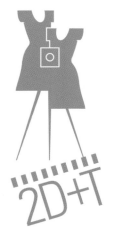

7.

1 - 7
Design Firm Red Square Design

1. Client   Swig Burris
    Designer   Nadine Hajjar

2. Client   Cedar Corp.
    Designers   Lev Zeitlin & Nadine Hajjar

3. Client   Free Time
    Designer   Lev Zeitlin

4. Client   Middle East Capital Group
    Designers   Lev Zeitlin & Nadine Hajjar

5. Client   Borja Veciana
    Designer   Lev Zeitlin

6. Client   Société Moderne D'Enterprise
                 et de commerce (SMEC)
    Designer   Lev Zeitlin

7. Client   Two Dresses and a Tripod
    Designer   Lev Zeitlin

(opposite)
Design Firm Walsh & Associates

    Designers   Miriam Lisco, Iskra Johnson
                 & Mark Ely

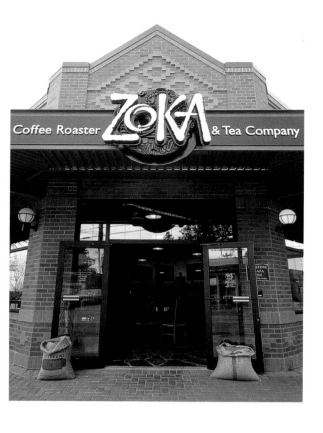

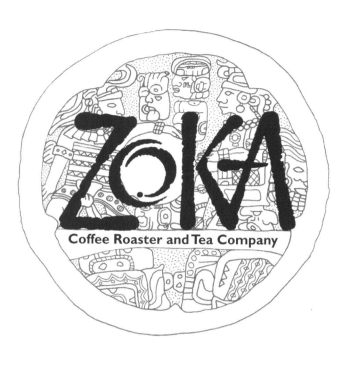

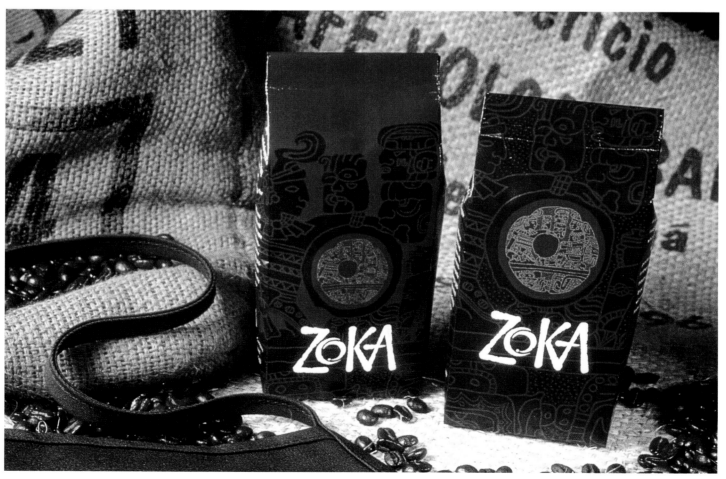

193

1.

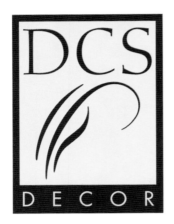

2.

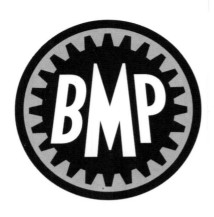

3.

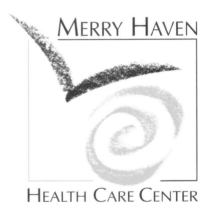

4.

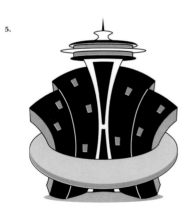

5.

6.

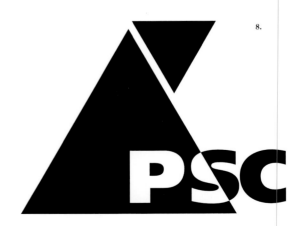

7.

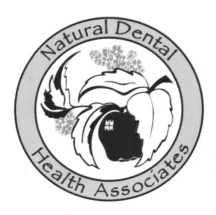

8.

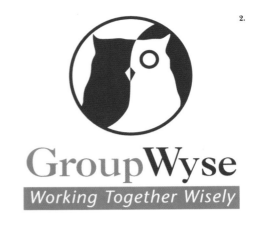

9.

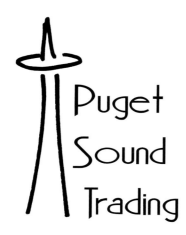

Puget Sound Trading

10.

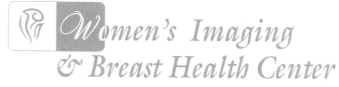

11.

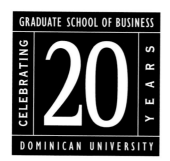

12.

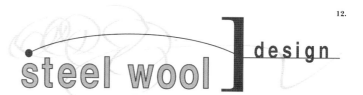

13.

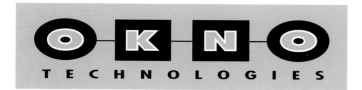

14.

OIL CAPITAL ELECTRIC

15.

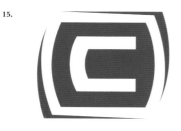

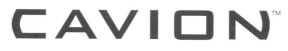

1 - 10		7. Client	Natural Dental
Design Firm	**Graphx Design**	Designers	Kari Baker & Donna Cooley
11 - 14			
Design Firm	**Steel Wool Design**	8. Client	Paradigm Search & Consulting
15		Designers	Alex Sobie & Patrick Smith
Design Firm	**Becker Design**		
		9. Client	Puget Sound Trading
1. Client	Buyken Metal Products	Designers	Alex Sobie & Kari Baker
Designers	Alex Sobie & Kari Baker		
		10. Client	Washington Imaging
2. Client	GroupWyse		Services, LLC
Designers	Alex Sobie & Patrick Smith	Designer	Kari Baker
3. Client	DCS Decor	11. Client	Dominican University
Designers	Alex Sobie, Kari Baker,	Designer	Kristy Lewis Andrew
	& Patrick Smith		
		12. Client	Steel Wool Design
4. Client	Inn at Lake Connamarra	Designer	Kristy Lewis Andrew
Designers	Kari Baker & Kaycia Ogata		
		13. Client	OKNO Technologies
5. Client	Jet City Bistro	Designer	Kristy Lewis Andrew
Designer	Kari Baker		
		14. Client	Oil Capital Electric
6. Client	Merry Haven	Designer	Kristy Lewis Andrew
Designers	Kari Baker & Donna Cooley		
		15. Client	Cavion
		Designers	Neil Becker

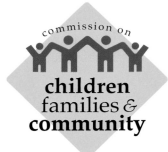

1.

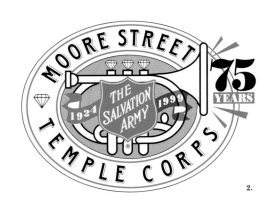

MOORE STREET TEMPLE CORPS
THE SALVATION ARMY
1924 1999
75 YEARS

2.

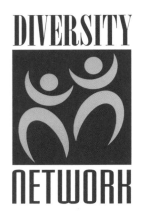

HOSPICE OF HUMBOLDT

3.

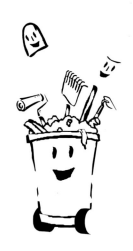

THE EVERY KID FUND

4.

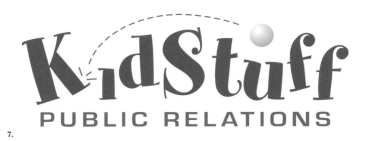

commission on
children families & community

5.

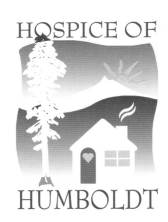

DIVERSITY NETWORK

6.

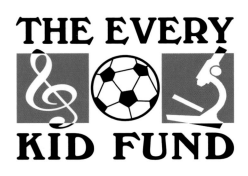

KidStuff
PUBLIC RELATIONS

7.

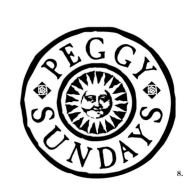

PEGGY SUNDAYS

8.

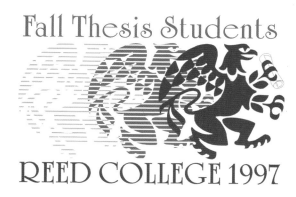

9.

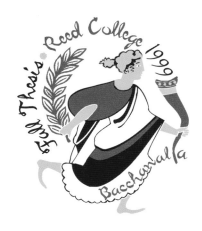

10.

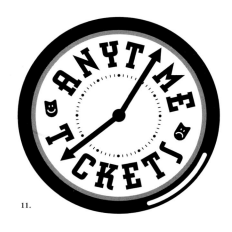

11.

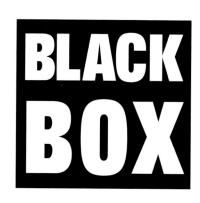

12.

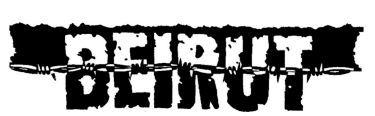

13.

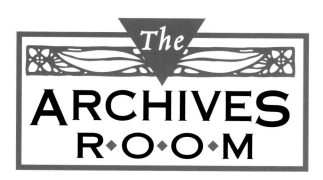

14.

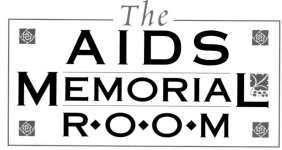

15.

(all)
Design Firm Jeff Fisher LogoMotives

1. Client	Peninsula Clean Team	
Designer	Jeff Fisher	
2. Client	Salvation Army/Moore St. Temple Corps	
Designer	Jeff Fisher	
3. Client	Hospice of Humboldt	
Designer	Jeff Fisher	
4. Client	TriAd (The Every Kid Fund)	
Designers	Jeff Fisher & Sue Fisher	
5. Client	Commission on Children, Families & Community	
Designer	Jeff Fisher	

6. Client	DiversityNetwork
Designer	Jeff Fisher
7. Client	KidStuff Public Relations
Designer	Jeff Fisher
8. Client	Peggy Sundays
Designer	Jeff Fisher
9, 10 Client	Reed College
Designer	Jeff Fisher
11 - 15 Client	triangle productions!
Designer	Jeff Fisher

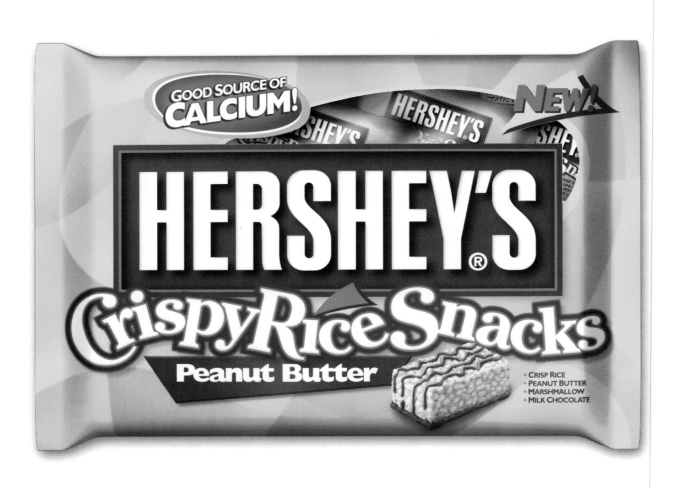

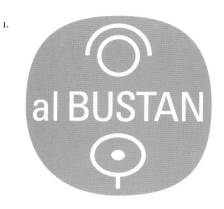

1.

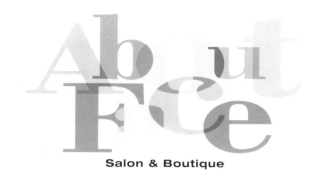

Salon & Boutique

2.

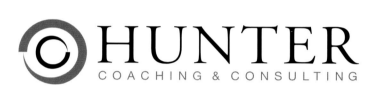

HUNTER
COACHING & CONSULTING

3.

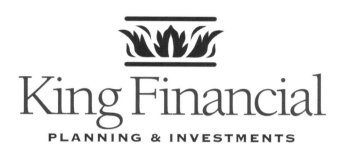

King Financial

PLANNING & INVESTMENTS

4.

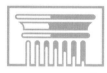

CUNA BROKERAGE SERVICES, INC.

A BROKER DEALER OF CUNA MUTUAL GROUP

5.

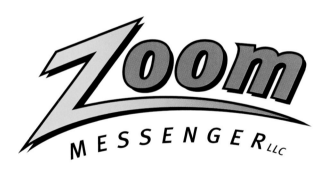

6.

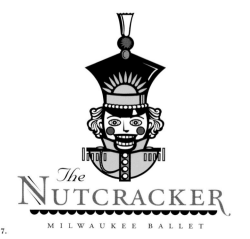

The NUTCRACKER

MILWAUKEE BALLET

7.

(opposite)

Design Firm   Zunda Design Group

Client   Hershey Chocolate U.S.A.
Designers   Jon Voss & Charles Zunda

1.
Design Firm   Red Square Design
2 - 7
Design Firm   Becker Design

1. Client   Al Bustan
    Designers   Lev Zeitlin & Nadine Hajjar

2. Client   About Face
    Designer   Neil Becker

3. Client   Hunter Coaching
                 and Consulting
    Designers   Neil Becker, Lisa Gaertig

4. Client   King Financial
    Designer   Neil Becker

5. Client   CUNA Brokerage Services, Inc.
    Designer   Neil Becker

6. Client   Zoom Messenger, llc
    Designer   Neil Becker

7. Client   Milwaukee Ballet
    Designer   Neil Becker

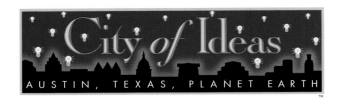

1.

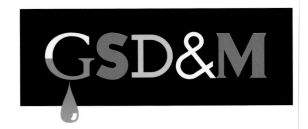

2.

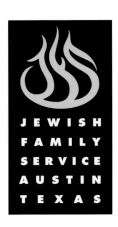

3.

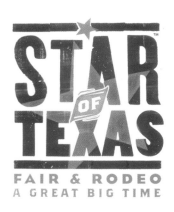

4.

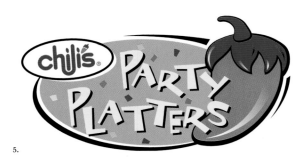

5.

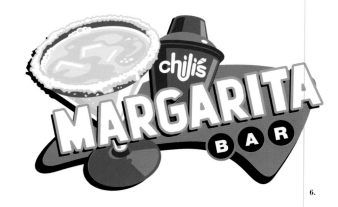

6.

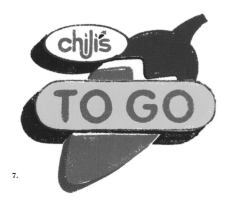

7.

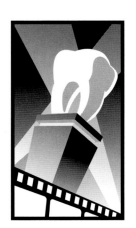

8.

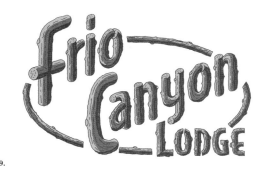

9.

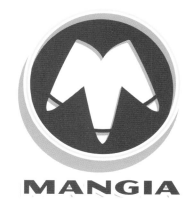

MANGIA

10.

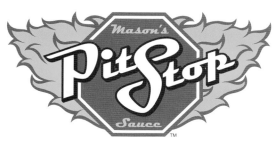

11.

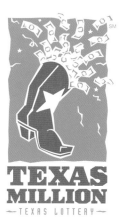

12.

SCRATCH OFFS
─ TEXAS LOTTERY ─

13.

TEXAS MILLION
─ TEXAS LOTTERY ─

14.

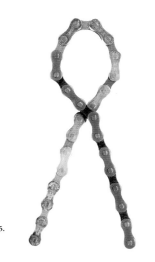

15.

(all)

Design Firm	**GSD&M**	
1. Client	City of Austin	
Designers	Marty Erhart & Tim McClure	
2. Client	GSD&M	
Designers	Marty Erhart & Heather Segrest	
3. Client	Jewish Family Service	
Designer	Marty Erhart	
4. Client	Star of Texas Fair & Rodeo	
Designer	Patrick Nolan	
5, 6		
Client	Chili's Grill & Bar	
Designer	Matt Mason	
7. Client	Chili's Grill & Bar	
Designers	Matt Mason & Paul Rogers	

8. Client	Dr. Larry "Hoppy" Lane, Dentist	
Designer	Matt Mason	
9. Client	Frio Canyon Lodge	
Designer	Matt Mason	
10. Client	Mangia Pizza	
Designer	Matt Mason	
11. Client	Mason's Pit Stop Sauce	
Designer	Matt Mason	
12. Client	Southwest Airlines	
Designer	Matt Mason	
13, 14		
Client	Texas Lottery Commission	
Designer	Matt Mason	
15. Client	Hill Country Ride for AIDS	
Designer	Marty Erhart	

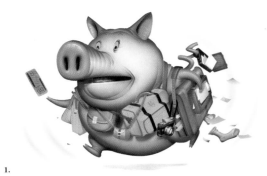

1.

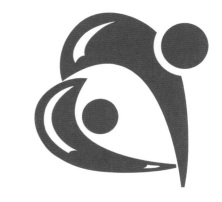

2.

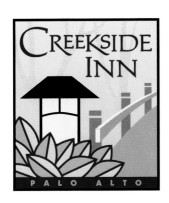

3.

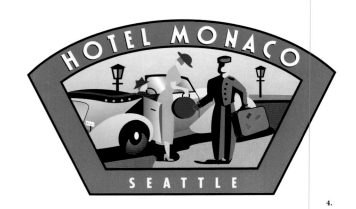

4.

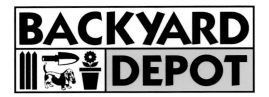

5.

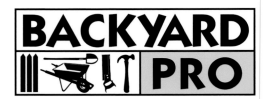

6.

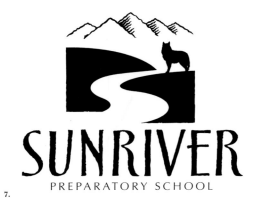

7.

1 - 2
Design Firm GSD&M
3 - 4
Design Firm Lori Powell Design Exploration
5 - 7
Design Firm Jeff Fisher LogoMotives

1. Client   Southwest Airlines
    Designers   Marty Erhart & Dale Minor

2. Client   Pennzoil/Avance
                  Educational Program
    Designer   Neyssan Moshref

3. Client   Greystone Hospitality
    Designer   Lori Powell

4. Client   Kimpton Group
    Designer   Lori Powell

5, 6
    Client   Backyard Depot
    Designers   Jeff Fisher

7. Client   TriAd
                  (Sunriver Preparatory School)
    Designers   Jeff Fisher & Sue Fisher

(opposite)
    Design Firm Kollberg/Johnson

    Client   Ambi Inc.
    Designers   Kollberg/Johnson

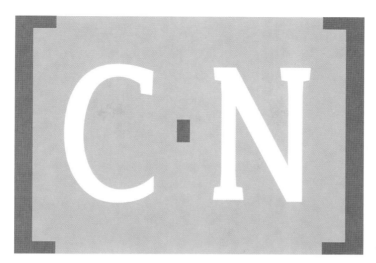

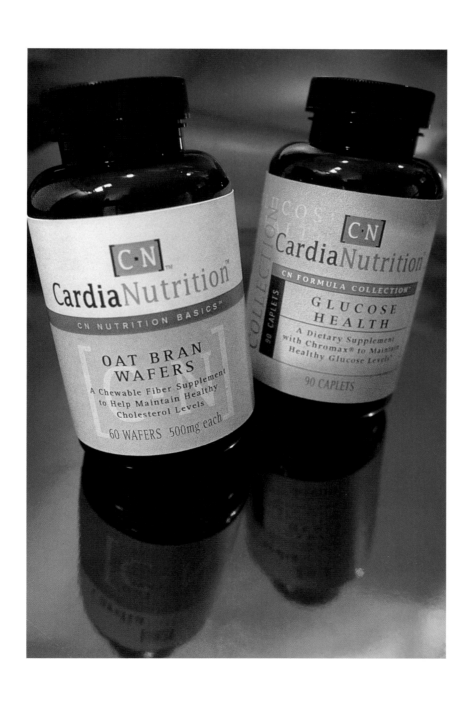

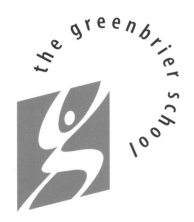

1.

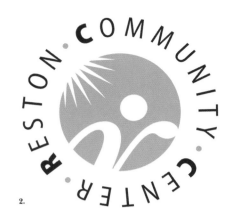

RESTON·COMMUNITY·CENTER· 2.

SYNTONICS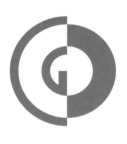

3.

K **KENNEDY CONSULTING LLC**

4.

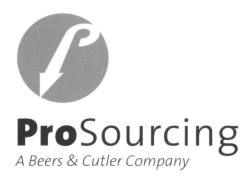

Cox Design Group llc

5.

namasté

6.

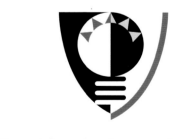

ProSourcing
A Beers & Cutler Company

7.

Jagtiani+Associates
Protecting your ideas

8.

204

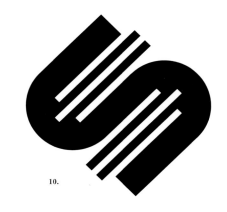

9.

10.

12.

GSS

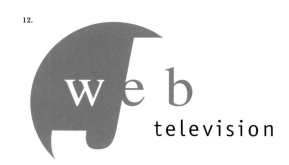

w e b
television

11.

SAYLORS
Dental Laboratory, Inc.

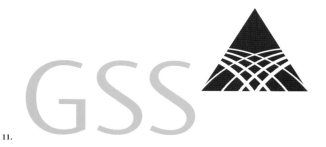

Pfeiffer®

13.

14.

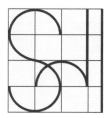

Re*w*ard®

15.

1 - 8, 11 - 13
  Design Firm Fuller Designs, Inc.
9
  Design Firm Swieter Design
10
  Design Firm Frank D'Astolfo Design
14 - 15
  Design Firm Chesapeake Group, Inc.

1. Client   Greenbrier School
   Designer   Doug Fuller

2. Client   Reston Community Center
   Designers   Doug Fuller & Aaron Taylor

3. Client   Syntonics
   Designers   Doug Fuller & Aaron Taylor

4. Client   Kennedy Consulting
   Designer   Minh Ta

5. Client   Cox Design Group
   Designer   Doug Fuller

6. Client   Namasté
   Designer   Doug Fuller

7. Client   Pro Sourcing
   Designer   Doug Fuller

8. Client   Jagtiani + Associates
   Designer   Doug Fuller

9. Client   Verve
   Designer   Mark Ford

10. Client   Simulprobe Technologies
    Designer   Frank D'Astolfo

11. Client   Global Systems & Strategies
    Designer   Doug Fuller

12. Client   J-Web Television
    Designer   Doug Fuller

13. Client   Saylors Dental Laboratory
    Designer   Minh Ta

14. Client   T. Marzetti Company
    Designer   John C. Sullivan

15. Client   Heinz Pet Products
    Designers Tina Collin & John C. Sullivan

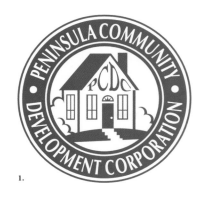

1.

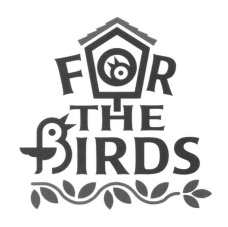

2.

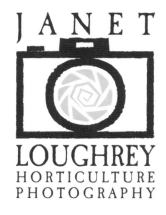

3.

Oregon Emerald

4.

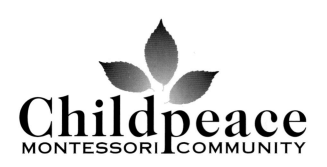

5.

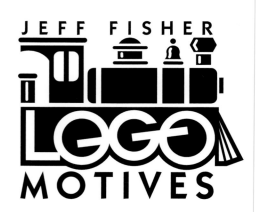

6.

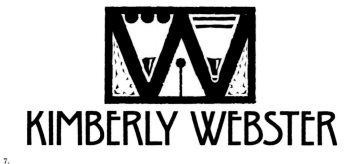

7.

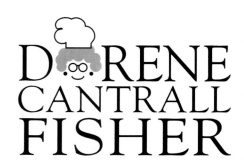

8.

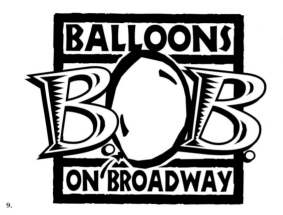

9.

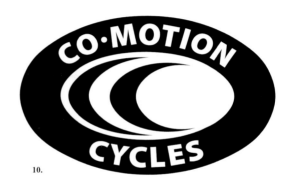

10.

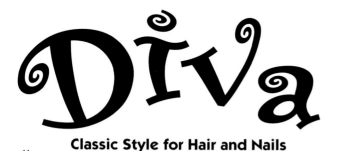

Classic Style for Hair and Nails

11.

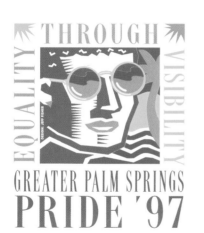

13.

12.

Our House
OF PORTLAND
10th
ANNIVERSARY
1988 · 1998

14.

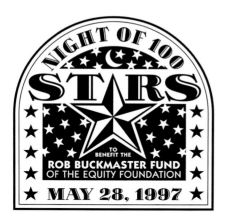

15.

1 - 15
Design Firm Jeff Fisher LogoMotives

1. Client   Portsmouth Community
          Development Corporation
   Designer   Jeff Fisher

2. Client   Junior League of Portland
   Designer   Jeff Fisher

3. Client   Childpeace Montessori
          Community
   Designer   Jeff Fisher

4. Client   Oregon Daily Emerald
   Designer   Jeff Fisher

5. Client   Janet Loughrey
          Horticulture Photography
   Designer   Jeff Fisher

6. Client   Jeff Fisher LogoMotives
   Designer   Jeff Fisher

7. Client   Kimberly Webster
   Designer   Jeff Fisher

8. Client   Dorene Cantrall Fisher
   Designer   Jeff Fisher

9. Client   Balloons on Broadway
   Designer   Jeff Fisher

10. Client   Co•Motion Cycles
   Designers   Jeff Fisher & Jerril Nilson

11. Client   Diva
   Designer   Jeff Fisher

12. Client   Pride Northwest, Inc.
   Designer   Jeff Fisher

13. Client   Rob Buckmaster Fund
   Designer   Jeff Fisher

14. Client   Our House of Portland
   Designer   Jeff Fisher

15. Client   Greater Palm Springs Pride, Inc.
   Designer   Jeff Fisher

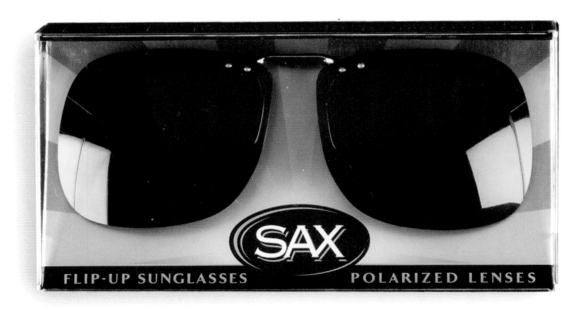

SAX FLIP-UP SUNGLASSES · POLARIZED LENSES

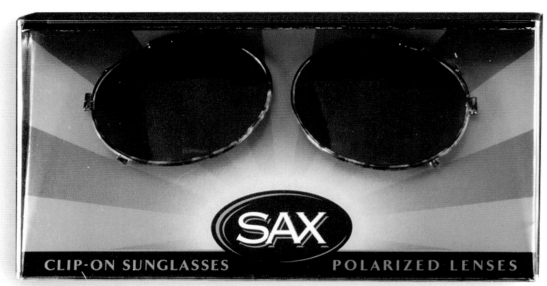

SAX CLIP-ON SUNGLASSES · POLARIZED LENSES

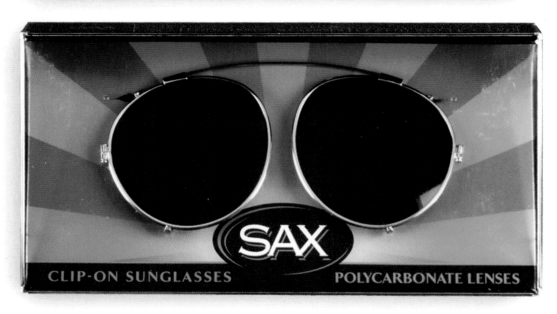

SAX CLIP-ON SUNGLASSES · POLYCARBONATE LENSES

1.
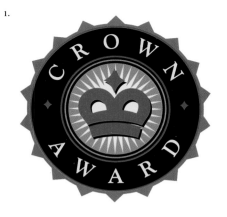

2.
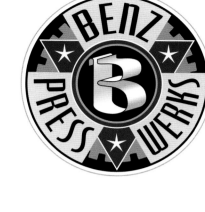

3.
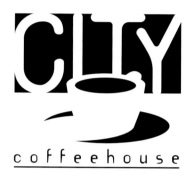

4.
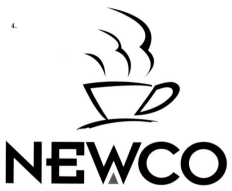

5.
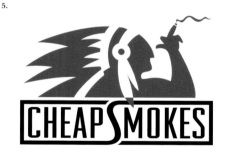

6.
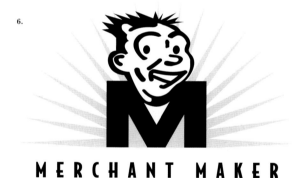

7.
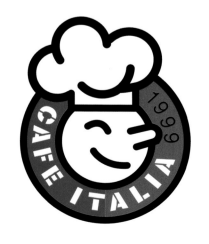

(opposite)
Design Firm Zunda Design Group

Client   Sax
Designers   Charles Zunda & Todd Nickel

1 - 7
Design Firm Bartels & Company, Inc.

1. Client   The Crown Awards
    Designers   Ron Rodemacher
                 & David Bartels

2. Client   Benz Press Werks
    Designers   Bob Thomas & David Bartels

3. Client   City Coffee House
    Designer   John Postlewait

4. Client   Newco, Inc.
    Designers   David Bartels &
                 Ron Rodemacher

5. Client   Cheap Smokes
    Designers   John Postlewait & David Bartels

6. Client   Cybermill
    Designers   David Bartels &
                 Ron Rodemacher

7. Client   Holy Redeemer Church
    Designers   Ron Rodemacher &
                 David Bartels

J J Gumberg Co.

2. VICTORIA + CO

1.

3.
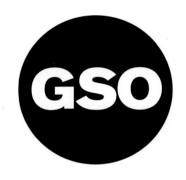

4.
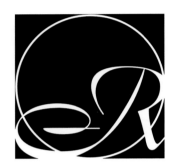

5.
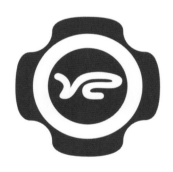

6.
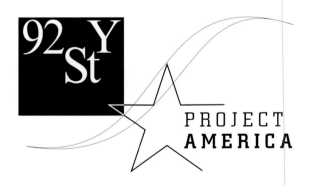

7.
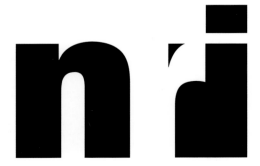

8.
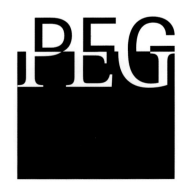

9.

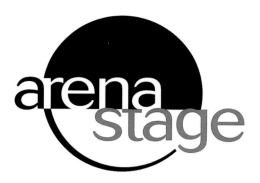

10.

11.

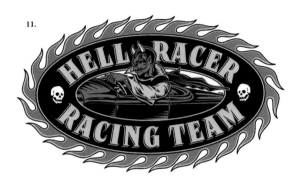

12.

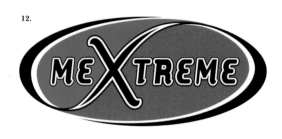

13.

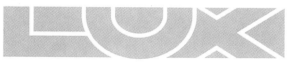

14.

15.

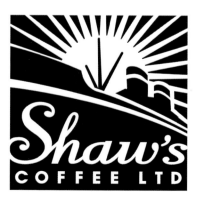

1 - 4, 6 - 8
Design Firm   Poulin + Morris
5
Design Firm   Swieter Design
9 - 13
Design Firm   Mires Design
14 - 15
Design Firm   Bartels & Co., Inc.

1. Client   J. J. Gumberg Co
    Designers   L. Richard Poulin
                  & Jonathan Posnett

2. Client   Victoria + Co
    Designers   Douglas Morris &
                  L. Richard Poulin

3. Client   GSO Graphics Inc.
    Designers   Douglas Morris &
                  Robert Patrick Festino

4. Client   Ridgeway Center
    Designer   Douglas Morris

5. Client   The Dr. Benjamin Remedy

6. Client   Bratskeir + Company
    Designers   Douglas Morris &
                  L. Richard Poulin

7. Client   National Reprographics, Inc.
    Designers   Douglas Morris &
                  L. Richard Poulin

8. Client   Planned Expansion Group Inc.
    Designer   Douglas Morris

9. Client   G.ball.com
    Designers   Scott Mires, Miguel Perez,
                  & Tracy Sabin

10. Client   Arena Stage
    Designers   Scott Mires & Miguel Perez

11. Client   Hell Racer
    Designers   José Serrano, Miguel Perez,
                  & Dan Thoner

12. Client   Schiedermayer & Assoc.
    Designers   José Serrano, Jeff Samaripa,
                  & Miguel Perez

13. Client   Lux Art Institute
    Designers   John Ball & Miguel Perez

14. Client   Magna Bank
    Designers   Ron Rodemacher
                  & David Bartels

15. Client   Shaw's Coffee Ltd.
    Designer   Brian Barclay

1.

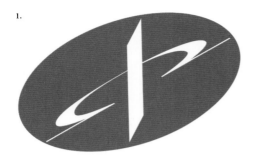

2. **Lightship**

3.

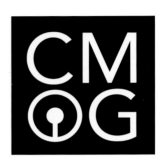

4.

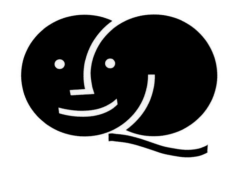

6.

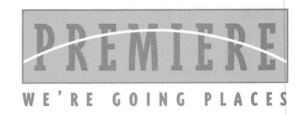

5.

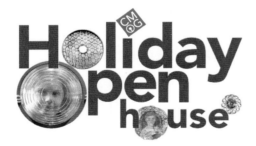

7.

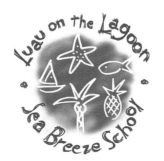

1 - 5
Design Firm Q. Cassetti
6 - 7
Design Firm Look

1. Client   Omega One Communications
   Designer   Q. Cassetti

2. Client   Lightship Telecom LLC
   Designer   Q. Cassetti

3. Client   Quest Diagnostics Incorporated
   Designer   Q. Cassetti

4. Client   Corning Museum of Glass
   Designers   Q. Cassetti & Rob Cassetti

5. Client   Corning Museum of Glass
   Designers   Q. Cassetti & Rob Cassetti

6. Client   Premiere, Limousine Company
   Designer   Betsy Todd

7. Client   Sea Breeze Preschool
   Designer   Betsy Todd

(opposite)
Design Firm DYNAPAC DesignGroup

   Client   Advance Plastics
   Designer   Lee A. Aellig

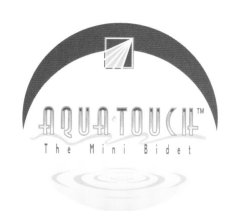

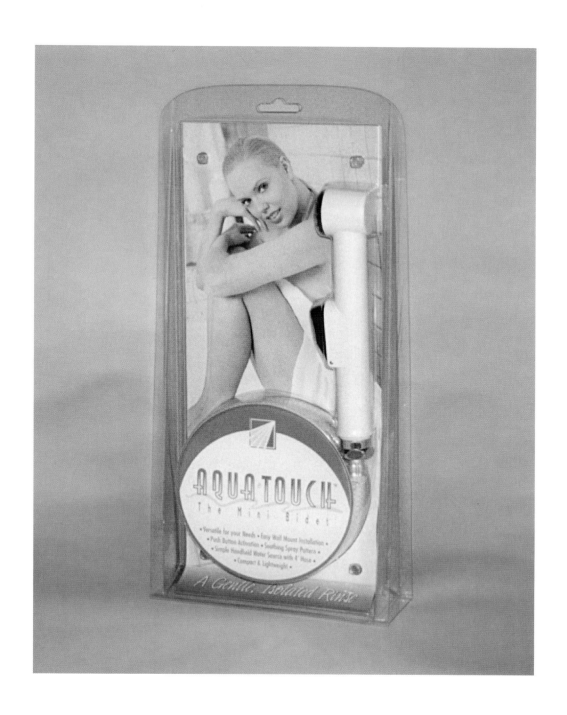

1.

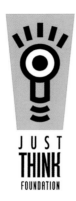

JUST THINK FOUNDATION

2.

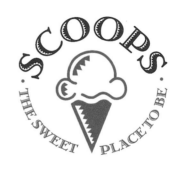

3.

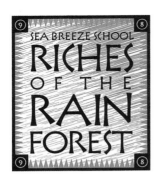

4.

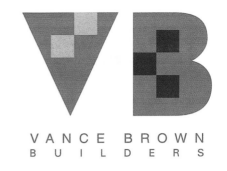

5.

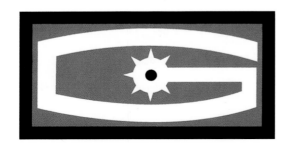

6.

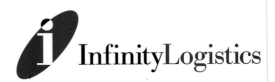

7.

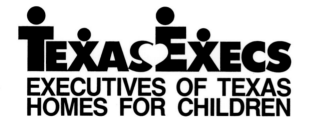

8.

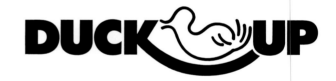

214

9.

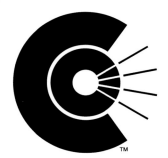

10.

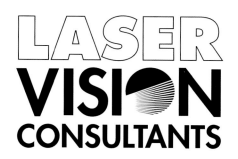

11.

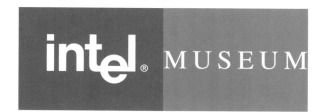

12.

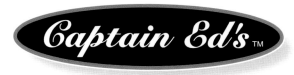

13.

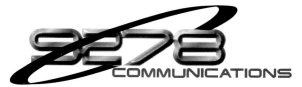

14.

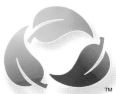

15.

ZOELLNER
ARTS
CENTER

LEHIGH University

1.

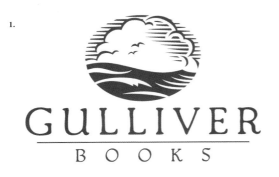

GULLIVER

B O O K S

2.

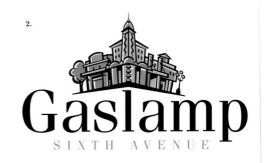

Gaslamp

S I X T H   A V E N U E

3.

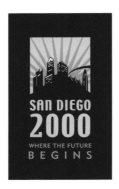

SAN DIEGO
2000
WHERE THE FUTURE
BEGINS

4.

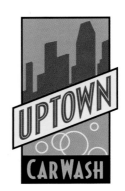

UPTOWN
CarWash

5.

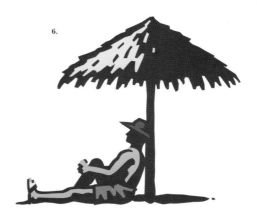

6.

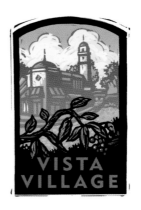

7.

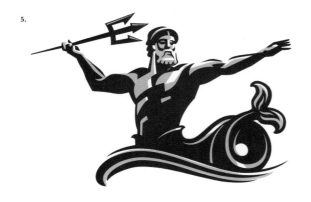

**EASTLAKE
TRAILS**

8.

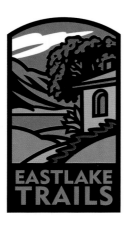

**VISTA
VILLAGE**

9.

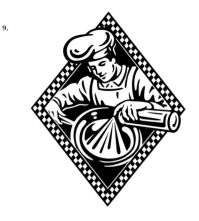

10.

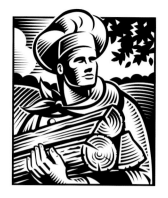

11.

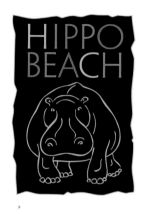

12.

13.

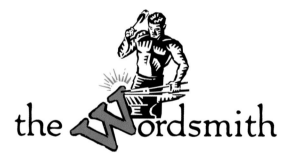

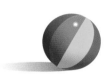

OCEANPLACE

14.

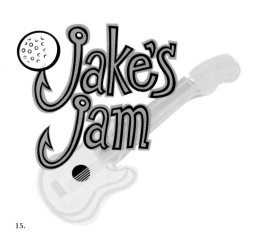

15.

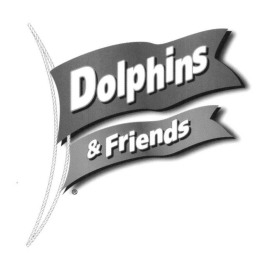

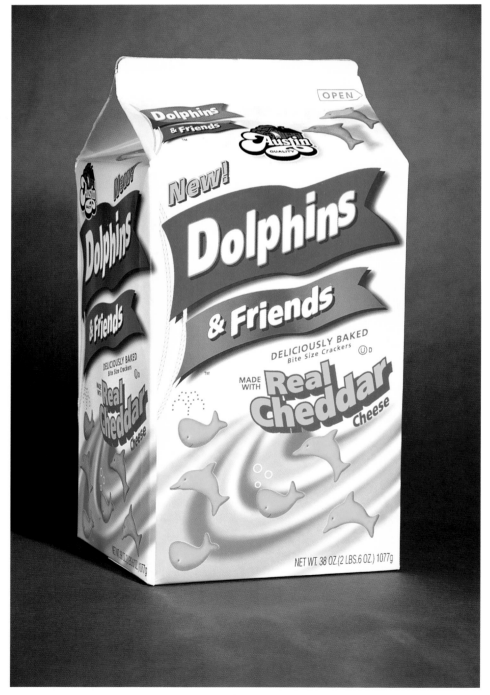

1.

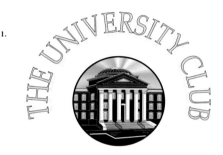

2.

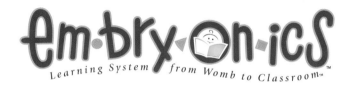

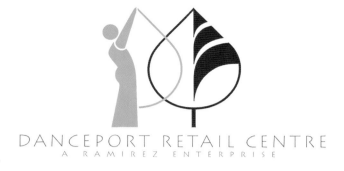

DANCEPORT RETAIL CENTRE
A RAMIREZ ENTERPRISE

3.

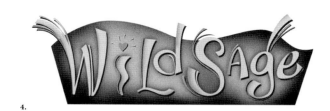

4.

5.

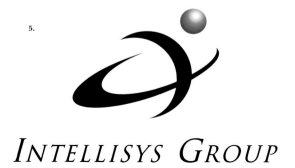

INTELLISYS GROUP

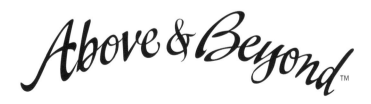

6.

BAUSCH
& LOMB
Surgical

7.

(opposite)
Design Firm Dixon & Parcels Associates, Inc.

Client   Austin Quality Foods

1
Design Firm Cathey Associates, Inc.
2 - 4, 6 - 7
Design Firm The Dupuis Group
5
Design Firm Callery & Company

1. Client   The University Club
    Designers   Matt Westapher
                 & Gordon Cathey

2. Client   Munchkin
    Designers   Bill Corridori, Jack Halpern,
                 & Nobuko Komine

3. Client   Firehouse Subs
    Designer   John Silva

4. Client   Local Squeeze
    Designers   Steven DuPuis &
                 Nobuko Komine

5. Client   Danceport
    Designer   Kelley Callery

6. Client   Van Kind Foods
    Designers   Bill Corridori, Nobuko Komine,
                 & Jack Halpern

7. Client   Bausch & Lomb Surgical
    Designers   Bill Corridori & Jack Halpern

1.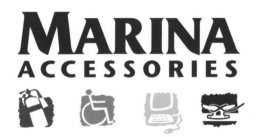

MARINA
ACCESSORIES

2.

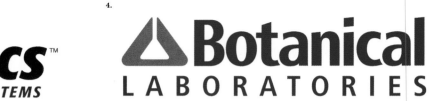

MONAGHAN
& COMPANY

BUILDING DOMINANT BRANDS

3.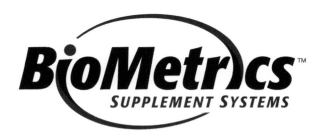

BioMetrics
SUPPLEMENT SYSTEMS

4.

▲**Botanical**
LABORATORIES

5. PACIFIC CREST

6.

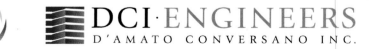 DCI · ENGINEERS
D'AMATO CONVERSANO INC.

7. MARK KROESE
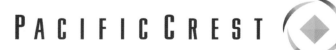
AdVenTuRe MeDiA

8.

Lagerlof
Bradley *Senecal*
& *Swift* LLP

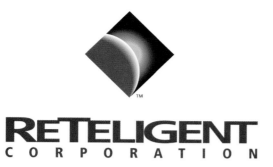

RETELIGENT
C O R P O R A T I O N

9.

10.

THE **ENLORE**TECHNOLOGY GROUP

11.

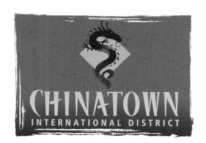

CHINATOWN
INTERNATIONAL DISTRICT

12.

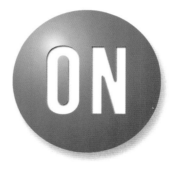

14.

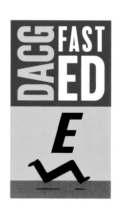

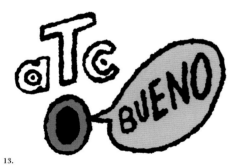

13.

15.

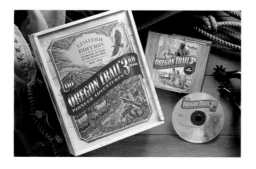

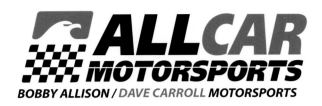

1.

2.
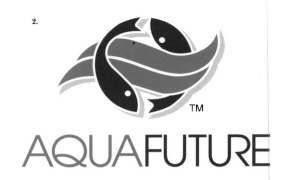

3.
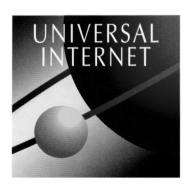

4.
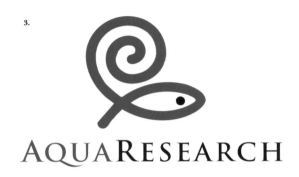

5.
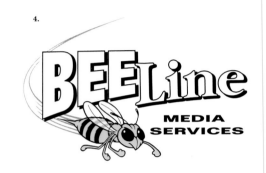

6.
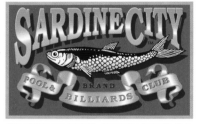

7.
UNIVERSAL INTERNET

1 - 7
Design Firm   The Wecker Group

1. Client   Allcar Motor Sports
    Designer   Robert Wecker

2. Client   Aqua Future, Inc.
    Designers   Robert Wecker & Matt Gnibus

3. Client   Aqua Future, Inc.
    Designers   Robert Wecker & Matt Gnibus

4. Client   Beeline Media Services
    Designer   Robert Wecker

5. Client   Blue Fin Billiards
    Designer   Robert Wecker

6. Client   Blue Fin Billiards
    Designer   Robert Wecker

7. Client   Universal Internet
    Designer   Robert Wecker

(opposite)
Design Firm   Lister Butler Consulting

    Client   Horizon Blue Cross Blue Shield
                   of New Jersey
    Designer   William Davis

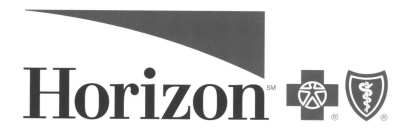

Horizon Blue Cross Blue Shield of New Jersey

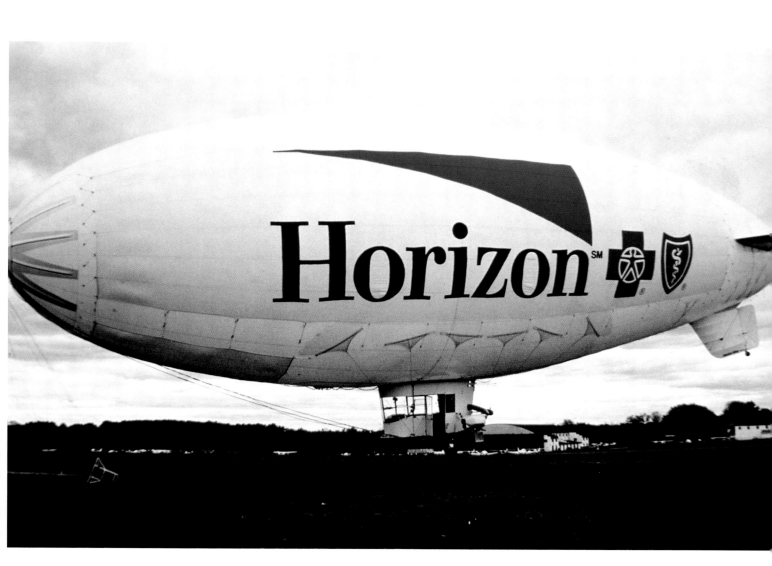

1.

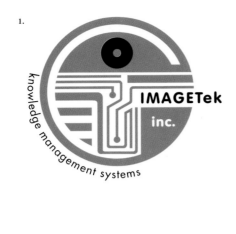

knowledge management systems

IMAGETek inc.

2.

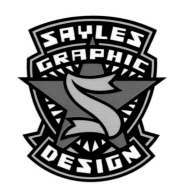

3.

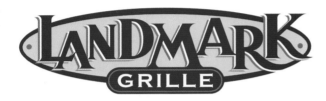

4.

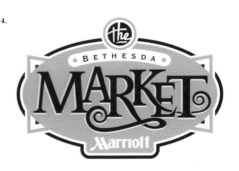

5.

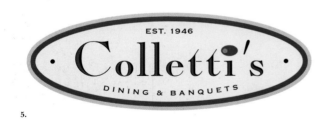

6.

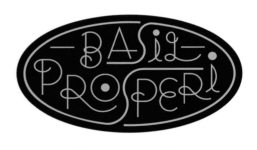

ristorante

7.

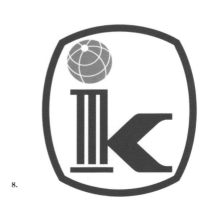

8.

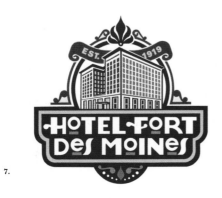

9.

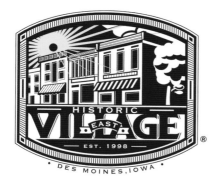

10.

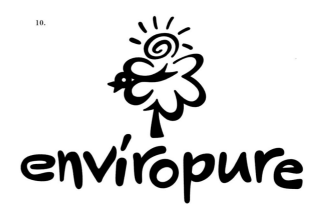

11.

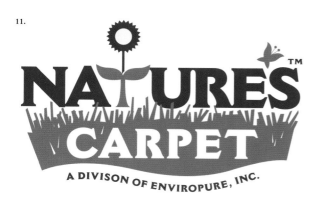

12.

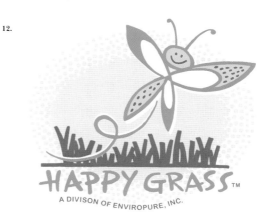

13.

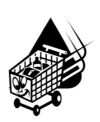

14.

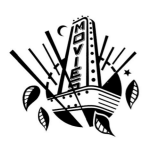
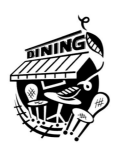
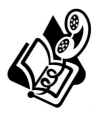

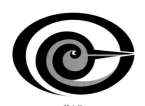

"Ariel"

15.

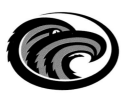

"Hawk"

(all)

	Design Firm	Sayles Graphic Design
1.	Client	ImageTek
	Designer	John Sayles
2.	Client	Sayles Graphic Design
	Designer	John Sayles
3.	Client	Hotel Fort Des Moines "Landmark Grille"
	Designer	John Sayles
4.	Client	Marriott "The Market"
	Designer	John Sayles
5.	Client	Colletti's Restaurant
	Designer	John Sayles
6.	Client	Basil Prosperi
	Designer	John Sayles
7.	Client	Hotel Fort Des Moines
	Designer	John Sayles
8.	Client	Krist Insurance
	Designer	John Sayles

9.	Client	East Side Neighborhood and Merchants Assn.
	Designer	John Sayles
10.	Client	McArthur Companies "EnviroPure"
	Designer	John Sayles
11.	Client	McArthur Companies "Nature's Carpet"
	Designer	John Sayles
12.	Client	McArthur Companies "Happy Grass"
	Designer	John Sayles
13.	Client	Chicago Tribune "Fall Round Up"
	Designer	John Sayles
14.	Client	Meredith Corporation "Successful Farming: Top Shops"
	Designer	John Sayles
15.	Client	Microware
	Designer	John Sayles

1.

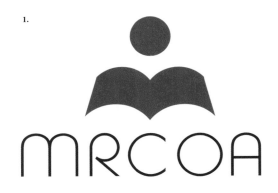

MRCOA

2.

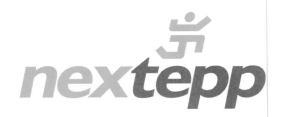
nextepp

3.

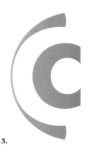

4.

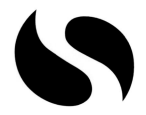

5.

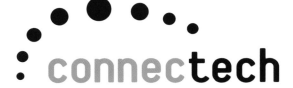
connectech

6.

Bank*Direct*™

7.

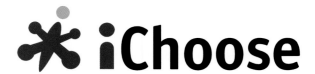
iChoose

8.

FirstStreet

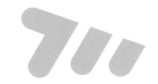

9.

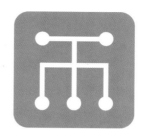

10.

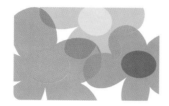

11.

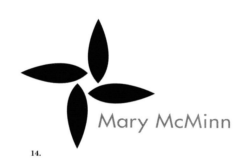

12.

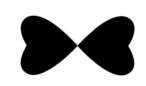

13.

Mary McMinn

14.

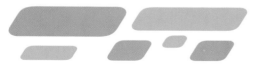

TECHNO-MATION

15.

1
Design Firm **Cathey Associates, Inc.**
2 - 15
Design Firm **Swieter Design**

1. Client   Media Research Corporation
of America
   Designers   Isabel Campos
& Gordon Cathey

2. Client   Nextepp
   Designer   Mark Ford

3. Client   Supre Inc.
   Designers   Mark Waggoner
& Carlos A. Perez

4. Client   Supre - Skin System
   Designer   Erica Brinker

5. Client   Connectech
   Designer   Mark Waggoner

6. Client   Bank Direct
   Designer   Carlos A. Perez

7. Client   iChoose
   Designers   Mark Waggoner, John Swieter,
& Carlos A. Perez

8. Client   First Street
   Designers   Ray Gallegos & Carlos A. Perez

9. Client   Techtonic
   Designer   Carlos A. Perez

10. Client   T-Mech
   Designer   Ray Gallegos

11. Client   Melissa Ronan
   Designer   Mark Waggoner

12. Client   Inertia
   Designer   Carlos A. Perez

13. Client   Dallas Heart Ball
   Designer   Ray Gallegos

14. Client   Mary McMinn
   Designer   Mark Waggoner

15. Client   Techno-Mation
   Designer   Carlos A Perez

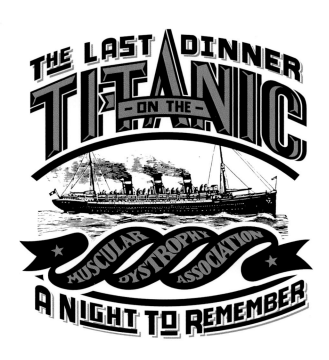

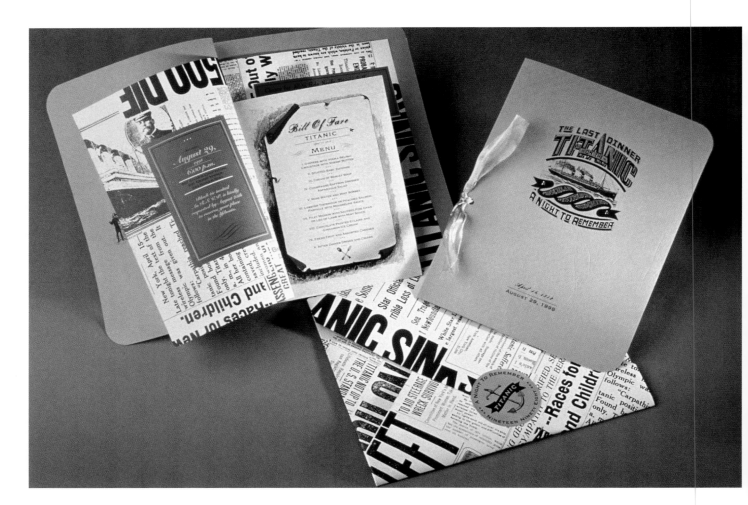

1.

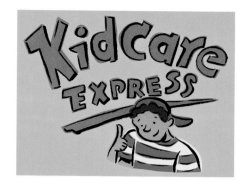

3.

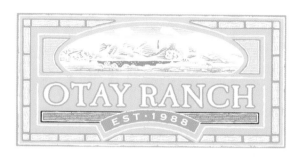

5.

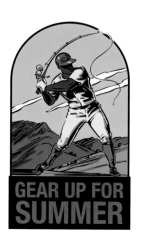

7.

2.

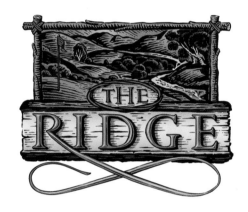

4.

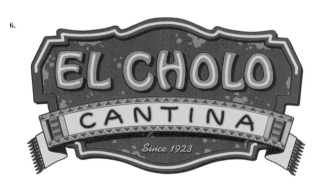

6.

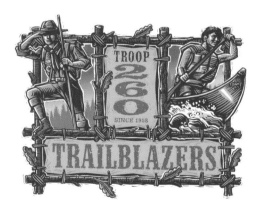

1.

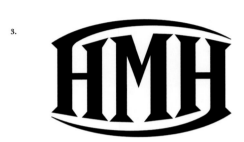

2.

3.

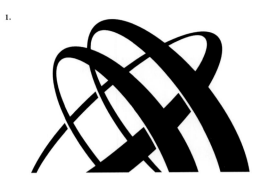

4.

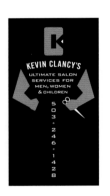

KEVIN CLANCY'S
ULTIMATE SALON
SERVICES FOR
MEN, WOMEN
& CHILDREN

5 0 3 • 2 4 6 • 1 4 2 8

5.

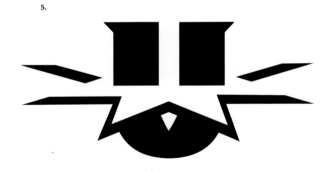

6.

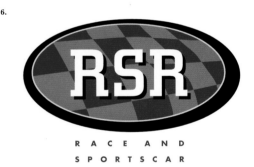

RSR

RACE AND
SPORTSCAR
RESTORATION

7.

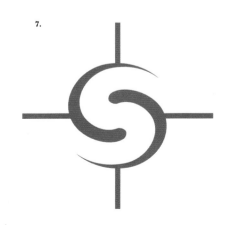

8.

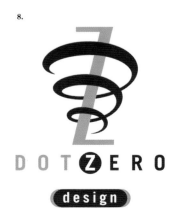

DOT ZERO
design

9.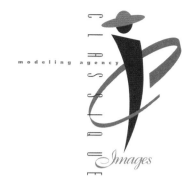

10.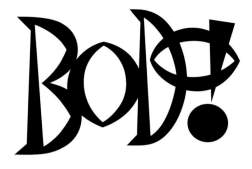

11.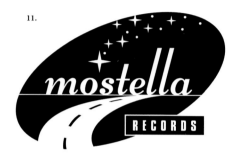

12.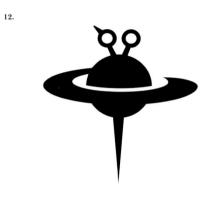

13.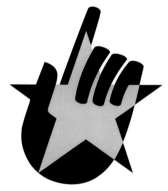

14.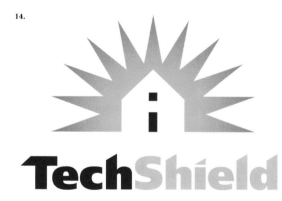

15.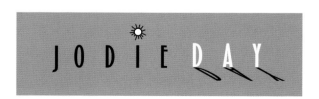

1.

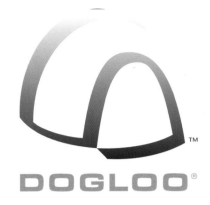

DOGLOO®
™

2.

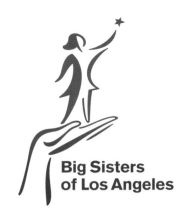

**Big Sisters
of Los Angeles**

3.

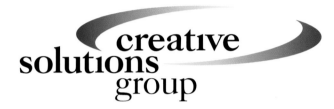

creative
solutions
group

4.

Black & Blu
E N T E R T A I N M E N T

5.

6.

C\\\C

7.

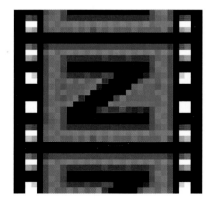

1 - 7
Design Firm Zamboo

1. Client   Dogloo
    Designer   Dave Zambotti

2. Client   Big Sisters of LA
    Designer   Dave Zambotti

3. Client   Creative Solutions Group
    Designer   Becca Bootes

4. Client   Black & Blu
    Designers   Dave Zambotti & Jeff Allison

5. Client   Premiere Dental
    Designers   Dave Zambotti & Becca Bootes

6. Client   CMC
    Designers   Becca Bootes & Dave Zambotti

7. Client   Zfilmmaker
    Designer   Dave Zambotti

(opposite)
Design Firm Sabingrafik, Inc.

    Client   Odyssey
    Designers   Lisa Peters & Tracy Sabin

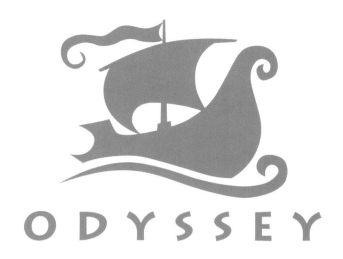

ODYSSEY

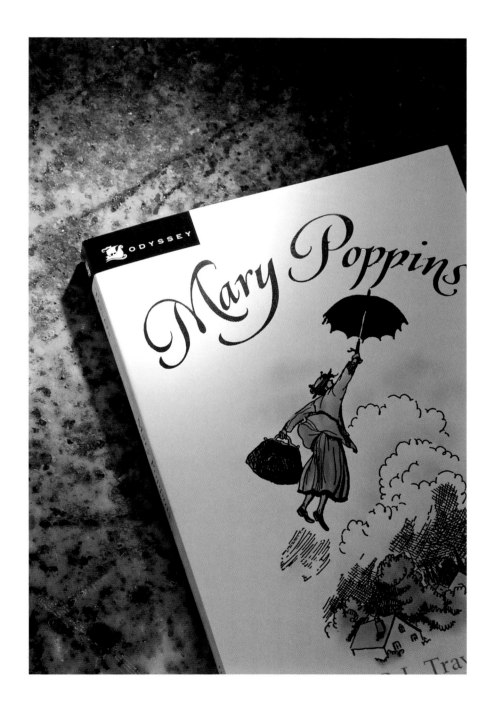

1.

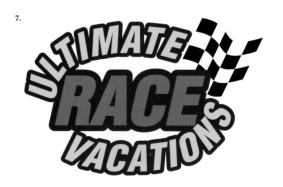

2.

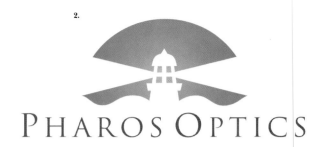

3.

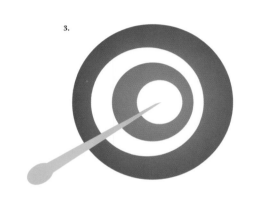

4.

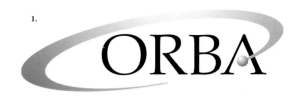

5.

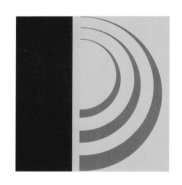

6.

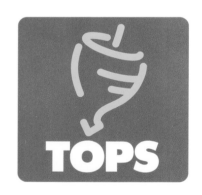

7.

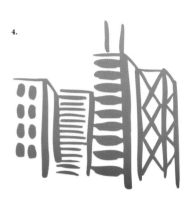

8.

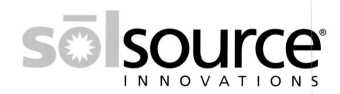

9.

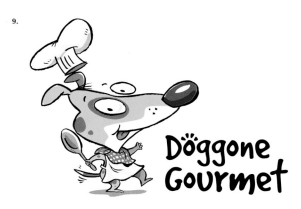

10.

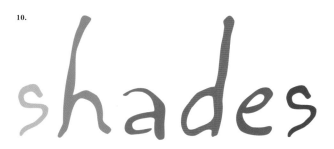

11.

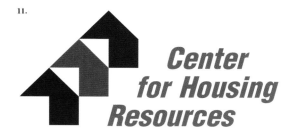

12.

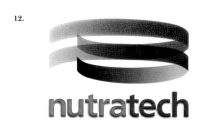

13.

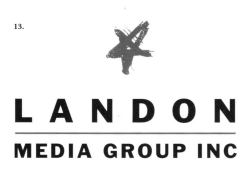

14.

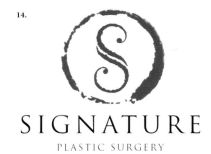

15.

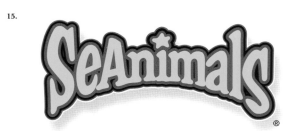

1 - 6, 8 - 9		
Design Firm	**Zamboo**	
7, 11		
Design Firm	**Cathey Associates, Inc.**	
10, 12 - 14		
Design Firm	**Lotas Minard Patton McIver**	
15		
Design Firm	**Dixon & Parcels Associates, Inc.**	

1. Client	ORBA	
Designer	Becca Bootes	
2. Client	Pharos Optics	
Designer	Becca Bootes	
3. Client	Baton Records	
Designer	Dave Zambotti	
4. Client	Windy City Productions	
Designer	Becca Bootes	
5. Client	Demand	
Designers	Dave Zambotti, Chris Go, & Becca Bootes	
6. Client	Tops	
Designer	Dave Zambotti	

7. Client	Ultimate Race Vacations	
Designer	Gordon Cathey	
8. Client	Solsource	
Designers	Becca Bootes, Chris Go, & Dave Zambotti	
9. Client	Doggone Gourmet	
Designers	Dave Zambotti & Chris Sharp	
10. Client	Dana (Shades)	
Designers	Kristin Moore-Gantz & Suzan Merritt	
11. Client	Center for Housing Resources	
Designer	Gordon Cathey	
12. Client	Nutratech Inc	
Designer	Daniela Ganem	
13. Client	Landon Media Group	
Designer	Yucel Erdogan	
14. Client	Signature Plastic Surgery	
Designer	Yucel Erdogan	
15. Client	Austin Quality Foods, Inc.	

1.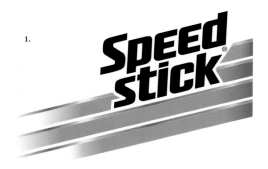

2.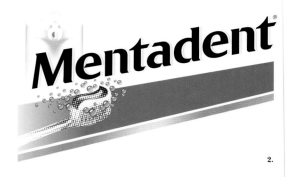

3.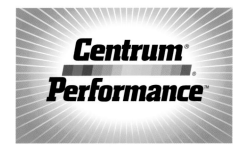

4.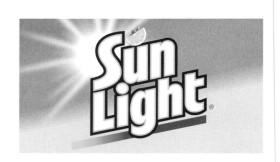

5.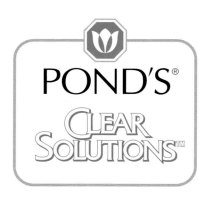

6.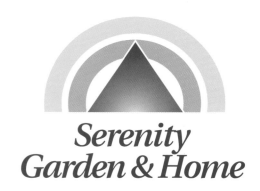

7.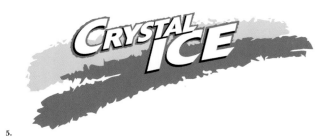

8.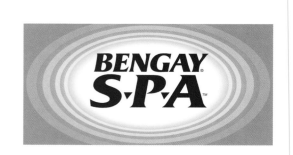

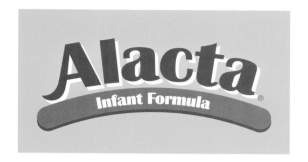

9.

STARR LITIGATION SERVICES, INC

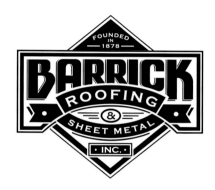

11.

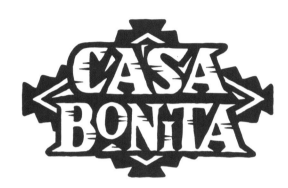

12.

14.

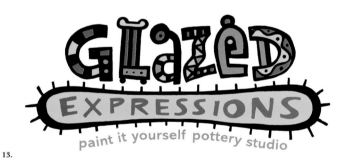

13.

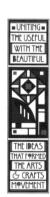

UNITING THE USEFUL WITH THE BEAUTIFUL

THE IDEAS THAT FORMED THE ARTS & CRAFTS MOVEMENT

15.

1 - 9
Design Firm Hans Flink Design Inc.
10 - 14
Design Firm Sayles Graphic Design
15
Design Firm Faine-Oller Productions, Inc.

1. Client   Colgate-Palmolive (Speed Stick)
    Designers   Mark Krukonis
                  & Susan Kunschaft

2. Client   Unilever HPC, USA
                  (Mentadent)
    Designer   Chang-Mei Lin

3. Client   Whitehall-Robins
                  (Centrum Performance)
    Designers   Chang-Mei Lin
                  & Susan Kunschaft

4. Client   Unilever HPC, USA (Sunlight)
    Designers   Michael Troian
                  & Harry Bertschmann

5. Client   Unilever HPC, USA
                  (Crystal Ice)
    Designers   Susan Kunschaft
                  & Chang-Mi Lin

6. Client   Serenity Garden & Home
    Designers   Loi Van Name & Hans D. Flink

7. Client   Unilever HPC, USA
                  (Pond's Clear Solutions)
    Designers   Chang Mei-Lin, Susan
                  Kunschaft, & Michael Troian

8. Client   Pfizer Inc. (Bengay SPA)
    Designer   Chang-Mei Lin

9. Client   Mead Johnson (Alacta)
    Designer   Susan Kunschaft

10. Client   Starr Litigation Services, Inc.
    Designer   John Sayles

11. Client   Barrick Roofing
    Designer   John Sayles

12. Client   Casa Bonita
    Designer   John Sayles

13. Client   Glazed Expressions
    Designer   John Sayles

14. Client   Pattee Enterprises
    Designer   John Sayles

15. Client   Coleson Foods, Inc.
    Designers   Catherine Oller, Barbara Faine,
                  Bruce Hale, & Steve Coppin

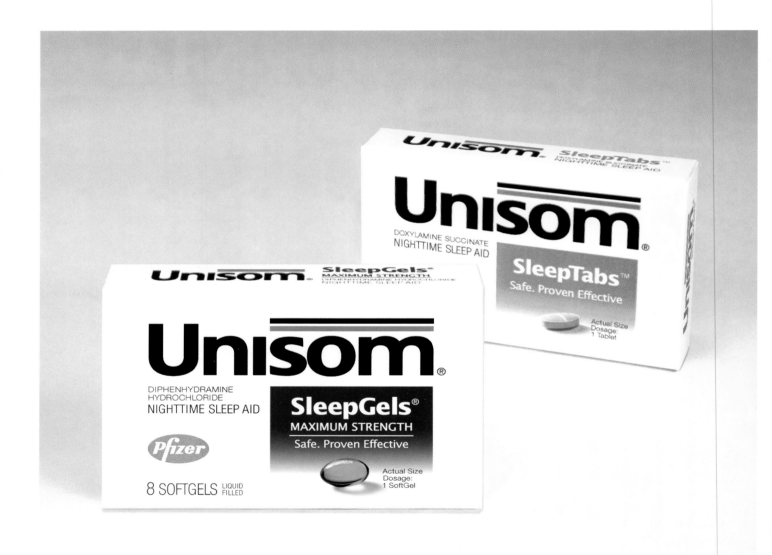

1.

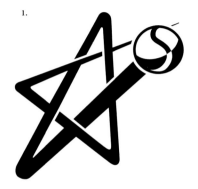

2.

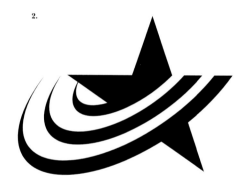

3.

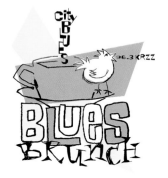

4.

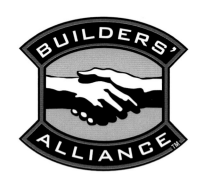

5.

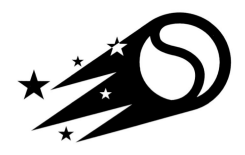

6.

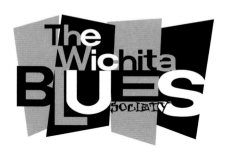

7.

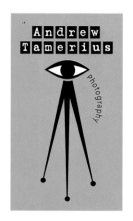

(opposite)
Design Firm **Hans Flink Design Inc.**

Client   Pfizer Inc. (Unisom)
Designers Michael Troian
           & Harry Berschmann

1 - 7
Design Firm **Dotzero Design**

1. Client   Star Advisors Softball Team
    Designers Jon Wippich & Karen Wippich

2. Client   Star Advisors Program Logo
    Designers Karen Wippich & Jon Wippich

3. Client   Star Advisors Night Flight Event
    Designers Jon Wippich & Karen Wippich

4. Client   HMH Advertising/
               Louisiana-Pacific
    Designer Jon Wippich

5. Client   The Wichita Blues Society,
               Blues Brunch
    Designers Karen Wippich & Jon Wippich

6. Client   Wichita Blues Society
    Designers Karen Wippich & Jon Wippich

7. Client   Andrew Tamerius Photography
    Designers Karen Wippich & Jon Wippich

1.

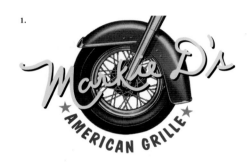

2.

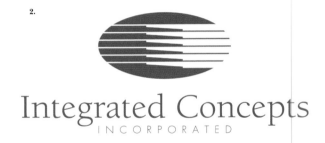
Integrated Concepts
INCORPORATED

3.

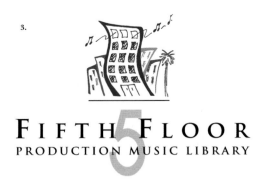

FIFTH **5** FLOOR
PRODUCTION MUSIC LIBRARY

4.

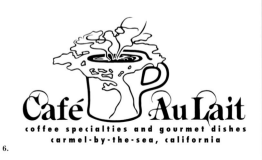

5.

Adamm's

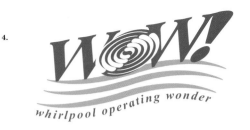
Café Au Lait
coffee specialties and gourmet dishes
carmel-by-the-sea, california

6.

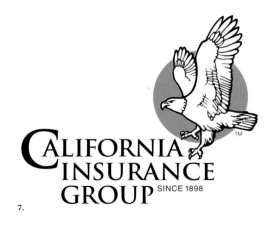
CALIFORNIA
INSURANCE
GROUP SINCE 1898

7.

CALIFORNIA
RESTAURANT
ASSOCIATION
EDUCATIONAL
FOUNDATION

8.

9.

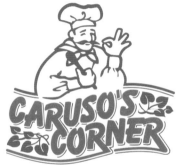

10.

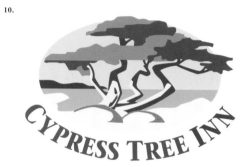

11.

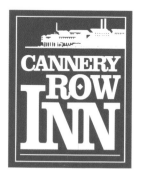

12.

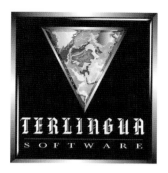

13.

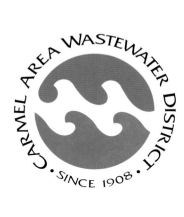

14.

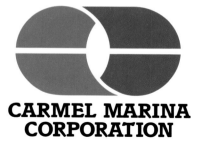

15.

1 - 5
Design Firm   Innovative Design & Advertising
6 - 11, 13 - 15
Design Firm   The Wecker Group
12
Design Firm   Maxi Harper Graphics

1. Client   Markie D's Restaurant
   Designers   Kim Crossett-Neumann
                 & Susan Nickey-Newton

2. Client   ITM
   Designers   Kim Crossett-Neumann
                 & Susan Nickey-Newton

3. Client   ABC-5th Floor Production
                 Music Library
   Designers   Kim Crossett-Neumann
                 & Susan Nickey-Newton

4. Client   vico
   Designers   Kim Crossett-Neumann
                 & Susan Nickey-Newton

5. Client   Adamm's Stained Glass
   Designers   Kim Crossett-Neumann, Susan
                 Nickey-Newton, & Dan Cotton

6. Client   Café au Lait Restaurant
   Designers   Robert Wecker

7. Client   California Insurance Group
   Designer   Robert Wecker

8. Client   California
                 Restaurant Association
   Designer   Robert Wecker

9. Client   Caruso's Corner
   Designer   Robert Wecker

10. Client   Cypress Tree Inn
    Designer   Robert Wecker

11. Client   Cannery Row Inn
    Designer   Robert Wecker
    Illustrator Mark Savee

12. Client   Terlingua
    Designer   Maxi Harper

13. Client   Carmel Area Waste
                 Management District
    Designer   Robert Wecker

14. Client   Carmel Marina Corporation
    Designer   Robert Wecker

15. Client   Carmel Valley Inn &
                 Tennis Resort
    Designer   Robert Wecker

1.

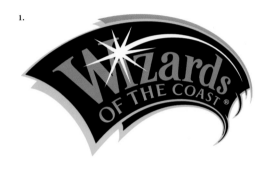

2.

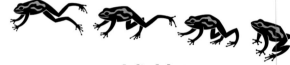

3.

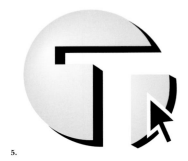

4.

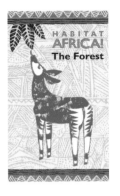

5.

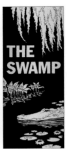

6.

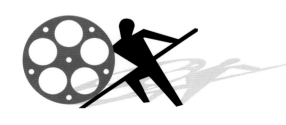

7.

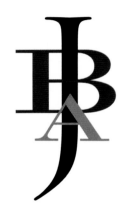

1
Design Firm Wizards/Spire Design
2 - 4
Design Firm Brookfield Zoo
5, 7
Design Firm Squires & Company
6

Designer Brandon Murphy

1. Client Wizards of the Coast

2, 3
    Client Brookfield Zoo
    Designer Hannah Jennings
    Illustrator Edith Emmengger

4. Client Brookfield Zoo
    Designers Andrew Murashige &
    Peter Skach
    Illustrator Jeff O'Connor

5. Client Techware Information Systems
    Designer Anna Magruder

6. Client Motion Projects
    Designer Brandon Murphy

7. Client Bill Jackson Associates
    Designer Christie Grotheim

(opposite)
    Design Firm Sayles Graphic Design

8. Client 1999 Iowa State Fair
    "Knock Yourself Out"
    Designer John Sayles

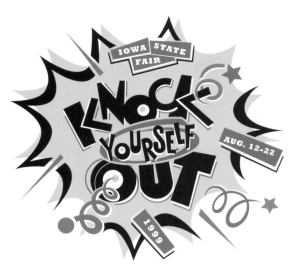

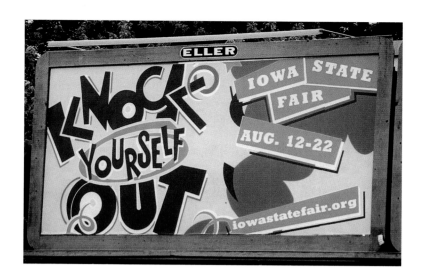

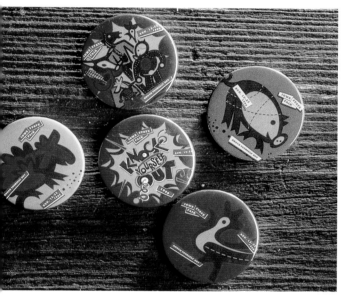

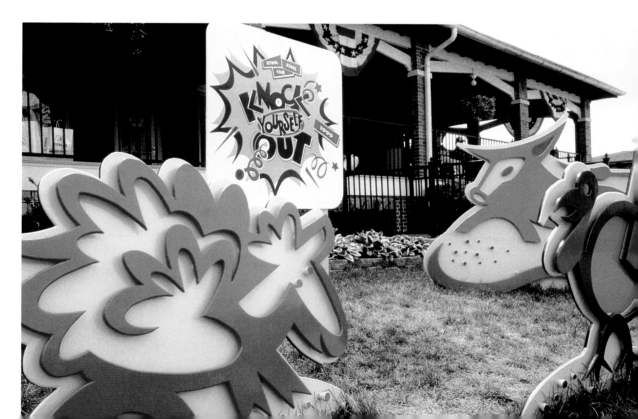

1.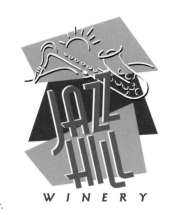

2.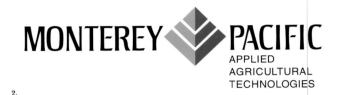

3.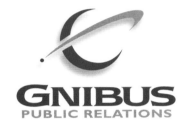

4.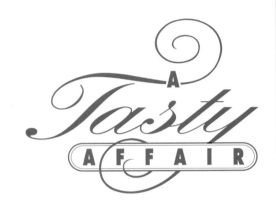

5.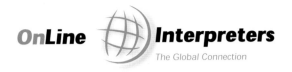

6.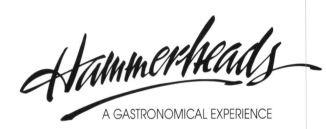

7.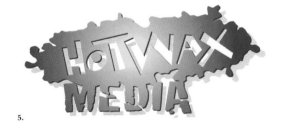

8.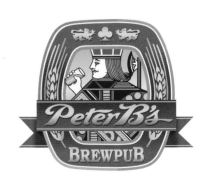

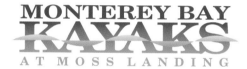

9.

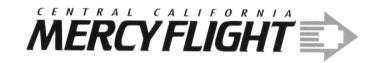

10.

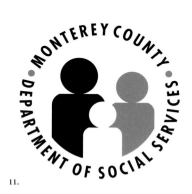

11.

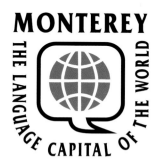

12.

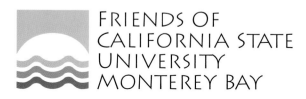

13.

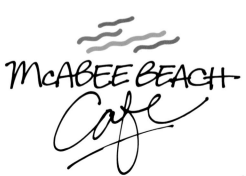

14.

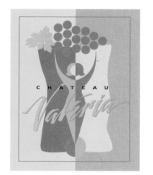

15.

(all)

	Design Firm	The Wecker Group
1.	Client	OnLine Interpreters, Inc.
	Designer	Robert Wecker
2.	Client	Monterey Pacific, Inc.
	Designer	Robert Wecker
3.	Client	Gnibus Public Relations
	Designer	Matt Gnibus
4.	Client	KAZU Public Radio
	Designer	Robert Wecker
5.	Client	Hot Wax Media
	Designer	Robert Wecker
6.	Client	Hammerheads Restaurant
	Designers	Robert Wecker & Mark Savee
7.	Client	CaskOne Vineyards
	Designer	Robert Wecker

8.	Client	Doubletree Monterey
	Designers	Robert Wecker & Matt Gnibus
9.	Client	Monterey Bay Kayaks
	Designers	Robert Wecker & Matt Gnibus
10.	Client	Mercy Flight/Central California
	Designer	Robert Wecker
11.	Client	Monterey County Department of Social Services
	Designer	Robert Wecker
12.	Client	City of Monterey
	Designer	Robet Wecker
13.	Client	CSU Monterey Bay
	Designer	Robert Wecker
14.	Client	McAbee Beach Cafe
	Designers	Robert Wecker & James Kyllo
15.	Client	Mink Vineyards
	Designer	Robet Wecker

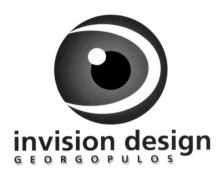

invision design
GEORGOPULOS

1.

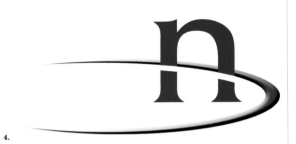

REDHANDRECORDS

2.

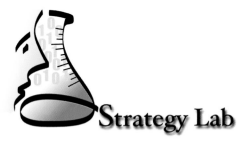

Strategy Lab

3.

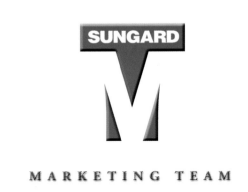

4.

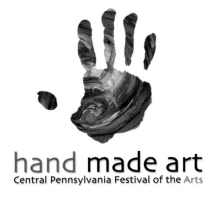

hand made art
Central Pennsylvania Festival of the Arts

5.

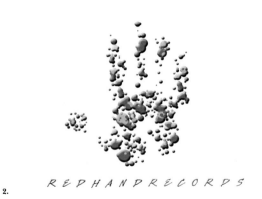

MARKETING TEAM

6.

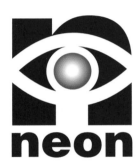

neon

7.

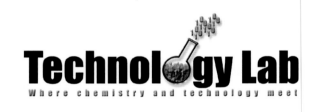

8.

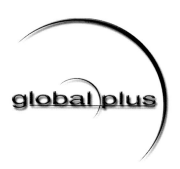

9.

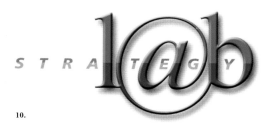

10.

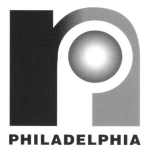

11.

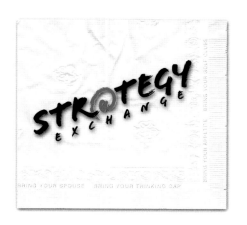

12.

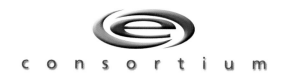

PHILADELPHIA
registered nurse
practitioner

13.

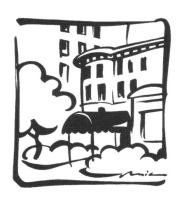

14.

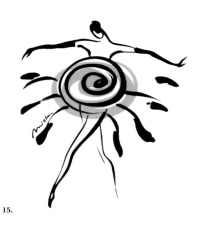

15.

1 - 13
Design Firm   Georgopulos Design
14, 15
Design Firm   Misha Design Studio

1. Client	Georgopulos Design	
Designer	Jonathan Georgopulos	
2. Client	Red Hand Records	
Designer	Jonathan Georgopulos	
3. Client	SunGard	
Designer	Jonathan Georgopulos	
4. Client	N	
Designer	Jonathan Georgopulos	
5. Client	Arts Fest 2000	
Designer	Jonathan Georgopulos	
6. Client	SunGard	
Designer	Jonathan Georgopulos	
7. Client	Neon	
Designer	Jonathan Georgopulos	

8. Client	SunGard
Designer	Jonathan Georgopulos
9. Client	Global Plus
Designer	Jonathan Georgopulos
10, 11	
Client	SunGard
Designer	Jonathan Georgopulos
12. Client	econsortium
Designer	Jonathan Georgopulos
13. Client	PHL Nurse Association
Designer	Jonathan Georgopulos
14. Client	Brookline Dental Studio
Designer	Misha Lenn
15. Client	Boston Ballet
Designer	Misha Lenn

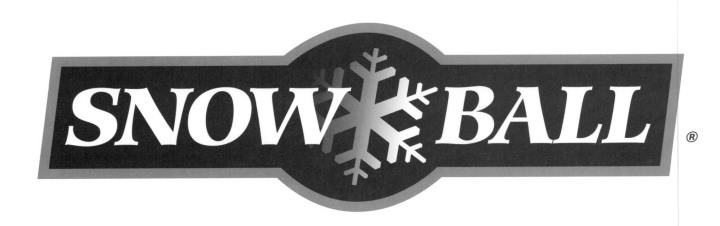

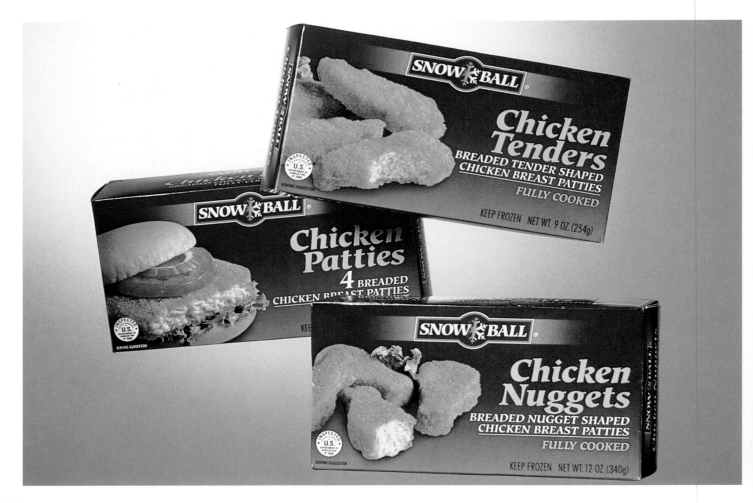

1.

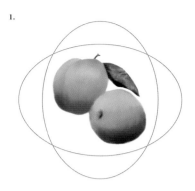

2.

3.

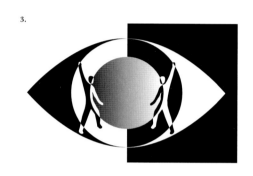

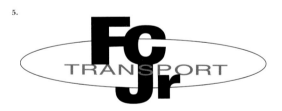
4.

5.

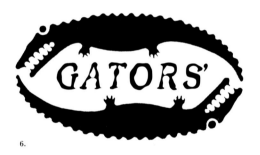

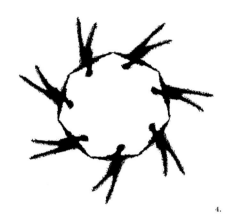
6.

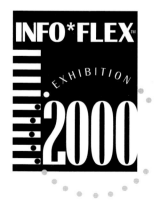
7.

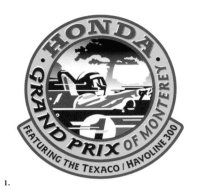

1.

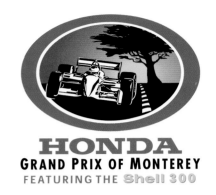

2.

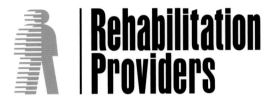

3.

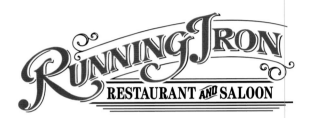

4.

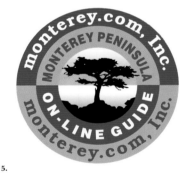

5.

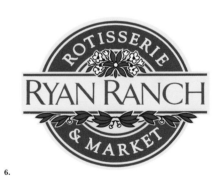

6.

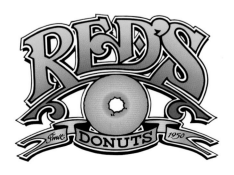

7.

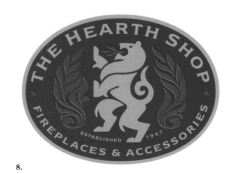

8.

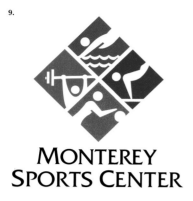

MONTEREY SPORTS CENTER

9.

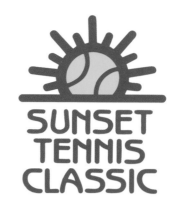

SUNSET TENNIS CLASSIC

10.

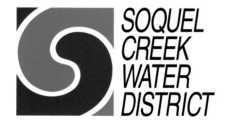

MONTEREY PENINSULA CHAMBER OF COMMERCE

11.

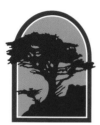

LIST ENGINEERING COMPANY

Mechanical Consultants

12.

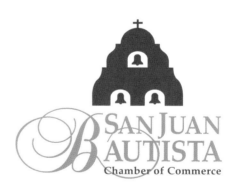

SOQUEL CREEK WATER DISTRICT

13.

San Juan Bautista Chamber of Commerce

14.

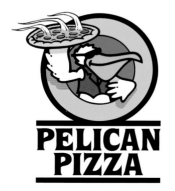

PELICAN PIZZA

15.

1 - 15
Design Firm The Wecker Group

1, 2					
	Client	Laguna Seca Raceway	9.	Client	Monterey Sports Center
	Designer	Robert Wecker		Designer	Robert Wecker
3.	Client	Rehabilitation Providers	10.	Client	Pacific Grove Rotary Club
	Designer	Robert Wecker		Designer	Robert Wecker
4.	Client	Running Iron Restaurant	11.	Client	Monterey Peninsula
	Designer	Robert Wecker			Chamber of Commerce
	Illustrator	Mark Savee		Designer	Robert Wecker
5.	Client	Monterey.com, Inc.	12.	Client	List Engineering Company
	Designer	Robert Wecker		Designer	Robert Wecker
6.	Client	Ryan Ranch Rotisserie	13.	Client	Soquel Creek Water District
	Designer	Robert Wecker		Designer	Robert Wecker
7.	Client	Red's Donuts	14.	Client	San Juan Bautista
	Designer	Robert Wecker			Chamber of Commerce
	Illustrator	Mark Savee		Designer	Robert Wecker
8.	Client	The Hearth Shop	15.	Client	Pelican Pizza
	Designer	Robert Wecker		Designer	Robert Wecker

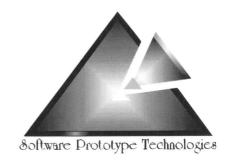

1.

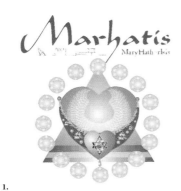

2.

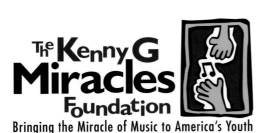

3.

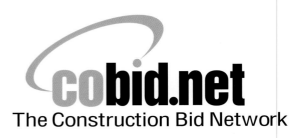

4.

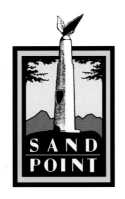

5.

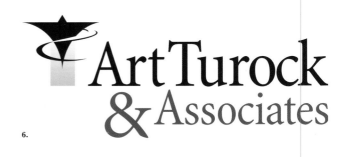

6.

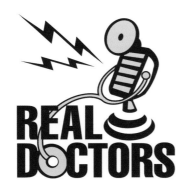

7.

1 - 2
Design Firm Maxi Harper Graphics
3 - 7
Design Firm Gable Design Group

1. Client   Marhatis: Spiritual-Healer
                 of Three Goddesses
    Designer   Maxi Harper

2. Client   SPT
    Designer   Maxi Harper

3. Client   Kenny G
    Designer   Damon Nakagawa

4. Client   cobid.net
    Designer   Damon Nakagawa

5. Client   Glenn Sound
    Designers   Damon Nakagawa
                & Ayumi Inoue

6. Client   Art Turock & Associates
    Designers   Tony Gable & Damon Nakagawa

7. Client   City of Seattle
    Designers   Tony Gable & Damon Nakagawa

(opposite)
Design Firm DYNAPAC Design Group

    Client   Harbor Lights Candle Shop
    Designer   Lee A. Aellig

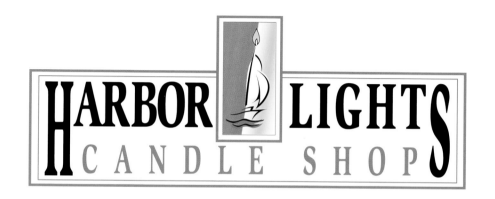

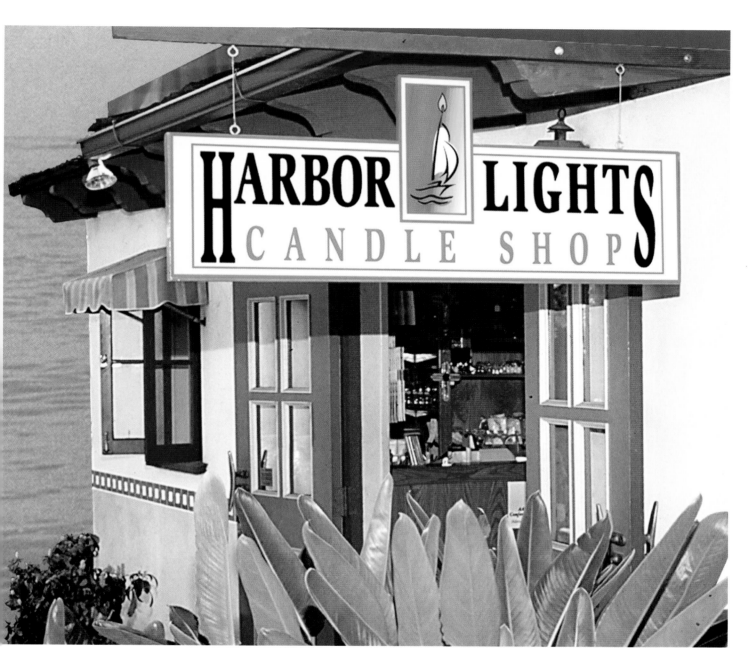

Rubbish

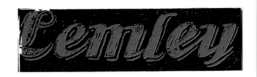

1.

2.

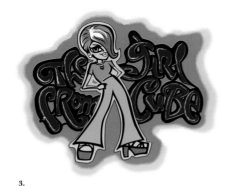

3.

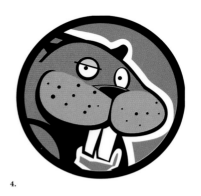

4.

APPLIANT

5.

jacknabbit.com

6.

Lingo

7.

8.

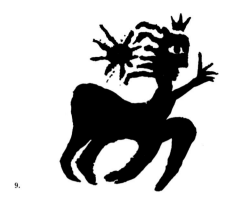

9.

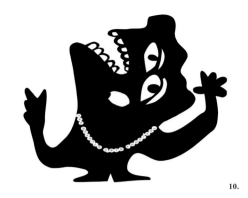

10.

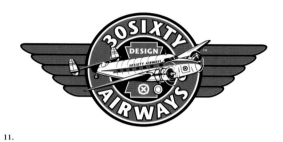

11.

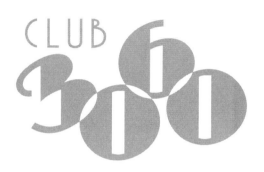

12.

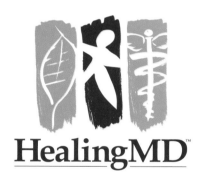

HealingMD™

13.

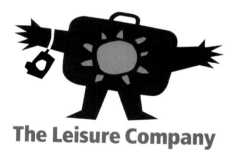

The Leisure Company

14.

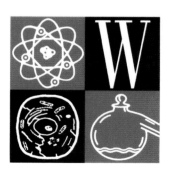

15.

distilled images

a picture's worth

1.

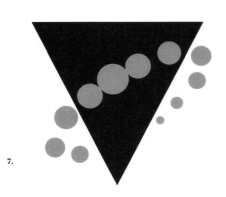

2.

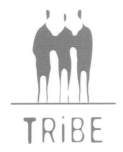

TRiBE

[m o v i n g]

Pictures

3.

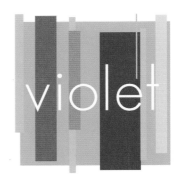

4.

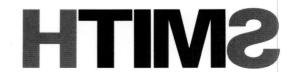

5.

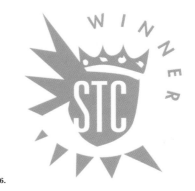

6.

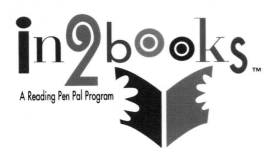

7.

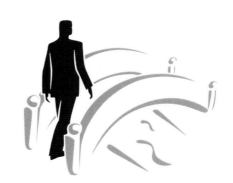

8.

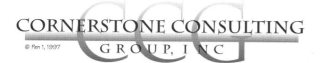

9.

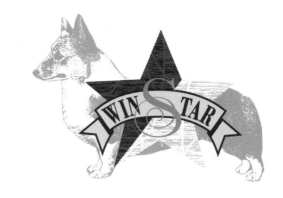

10.

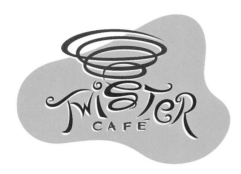

11.

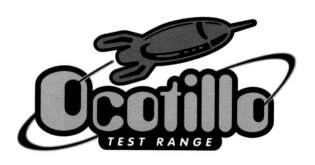

12.

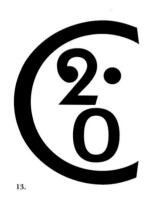

13.

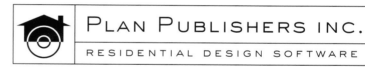

14.

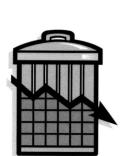

15.

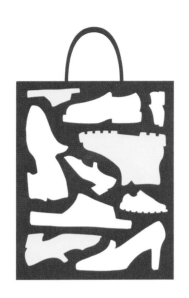

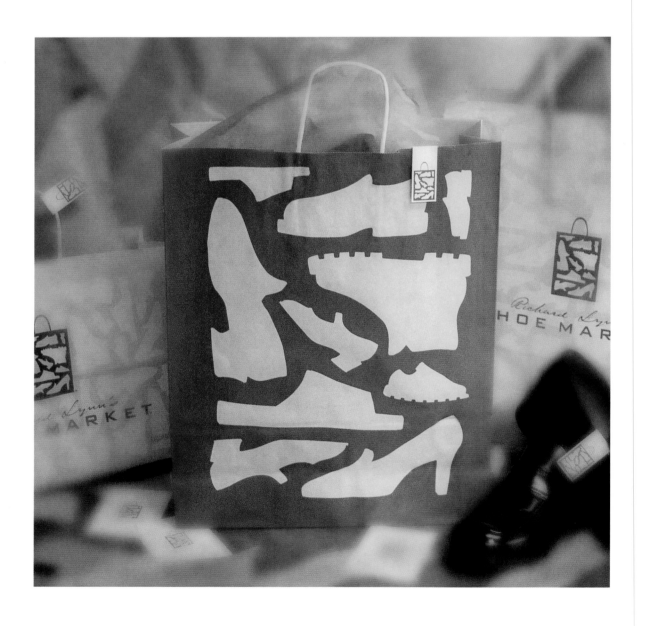

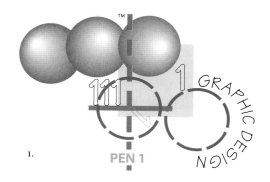

1.

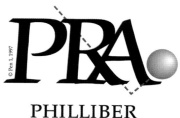

2.

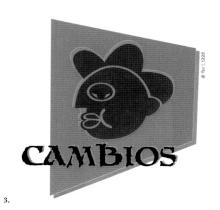

3.

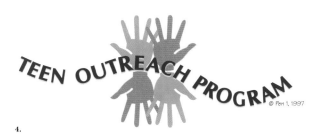

4.

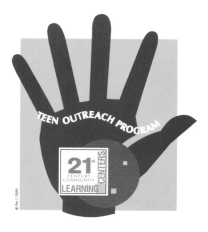

5.

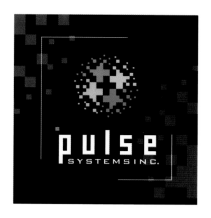

6.

7.

(opposite)
Design Firm **Insight Design Communications**

Client   Richard Lynn's Shoe Market
Designers   Sherrie & Tracy Holdeman

1 - 5
Design Firm **Pen 1**

6
Design Firm **Insight Design Communications**

7
Design Firm **Walsh & Associates, Inc.**

1. Client   Pen 1
   Designer   Karen Bahadori

2. Client   Philliber Research Associates
   Designer   Karen Bahadori

3. Client   Teen Outreach Program/
               Cambios
   Designers   Karen Bahadori &
               Alicia Colina-Ashby

4, 5
   Client   Teen Outreach Program
   Designer   Karen Bahadori

6. Client   Pulse System Inc.
   Designers   Sherrie & Tracy Holdeman

7. Client   Fran's Chocolates Ltd.
   Designer   Miriam Lisco

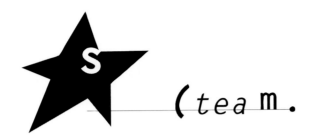

1.

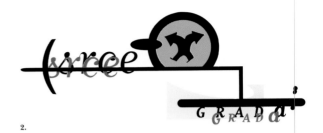

2.

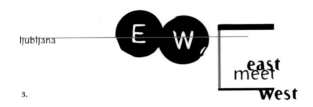

3.

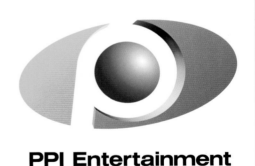

4.

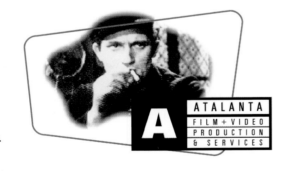

5.

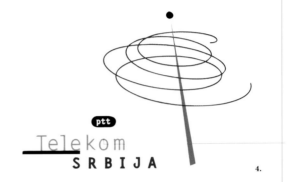

PPI Entertainment

6.

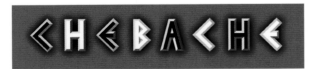

7.

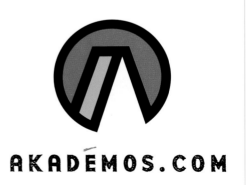

AKADEMOS.COM

8.

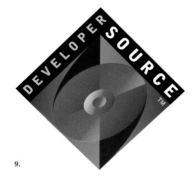

9.

SHIMIƵU — SHIMIZU DESIGN STUDIO INC.

10.

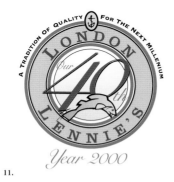

11.

Harvest Moon ™

The best meals under the moon.

12.

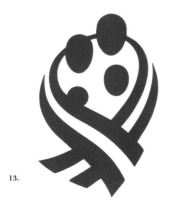

13.

ASSASSINS

14.

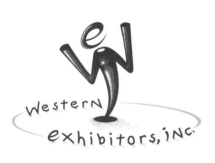

15.

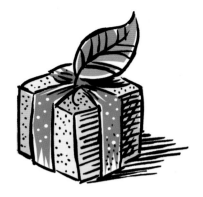

1.

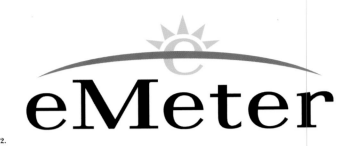

2.

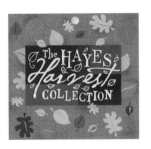

3.

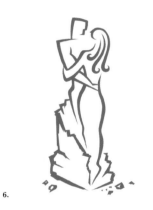

4.

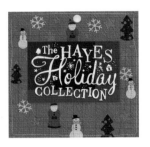

5.

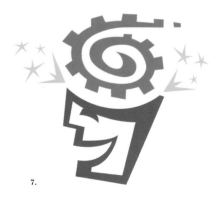

6.

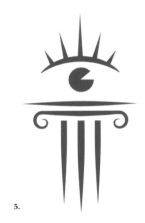

7.

(all)
Design Firm Insight Design Communications

1. Client   gardenandholiday.com
    Designers   Sherrie and Tracy Holdeman

2. Client   eMeter
    Designers   Sherrie and Tracy Holdeman

3, 4
    Client   The Hayes Co.
    Designers   Sherrie and Tracy Holdeman

5. Client   Howard's Optique
    Designers   Sherrie and Tracy Holdeman

6. Client   Physique Enhancement
    Designers   Sherrie and Tracy Holdeman

7. Client   Gear Up
    Designers   Sherrie and Tracy Holdeman

(opposite)
Design Firm Whitney Stinger, Inc.

    Client   Bone Daddy +
                 The Blues Shakers
    Designers   Mike Whitney & Karl Stinger

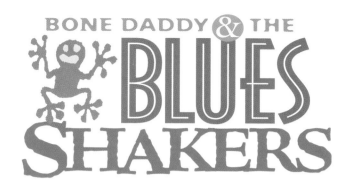

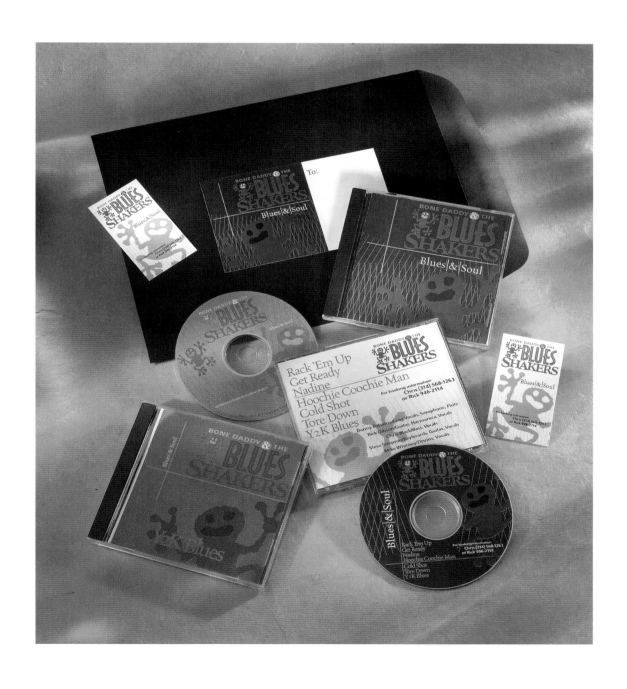

d'MUIR

1.

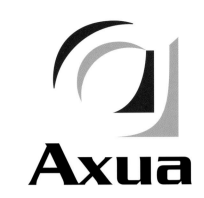

Axua

2.

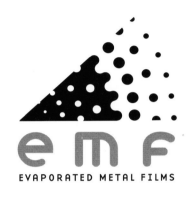

emf
EVAPORATED METAL FILMS

3.

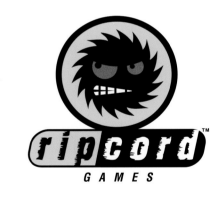

G★ball

4.

im●de
retrievalsystems

5.

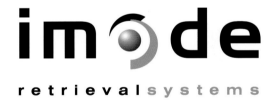

ripcord™
GAMES

6.

3|2
CollegeAvenue

7.

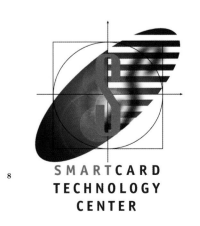

SMARTCARD
TECHNOLOGY
CENTER

8.

264

The Replication Challenge:

Lessons Learned from the
National Replication Project for
the Teen Outreach Program (TOP)

9.

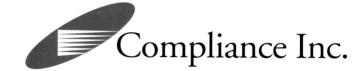

10.

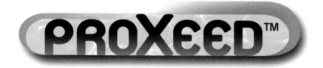

11.

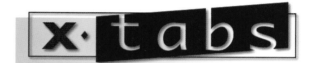

12.

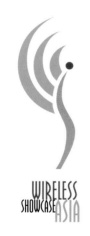

13.

14.

HOLY

TRINITY

CATHOLIC

CHURCH

1787 ANNO DOMINI

ACURA

CLASSIC

15.

1 - 7		
Design Firm	**Iron Design**	
8, 10 - 14		
Design Firm	**Tim Kenney Design Partners**	
9		
Design Firm	**Pen 1**	
15		
Design Firm	**Lawson Design**	

	Client	Marietta Corp.
1.	Designer	Todd Edmonds
2.	Client	AXUA
	Designer	Todd Edmonds
3.	Client	Evaporated Metal Films Corp.
	Designer	Todd Edmonds
4.	Client	Momentum Media
	Designer	Jim Keller
5.	Client	Imode Retrieval Systems
	Designer	Todd Edmonds
6.	Client	Rip Cord Games
	Designer	Jim Keller
7.	Client	Integrated Acquisitions & Development
	Designer	Todd Edmonds

8.	Client	GSA (General Services Administration)
	Designer	Tim Kenney
9.	Client	Teen Outreach Program
	Designer	Karen Bahadori
10.	Client	Compliance Inc.
	Designer	Tim Kenney
11.	Client	Sigma-Tau Pharmaceuticals, Inc. (proXeed)
	Designer	Tim Kenney
12.	Client	New Dominion Resources Corporation (x-tabs)
	Designer	Monica Banko
13.	Client	PCIA (Personal Communications Industry Association)
	Designer	Charlene Gamba
14.	Client	Holy Trinity Catholic Church
	Designer	Tim Kenney
15.	Client	Rubin Postaer & Assoc. (Acura)
	Designers	Jeff Lawson & Bob Francis

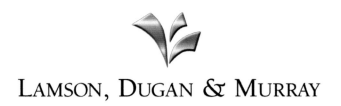

LAMSON, DUGAN & MURRAY

1.

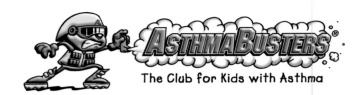

2.

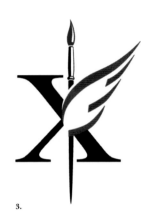

3.

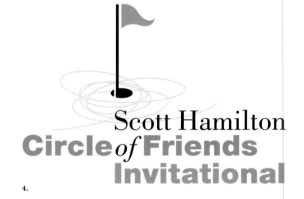

4.

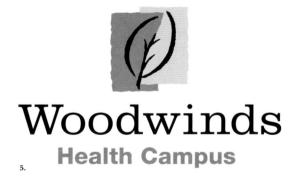

Woodwinds

Health Campus

5.

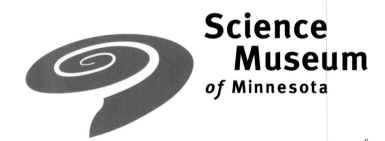

6.

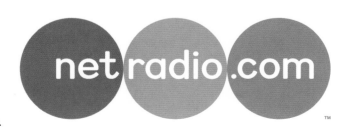

7.

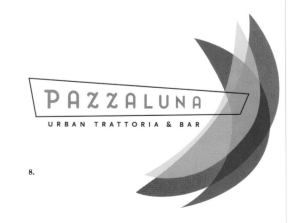

8.

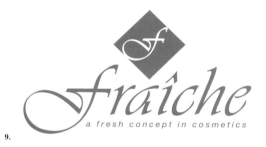

9.

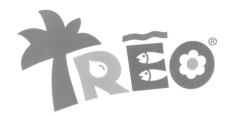

COMMERCIAL REAL ESTATE
1776 BROADWAY ■ SUITE 2000 ■ NEW YORK, NY 10019

10.

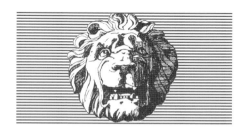

11.

12.

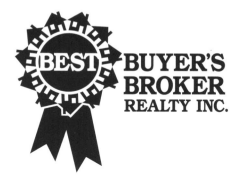

13.

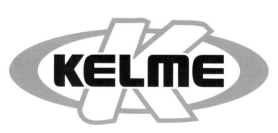

14.

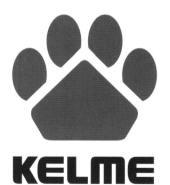

15.

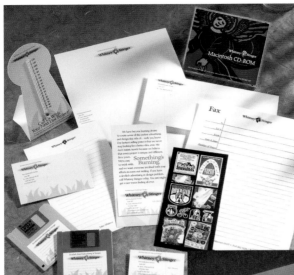

Devilish Good Advertising & Design

Whitney ☻ Stinger

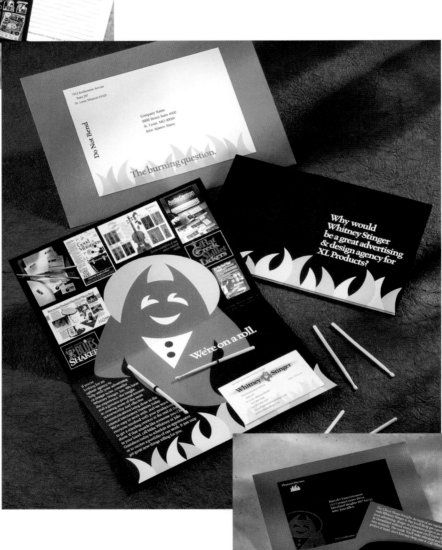

1.

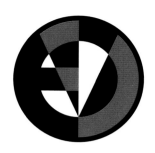

EVD Advertising

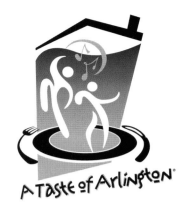

2.

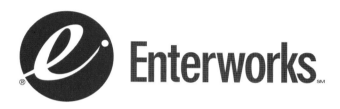

3.

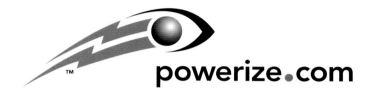

4.

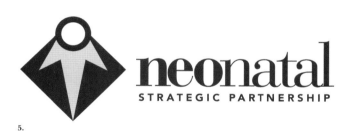

5.

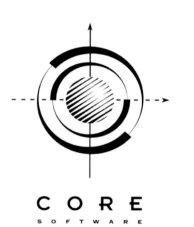

6.

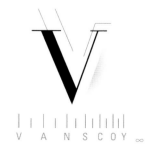

7.

(opposite)
Design Firm Whitney Stinger

Client   Whitney Stinger, Inc
Designers   Mike Whitney & Karl Stinger

1 - 5
Design Firm EVD Advertising
6, 7
Design Firm Curry Design Associates

1. Client   EVD Advertising
   Designers   Rachel Deutsch & David Street

2. Client   Taste of Arlington
   Designers   Rachel Deutsch & Marc Foelsch

3. Client   Enterworks
   Designers   Rachel Deutsch, Blake Stenning,
               & Marc Foelsch

4. Client   Powerize
   Designers   Rachel Deutsch &
               Tom Cosgrove

5. Client   Neonatal Strategic Partnership
   Designers   Rachel Deutsch & Marc Foelsch

6. Client   Core Software Technology
   Designer   Jason Scheideman

7. Client   VanScoy Photography
   Designer   Jason Scheideman

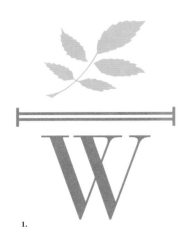

1.

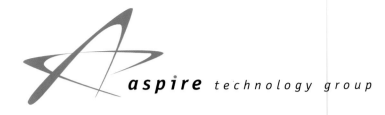

2.

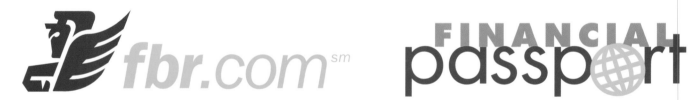

3.

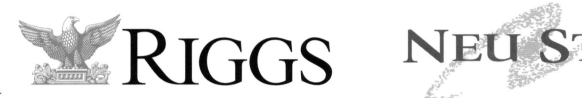

4.

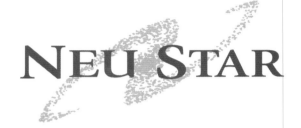

5.

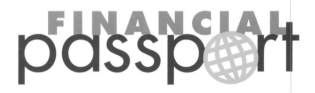

6.

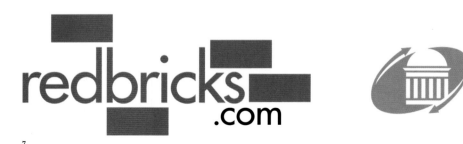

7.

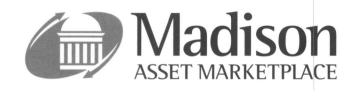

8.

WINGATE
UNIVERSITY

9.

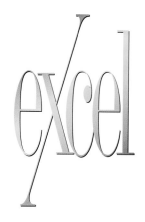

10.

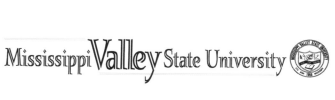

11.

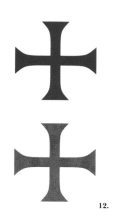

12.

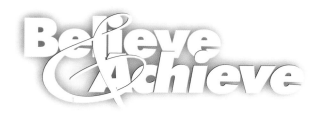

13.

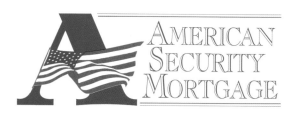

14.

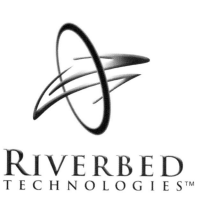

15.

1 - 8
Design Firm Iconixx
            (Iconixx Web Development)
9 - 14
Design Firm Steve Thomas
            Marketing Communications
15
Design Firm EVD Advertising

1. Client   The Mark Winkler Company
    Designers   Gretchen Frederick &
                Anjeanette Agro

2. Client   Aspire Technology Group
    Designers   John Cabot Lodge &
                Robin Clay Diamond

3. Client   Riggs Bank NA
    Designers   John Cabot Lodge &
                Andrew Johnson
    Illustrator Mark Summers

4. Client   Neu Star, Inc.
    Designers   John Cabot Lodge &
                Lara Santos

5. Client   FBR.com
    Designer   Andrew Johnson

6. Client   Pace Financial Network, LLC
    Designers   John Cabot Lodge &
                Lara Santos

7. Client   Redbricks.com
    Designers   John Cabot Lodge &
                Lara Santos

8. Client   Madison Asset Marketplace
    Designers   John Cabot Lodge, Mary
                Parsons, & Chuck Sundin

9. Client   Wingate University
    Designer   Steve Thomas

10. Client   UNC Charlotte
    Designer   Steve Thomas

11. Client   Mississippi Valley State
                University
    Designer   Steve Thomas

12. Client   Church of the Beloved
    Designer   Steve Thomas

13. Client   Charlotte Country Day School
    Designers   Steve Thomas & Dan Wold

14. Client   American Security Mortgage
    Designer   Steve Thomas

15. Client   Riverbed Technologies
    Designers   Rachel Deutsch &
                Marc Foelsch

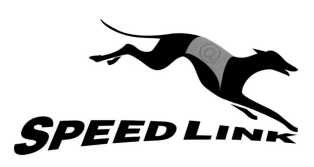

1.

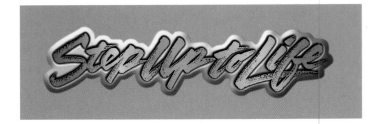

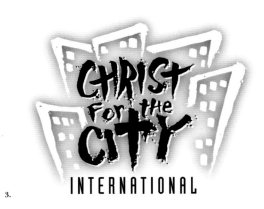

3.

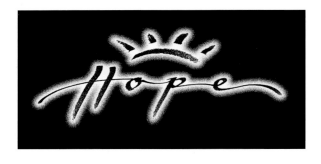

2.

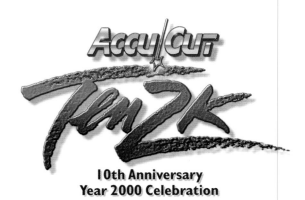

4.

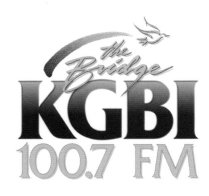

5.

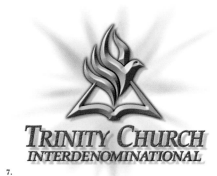

6.

7.

1
Design Firm   **California Design International**

2 - 7
Design Firm   **Dotzler Creative Arts**

1. Client   Diamond Lane Communication
   Designers   Linda Kelley & Dan Liew

2. Client   Step Up To Life

3. Client   Christ For The City

4. Client   Accu-Cut

5. Client   Hope Center

6. Client   KGBI

7. Client   Trinity Church

(opposite)
Design Firm   **Templin Brink Design**

   Client   Classic Company
   Designer   Joel Templin

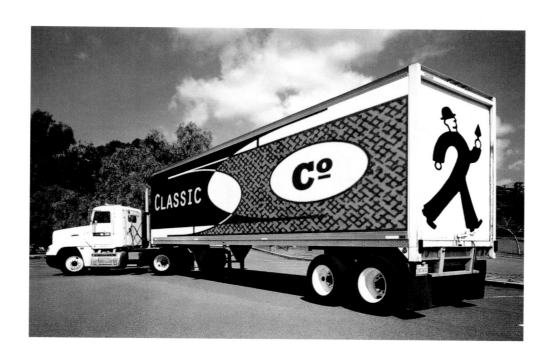

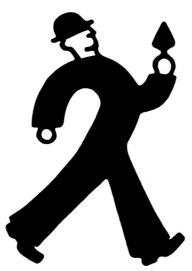

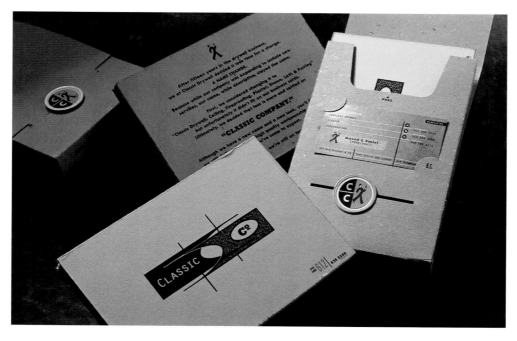

273

TRUEVISION

1.

TRUEVISION
FOUNDATION

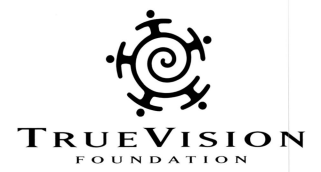

2.

formfunction

3.

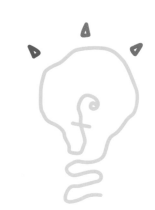

4.

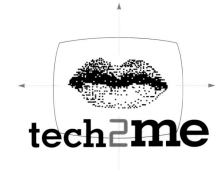

tech2me

5.

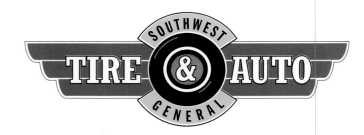

6.

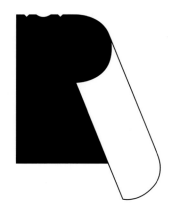

7.

SAGE

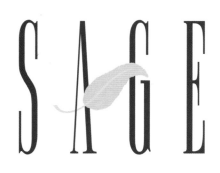

8.

274

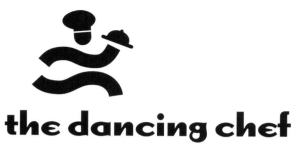

the dancing chef

9.

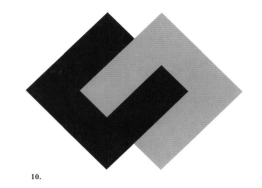

10.

T H E
A R T
I C H
O K E
C A F E

11.

RAA

12.

NATIONAL
ATOMIC
MUSEUM

13.

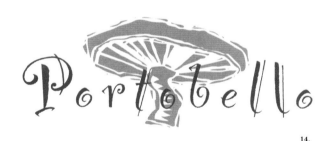

Portobello

14.

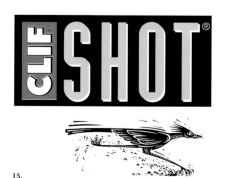

15.

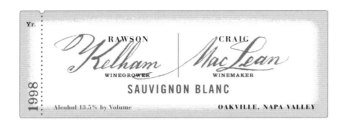

1.

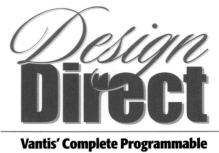

Vantis' Complete Programmable
Logic Software Solution

2.

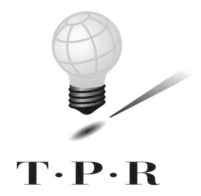

T·P·R

3.

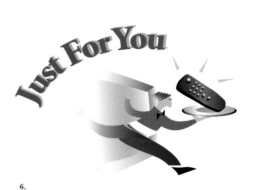

**Real Estate
Energy Solutions**

4.

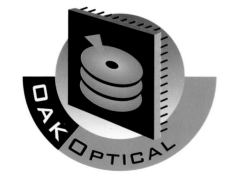

PENSARE™

5.

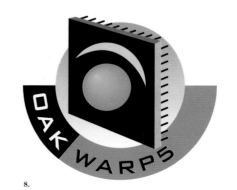

6.

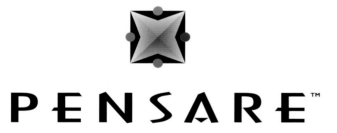

7.

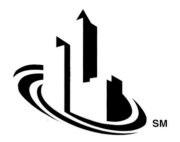

8.

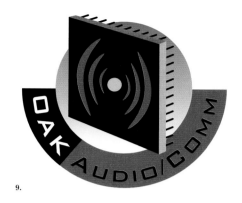

9.

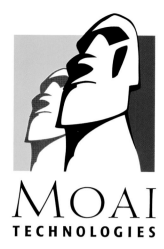

MOAI
TECHNOLOGIES

10.

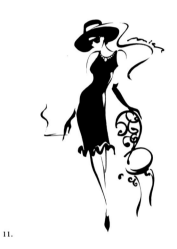

11.

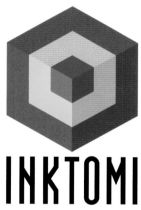

INKTOMI

12.

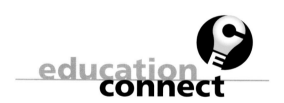

education
connect

13.

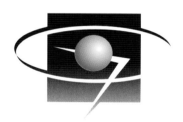

GALIL
WE MOVE THE WORLD

14.

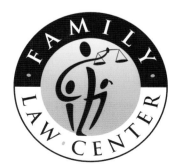

15.

1
Design Firm **Templin Brink Design**
2 - 10, 12 - 15
Design Firm **California Design International**
11
Design Firm **Misha Design Studio**

1. Client	Kelham MacLean Winery	
Designer	Gaby Brink	

2. Client   Vantis
Designers Linda Kelley & Brian Sasville

3. Client   Trainer Public Relation
Designers Linda Kelley & Dan Liew

4. Client   PG & E Energy Services
Designers Linda Kelley &
             Chelsea Hernandez

5. Client   Pensare
Designers Linda Kelley & Suzy Leung

6. Client   On Command—Just For You
Designers Chris Ardito & Dan Liew

7 - 9
Client   Oak Technology
Designers Linda Kelley & Suzy Leung

10. Client   MOAI
Designers Linda Kelley & Dan Liew

11. Client   The Little Black Dress/
             Fashion Show '98
Designer   Misha Lenn

12. Client   INKTOMI
Designer   Linda Kelley

13. Client   Education Connect
Designers Chris Ardito & Brian Sasville

14. Client   Galil
Designers Chris Ardito & Calvin Lew

15. Client   Family Law Center
Designers Linda Kelley & Dan Liew

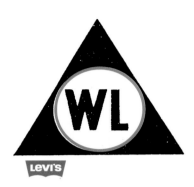

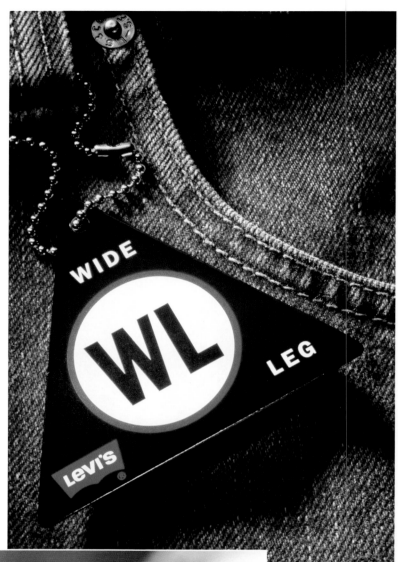

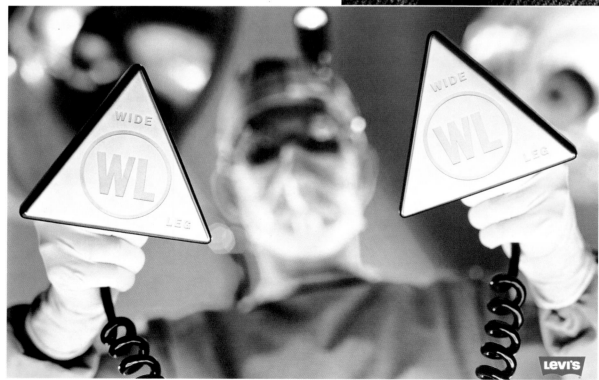

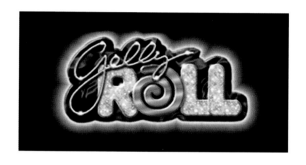

1.

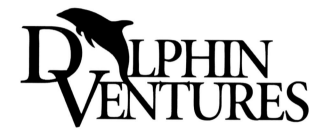

2.

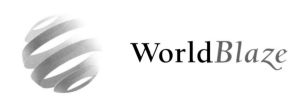

3.

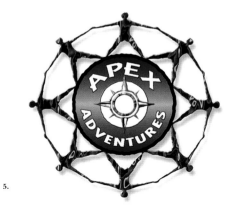

4.

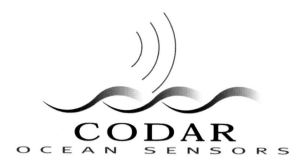

5.

WorldBlaze

6.

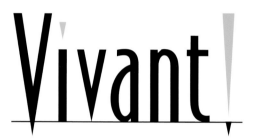

7.

(opposite)
Design Firm Foote, Cone, & Belding

Client   Levi Strauss & Co.
Designer Joel Templin

1 - 5
Design Firm Gunion Design
6, 7
Design Firm California Design International

1. Client   Sakura of America
   Designer Jefrey Gunion

2. Client   Dolphin Ventures
   Designer Jefrey Gunion

3. Client   Codår Ocean Sensors
   Designer Jefrey Gunion

4. Client   Life Action Partnership, Inc.
   Designer Jefrey Gunion

5. Client   Apex Adventures
   Designer Jefrey Gunion

6. Client   World Blaze
   Designers Linda Kelley & Dan Liew

7. Client   Vivant!
   Designers Linda Kelley & Brian Sasville

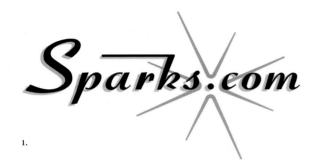

1.

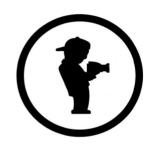

2.

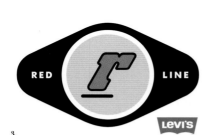

3.

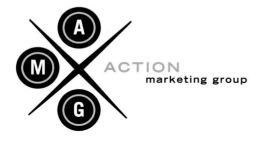

4.

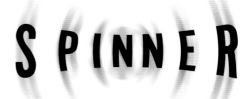

5.

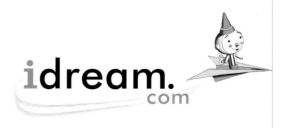

6.

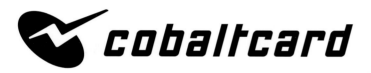

7.

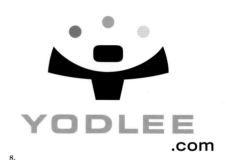

8.

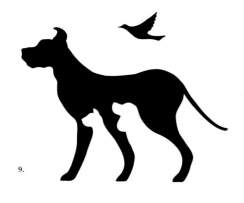

9.

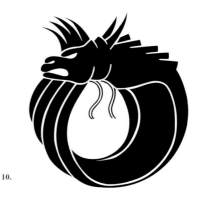

10.

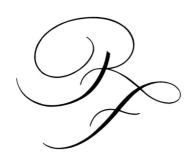

11.

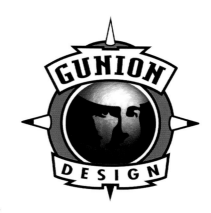

12.

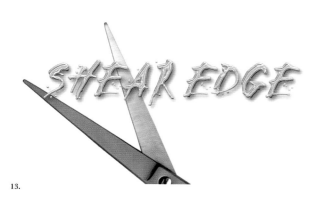

13.

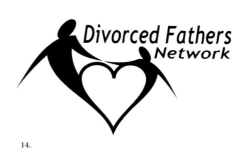

14.

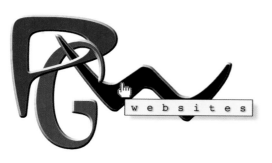

15.

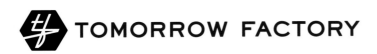 TOMORROW FACTORY

1.

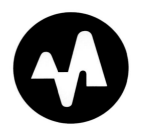

2.

phoenix▶pop

3.

AMAZ◯N.COM

4.

CUT FROM THE ORIGINAL CLOTH™

DOCKERS® **K-1** KHAKIS

Cramerton Army Cloth
Adopted, U.S. Army.
1932

5.

Designed by
SOUTHPARK FABRICATORS San Francisco, CA
tel 415-897-6622

6.

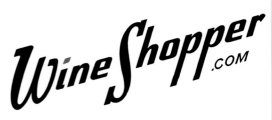

7.

1 - 7
Design Firm Templin Brink Design

1. Client   Tomorrow Factory
   Designer   Joel Templin

2. Client   Warren Miller
   Designers Joel Templin, Paul Howalt,
              & Gaby Brink

3. Client   Phoenix- Pop
   Designer   Joel Templin

4. Client   Amazon.com
   Designer   Joel Templin

5. Client   Dockers Khakis
   Designer   Gaby Brink

6. Client   Southpark Fabricators
   Designer   Gaby Brink

7. Client   WineShopper.com
   Designers Gaby Brink & Joel Templin

(opposite)
Design Firm Insight Design
              Communications

Client   With A Twist
Designers Sherrie Holdeman
           & Tracy Holdeman

282

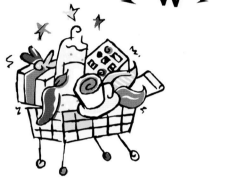

f o o d a n d g i f t s . c o m

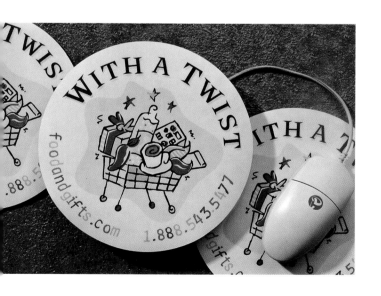

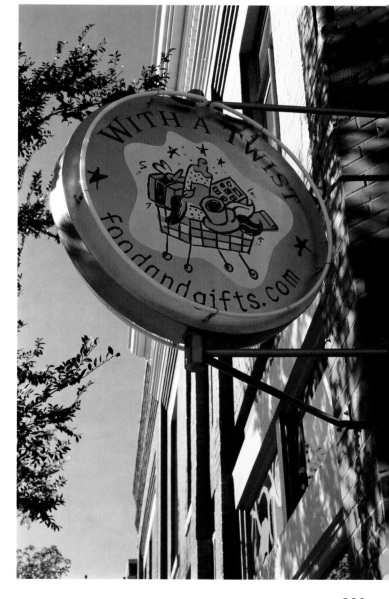

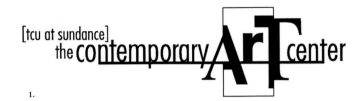

1.

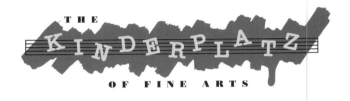

2.

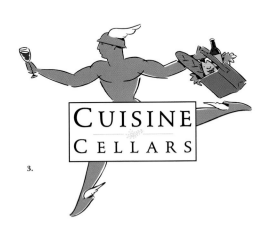

3.

AGRÍAMERICA

4.

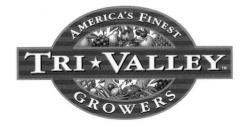

5.

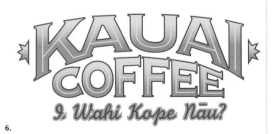

6.

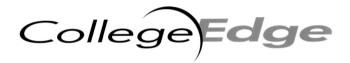

7.

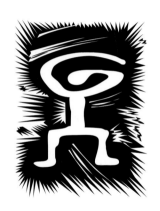

8.

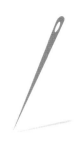

Lucille & Henry
Home Textiles

9.

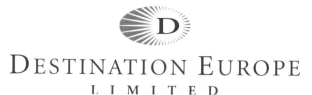

10.

SANTANA ROW

11.

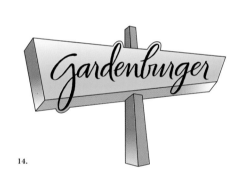

12.

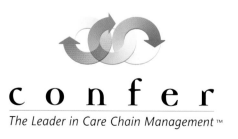

DESTINATION
HOTELS & RESORTS

13.

Gardenburger

14.

confer
The Leader in Care Chain Management ™

15.

1 - 2
Design Firm Michael Niblett Design
3 - 14
Design Firm Design Tribe
15
Design Firm California Design International

1. Client   The TCU Contemporary
                 Art Center
   Designer   Michael Niblett

2. Client   The Kinderplatz of Fine Arts
   Designer   Michael Niblett

3. Client   Cuisine Cellars
   Designer   Mark Marinozzi

4. Client   Agri America
   Designers   Mark Mavinozzi & Gary Blum

5. Client   Tri Valley Growers
   Designers   Mark Marinozzi & Gary Blum

6. Client   Kauai Coffee
   Designers   Mark Marinozzi & Gary Blum

7. Client   College Edge
   Designers   Dennis Pettigrew &
                 Mark Marinozzi

8. Client   Design Tribe
   Designer   Mark Marinozzi

9. Client   Lucille & Henry
   Designers   Mark Marinozzi
                 & Renee McElroy

10. Client   Destination Europe Limited
    Designers   Dennis Pettigrew
                 & Mark Marinozzi

11. Client   Federal Realty Investment Trust
    Designers   Erik Schmitt, Dennis Pettigrew,
                 & Mark Marinozzi

12. Client   Max Photography
    Designer   Mark Marinozzi

13. Client   Destination Hotels & Resorts
    Designers   Dennis Pettigrew
                 & Mark Marinozzi

14. Client   Garden Burger
    Designers   Mark Marinozzi &
                 Renee McElroy

15. Client   Confer
    Designers   Chris Ardito & Dan Liew

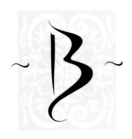

1.

BALLENTINE
D E S I G N S

2.
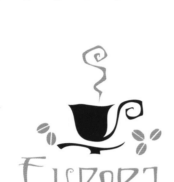

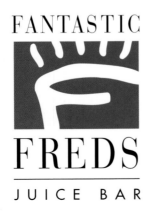

3.

ESPRESSO BARS

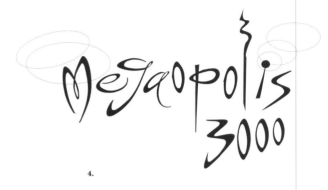

4.

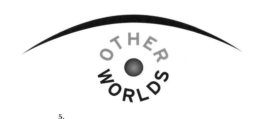

5.

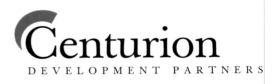

6.

FANTASTIC
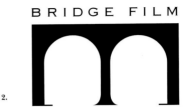
FREDS

7. JUICE BAR

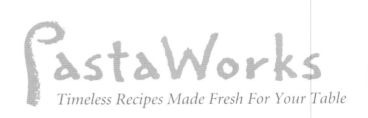

8.

M E A D O W B A N K   E S T A T E S

9.

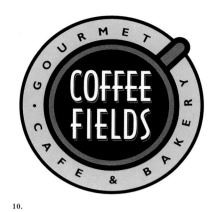

10.

SJ Corio Company

AUCTIONS   APPRAISALS   LIQUIDATIONS

11.

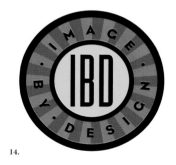

B A Y O U

C A R D I O T H O R A C I C

SURGERY ASSOCIATES, LTD

12.

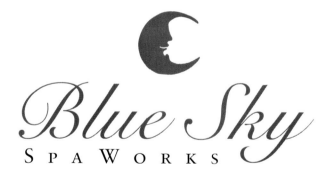

Blue Sky

S P A W O R K S

13.

IBD

14.

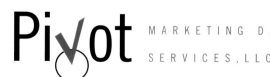

MARKETING DATA

SERVICES, LLC.

15.

1 - 5
Design Firm   Monica Reskala
6 - 15
Design Firm   Creative Vision Design Co.

1.	Client	Ballentine Designs
	Designer	Monica Reskala
2.	Client	Bridge Film
	Designer	Monica Reskala
3.	Client	Europa Espresso Bars
	Designer	Monica Reskala
4, 5	Client	Zeum
	Designer	Monica Reskala
6.	Client	S.J. Corio, Company
	Designer	Greg Gonsalves
7.	Client	Native, Inc.
	Designer	Greg Gonsalves

8.	Client	PastaWorks
	Designer	Greg Gonsalves
9.	Client	Empson U.S.A.
	Designer	Greg Gonsalves
10.	Client	Coffee Fields
	Designer	Greg Gonsalves
11.	Client	S.J. Corio Company
	Designer	Greg Gonsalves
12.	Client	Bayou C.S.A.
	Designer	Greg Gonsalves
13.	Client	Blue Sky Spaworks
	Designer	Greg Gonsalves
14.	Client	Image By Design
	Designer	Greg Gonsalves
15.	Client	Pivot, LLC.
	Designer	Greg Gonsalves

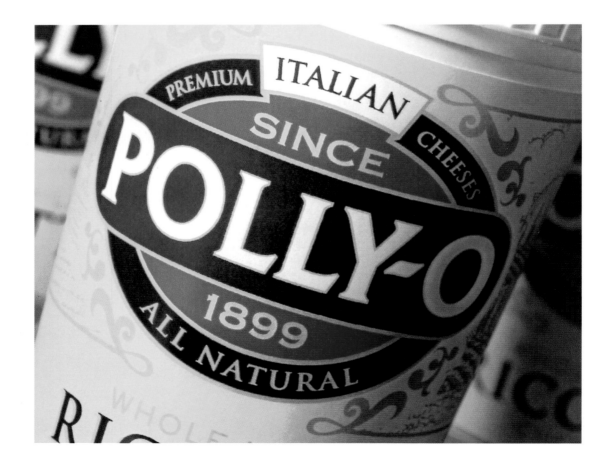

1.

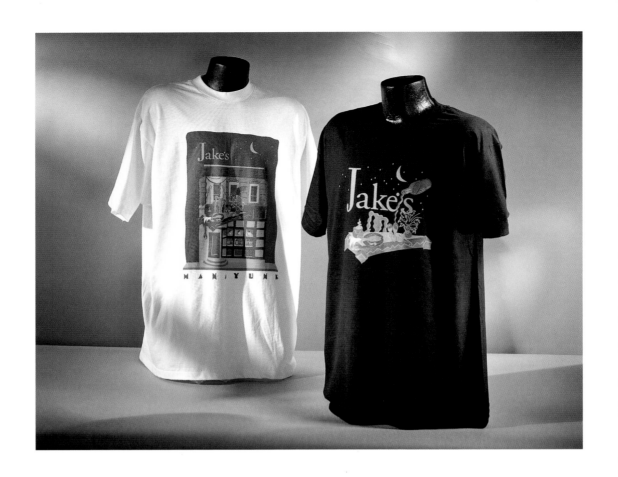

2.

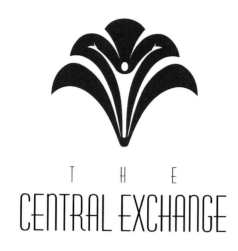

THE
CENTRAL EXCHANGE

3.

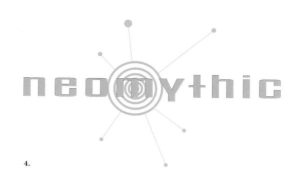

4.

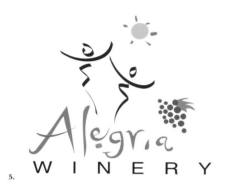

WINERY

5.

SCHELLING

6.

SCOTT'S
SEAFOOD

7.

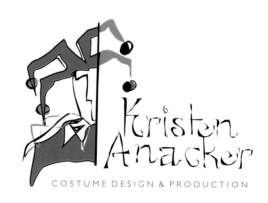

COSTUME DESIGN & PRODUCTION

8.

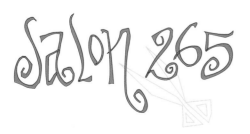

9.

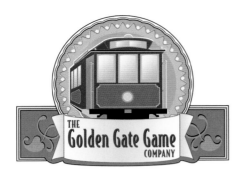

1.

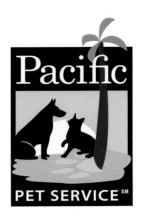

2.

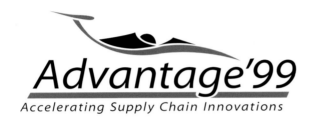

3.

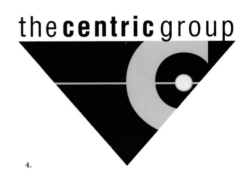

4.

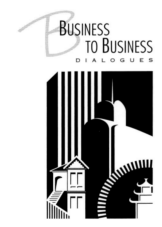

5.

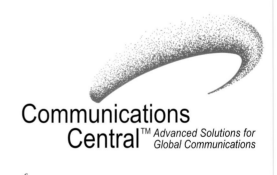

6.

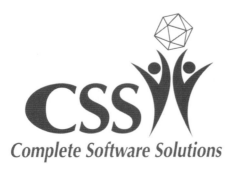

7.

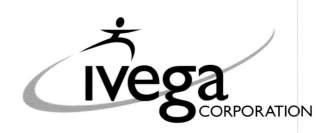

8.

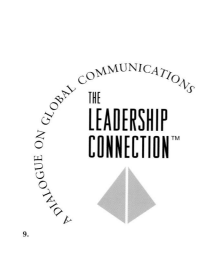

9.

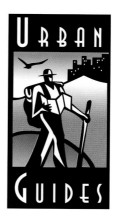

10.

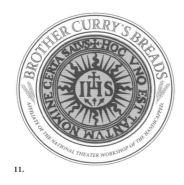

11.

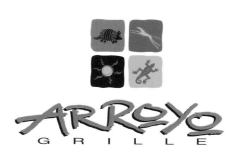

12.

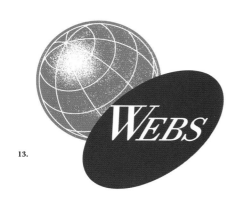

13.

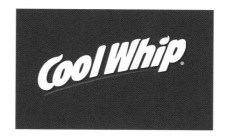

14.

15. **CHASE FUNDS**

1 - 10			7. Client	CSS, Complete Software Solutions
Design Firm	McKenzie & Associates, Inc.		Designers	Jean McKenzie & Debbi Murzyn
11, 12, 14, 15				
Design Firm	Hanson Associates, Inc.		8. Client	Ivega Corporation
13			Designers	Jean McKenzie & Debbi Murzyn
Design Firm	Studio Morris			
			9. Client	Ernst & Young
1. Client	The Golden Gate Game Company		Designers	Jean McKenzie, Debbie Murzyn, & Jenny Kolcun
Designers	Jean McKenzie & Misho Stawnecky			
			10. Client	Urban Guides
2. Client	Pacific Pet Service		Designers	Jean McKenzie, Debbie Murzyn, & Ada Lee
Designers	Jean McKenzie & Misho Stawnecky			
			11. Client	National Theater Workshop of the Handicapped
3. Client	Ernst & Young		Designers	Tobin Beck, Christy Beck, & Rose Dominiano
Designers	Jean McKenzie, Shannon Sanders, & Brad Walton			
			12. Client	Kraft Foods
4. Client	Ernst & Young		Designer	Christy Beck
Designers	Jean McKenzie & Jonina Skaggs			
			13. Client	WEBS—Foreign Fund, Inc.
5. Client	The City of Hope		Designer	Kaoru Sato
Designers	Jean McKenzie, Debbie Murzyn, & Shannon Sanders			
			14. Client	Arroyo Grille
			Designer	Tobin Beck
6. Client	Ernst & Young			
Designers	Jean McKenzie, Debbie Murzyn, & Daniel McClain		15. Client	Chase Manhattan Bank
			Designers	Tobin Beck & Christy Beck

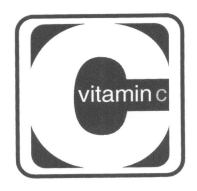

1.

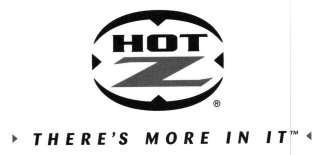

2.

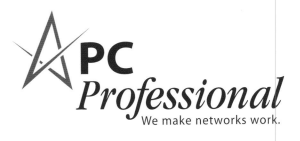

3.

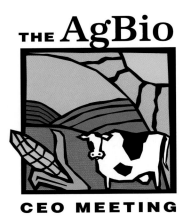

4.

BAY AREA
WATER TRANSIT
INITIATIVE

charting the course

5.

THE AgBio

CEO MEETING

6.

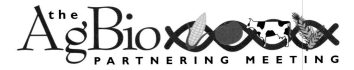

7.

1
Design Firm **Elektra Entertainment**
2, 3
Design Firm **Miriello Grafico Inc.**
4 - 7
Design Firm **McKenzie & Associates, Inc.**

1. Client   Vitamin C
    Designer   Alli Truch

2. Client   Hot Z
    Designer   Chris Keeney

3. Client   ezlink
    Designer   Michelle Aranda

4. Client   PC Professional
    Designers   Jean McKenzie &
                 Debbi Merzyn

5. Client   Bay Area Water Transit
                 & Initiative
    Designers   Dan Wen & Debbi Merzyn

6. Client   Burrill & Company
    Designers   Jean McKenzie & Debbi Merzyn

7. Client   Burrill & Company
    Designers   Jean McKenzie & Debbi Merzyn

(opposite)
Design Firm **Hanson Associates, Inc.**

    Client   The Eyeglass Works
    Designer   Mary Zook

the eyeglass works

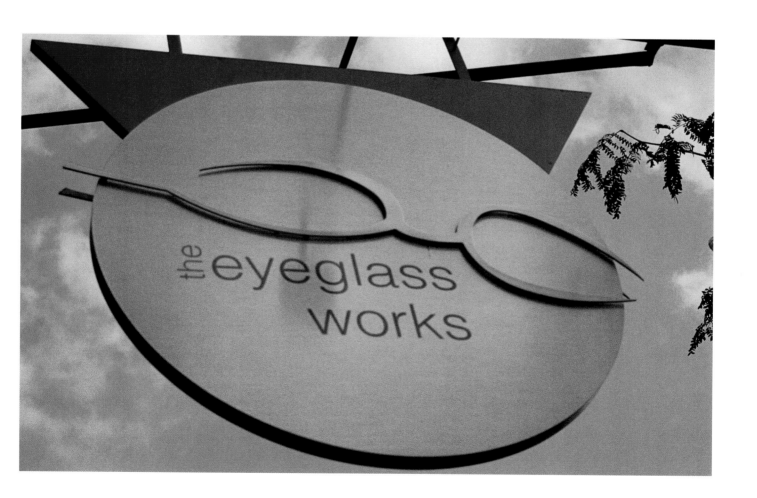

ALTEK

INNOVATIVE
MANUFACTURING
SOLUTIONS

1.

2.

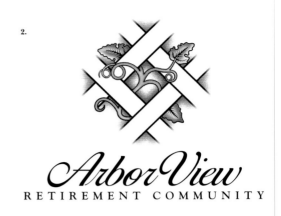

ArborView

RETIREMENT COMMUNITY

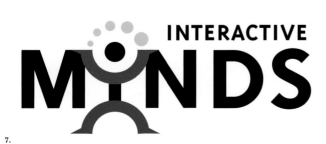

Inland Northwest Cancer Centers

The hope to cure. The promise to care.

3.

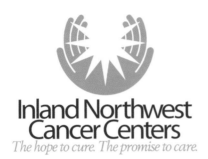

AISLE *of* VIEW

A WEDDING FROM YOUR POINT OF VIEW

4.

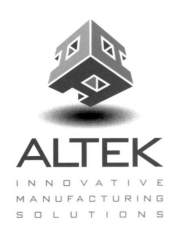

E-SYNC networks, inc.

5.

CHRIS L. CHAFFIN, DDS

GENERAL, COSMETIC & IMPLANT DENTISTRY

6.

INTERACTIVE
M NDS

7.

Vubox

8.

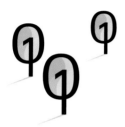

Application
Park™

9.

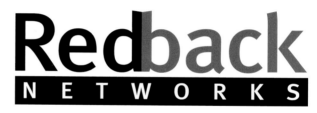

10.

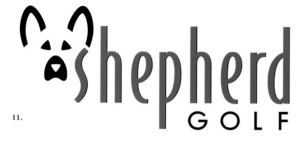

Shepherd
GOLF

11.

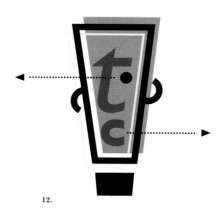

12.

14.

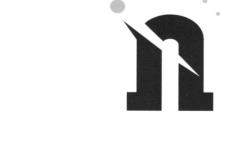

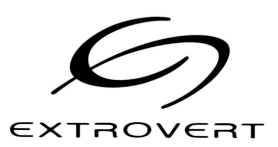

EXTROVERT

13.

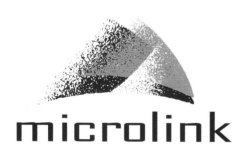

microlink

15.

1 - 3, 6
Design Firm **Klundt Hosmer Design**
4
Design Firm **Graphica**
Communication Solutions
5
Design Firm **The Wyant Symbol Group**
7, 10, 11
Design Firm **Long Design**
8, 9
Design Firm **Vubox**
12 - 15
Design Firm **Miriello Grafico Inc.**

1. Client Altek
Designers Darin Klundt & Tracey Carlson

2. Client ArborView Retirement
 Community
Designers Darin Klundt & Brian Gage

3. Client Inland Northwest
 Cancer Centers
Designers Darin Klundt &
 Shirlee Bonifield

4. Client Aisle of View
Designer Craig Terrones

5. Client E - Sync Network Systems
Designers Julia Wyant & Paul Neel

6. Client Chris L. Chaffin, DDS
Designers Darin Klundt & Amy Gunter

7. Client Interactive Minds
Designer Jennifer Long

8. Client Vubox
Designer Robin Awes

9. Client Application Park
Designer Robin Awes

10. Client Redback Networks
Designer Jennifer Long

11. Client Shepherd Golf
Designer Jennifer Long

12. Client Technically Correct
Designer Dennis Garcia

13. Client Extrovert
Designer Liz Bernal

14. Client Newport Communications
Designers Chris Keeney & Dennis Garcia

15. Client Microlink
Designer Chris Keeney

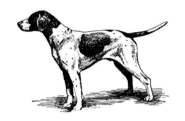

Dog Goods, Ltd.

1.

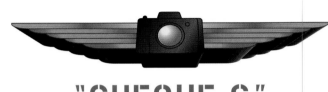

2.

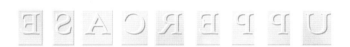

3.

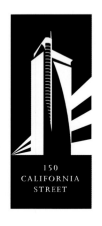

THE EQUITABLE BUILDING

4.

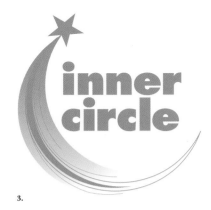

5.

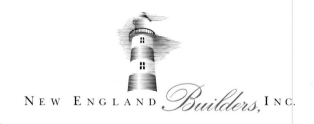

6.

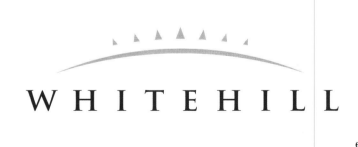

7.

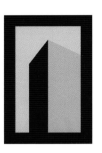

8.

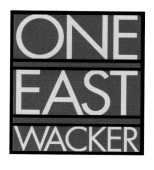

9.

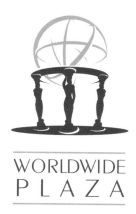

WORLDWIDE PLAZA

10.

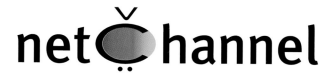

11.

12.

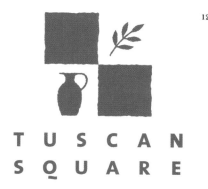

TUSCAN SQUARE

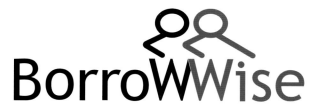

BorroWWise

13.

electricminds

14.

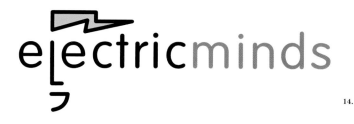

arzoon

15.

1 - 10
Design Firm Pivot Design, Inc.
11, 13 - 15
Design Firm Long Design
12
Design Firm Studio Morris

1. Client   Dog Goods, Ltd.
    Designer   Elizabeth Johnson

2. Client   Cheque 6
                Aviation Photography
    Designer   Brock Haldeman

3. Client   Focal Communications Corp.
    Designer   Bonnie Cauble

4. Client   Jones Lang LaSalle
    Designer   Brock Haldeman

5. Client   Equity Office
    Designer   Brock Haldeman

6. Client   Whitehill Technologies
    Designer   Brock Haldeman

7. Client   Uppercase Books
    Designer   Elizabeth Johnson

8. Client   New England Builders, Inc.
    Designer   Tim Hogan

9. Client   Jones Lang LaSalle
    Designer   Brock Haldeman

10. Client   Jones Lang LaSalle
    Designer   Brock Haldeman

11. Client   NetChannel
    Designer   Jennifer Long

12. Client   Tuscan Square
    Designers   Patricia Kovic & Jeff Morris

13. Client   BorrowWise
    Designer   Jennifer Long

14. Client   Electric Minds
    Designer   Jennifer Long

15. Client   arzoon.com
    Designer   Jennifer Long

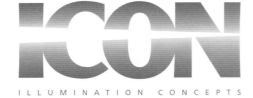

1.

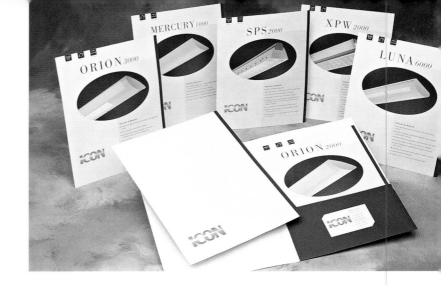

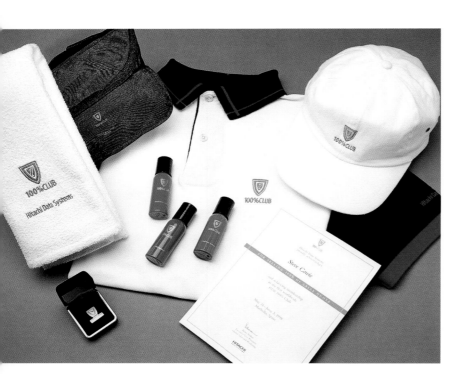

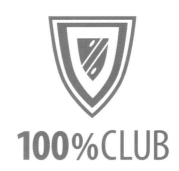

100%CLUB

2.

Navigator

INVESTMENTS

3.

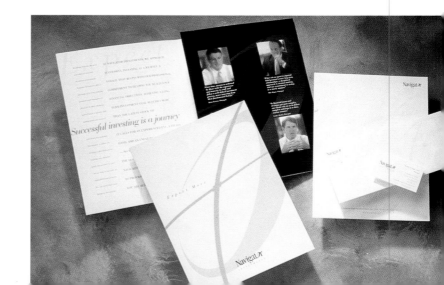

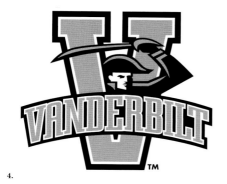

4.

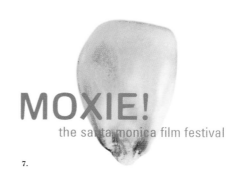

5.

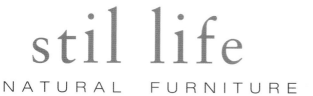

6.

MOXIE!
the santa monica film festival

7.

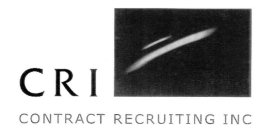

8.

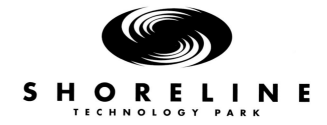

9.

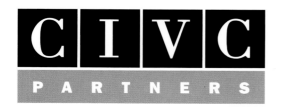

10.

1, 3
Design Firm **Adkins/Balhunas**
2
Design Firm **Hitachi Data Systems**
4
Design Firm **Rickabaugh Graphics**
5 - 8
Design Firm **Insyght**
9, 10
Design Firm **Pivot Design, Inc.**

1. Client   Illumination Concepts
   Designers   Jerry Balchunas,
                Susan DeAngelis &
                Michelle Phaneuf

2. Client   Hitachi Data Systems
   Designer   Lilia Chu

3. Client   Navigator Investments
   Designers   Jerry Balchunas,
                Michelle Phaneuf &
                Matt Fernbuger

4. Client   Vanderbilt University
   Designers   Eric Rickabaugh & Dave Cap

5. Client   Insyght
   Designer   Fabian Geyrhalter

6. Client   Nadeau
   Designer   Fabian Geyrhalter

7. Client   Moxie! The Santa Monica
                Film Festival
   Designer   Fabian Geyrhalter

8. Client   Contract Recruiting
   Designer   Fabian Geyrhalter

9. Client   Equity Office
   Designer   Brock Haldman

10. Client   CIVC Partners
    Designer   Holle Anderson

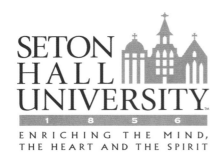

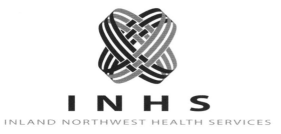

1.

2.

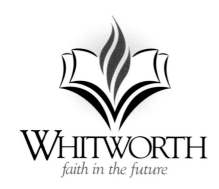

3.

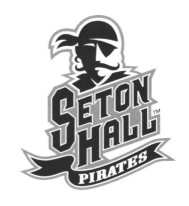

4.

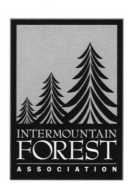

5.

6.

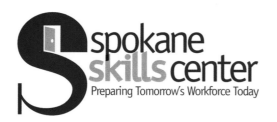

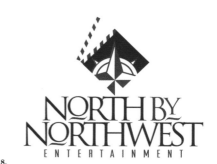

7.

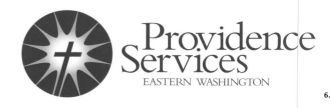

8.

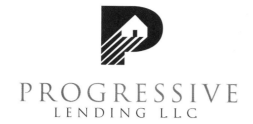

PROGRESSIVE
LENDING LLC

9.

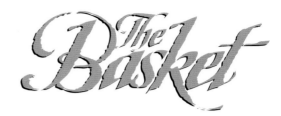

10.

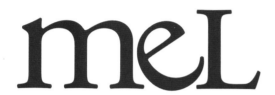

11.

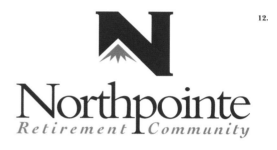

12.

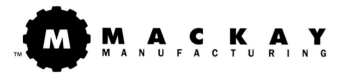

13.

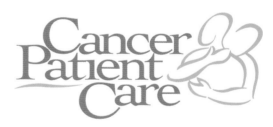

14.

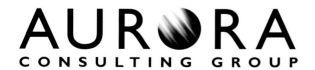

15.

1, 2
Design Firm **Rickabaugh Graphics**
3 - 15
Design Firm **Klundt Hosmer Design**

1. Client   Seton Hall University
   Designer   Eric Rickabaugh

2. Client   Seton Hall University
   Designers Eric Rickabaugh & Dave Cap

3. Client   Inland Northwest
             Health Services
   Designers Darin Klundt & Henry Ortega

4. Client   Intermountain Forest Assoc.
   Designers Darin Klundt & Amy Gunter

5. Client   Whitworth
   Designers Brian Gage & Darin Klundt

6. Client   Providence Services of E.W.
   Designers Darin Klundt & Henry Ortega

7. Client   Spokane Skills Center
   Designers Darin Klundt & Amy Gunter

8. Client   North by Northwest
             Entertainment
   Designers Darin Klundt & Brian Gage

9. Client   Progressive Lending
   Designers Darin Klundt &
             Judy Heggum-Davis

10. Client   The Basket
    Designer Brian Cage

11. Client   Mel
    Designers Brian Gage & Darin Klundt

12. Client   North Pointe
             Retirement Community
    Designers Darin Klundt & Brian Gage

13. Client   MacKay Manufacturing
    Designers Darin Klundt & Brian Gage

14. Client   Cancer Patient Care
    Designers Darin Klundt & Amy Gunter

15. Client   Aurora Consulting Group
    Designers Darin Klundt , Judy
             Heggum-Davis, & Brian Gage

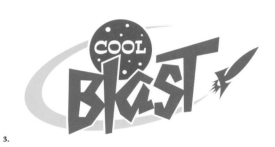

1.

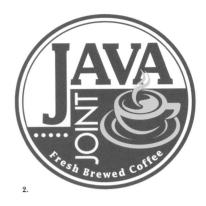

2.

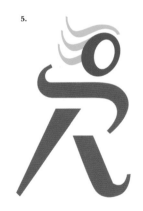

3.

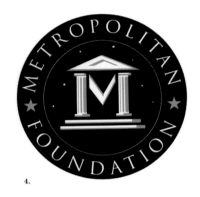

4.

5.

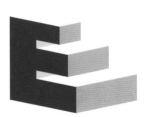

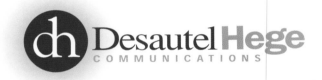

6.

7.

1 - 3
Design Firm   Babcock, Schmid, Louis,
& Partners
4
Design Firm   Iron Design
5
Design Firm   Long Design
6, 7
Design Firm   Klundt Hosmer Design

1. Client   Minit Mart
    Designers   Babcock, Schmid, Louis,
                 & Partners

2. Client   Minit Mart
    Designers   Babcock, Schmid, Louis,
                 & Partners

3. Client   Minit Mart
    Designers   Babcock, Schmid, Louis,
                 & Partners

4. Client   Metropolitan Foundation
    Designer   Todd Edmonds

5. Client   Rhonda Abrams
    Designer   Jennifer Long

6. Client   Desautel Hege Communications
    Designers   Darin Klundt & Henry Ortega

7. Client   Executive Lending Group
    Designers   Brian Gage & Darin Klundt

(opposite)
Design Firm   Wallace Church Ass., Inc.

    Client   Maxfli Golf Balls
    Designers   Stan Church, John Waski,
                 & Derek Samue

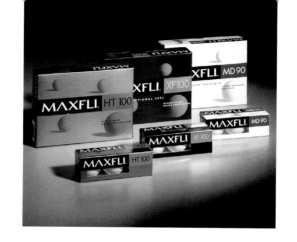

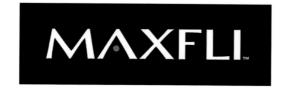

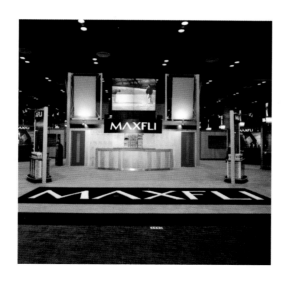

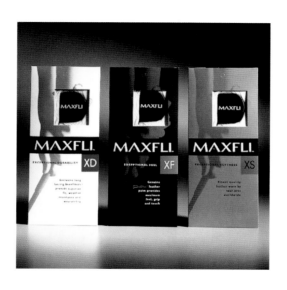

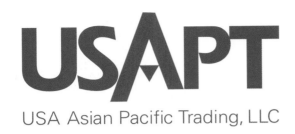

USA Asian Pacific Trading, LLC

1.

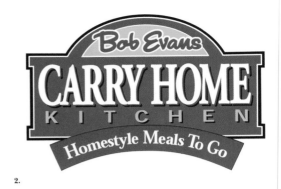

2.

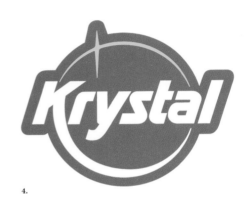

3.

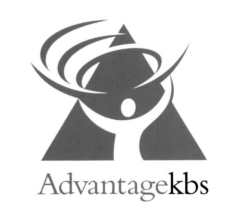

4.

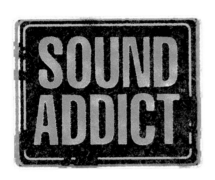

5.

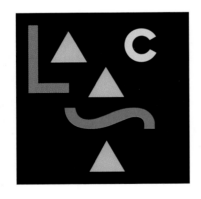

Advantagekbs

6.

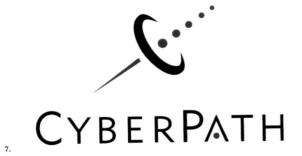

CYBERPATH

7.

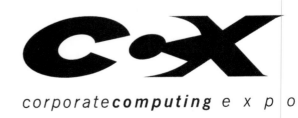

8.

304

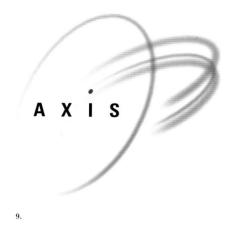

A X I S

9.

LYC⊙S®

10.

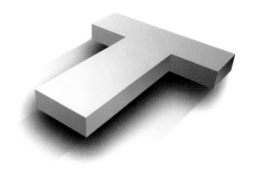

11.

g

12.

BUMBLE BEE®

13.

ADP® YEAR 2000 COMPLIANCE 2000 1999 PROGRAM

14.

OpenCon Systems, Inc.
WORLDWIDE COMMUNICATIONS SOLUTIONS

15.

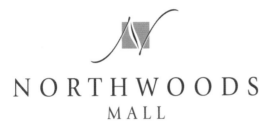

1.

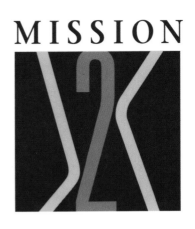

2.

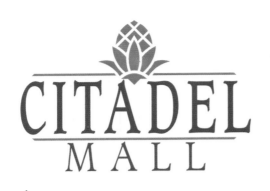

3.

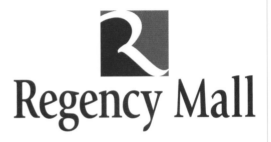

4.

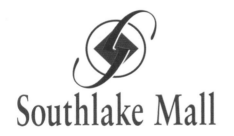

5.

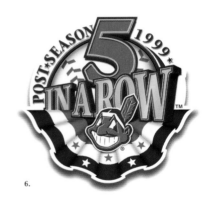

6.

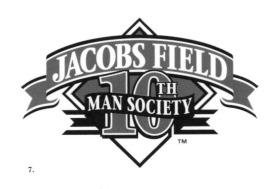

7.

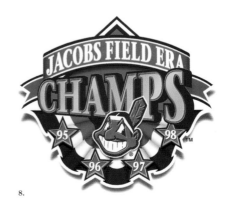

8.

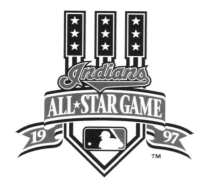

9.

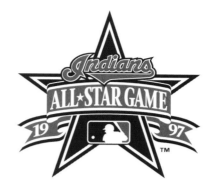

10.

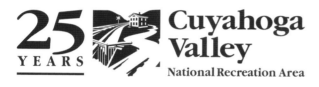

11.

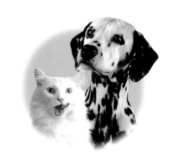

12.

BEACON PLACE

13.

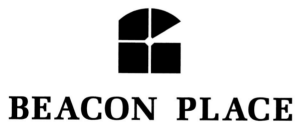

14.

15.

(all)

Design Firm Herip Associates

1. Client   The Richard E. Jacobs Group
   Designers Walter M. Herip, John R.
             Menter, & Rick Holb

2. Client   The Richard E. Jacobs Group
   Designers John R. Menter &
             Walter M. Herip

3. Client   The Richard E. Jacobs Group
   Designers John R. Menter, Rick Holb,
             & Walter M. Herip

4, 5
   Client   The Richard E. Jacobs Group
   Designers John R. Menter &
             Walter M. Herip

6 - 8
   Client   Cleveland Indians
   Designers John R. Menter &
             Walter M. Herip

9, 10
   Client   Major League Baseball
   Designers Walter M. Herip &
             John R. Menter

11. Client   CVNRA
   Designers Walter M. Herip

12. Client   Ernst & Young, LLP
   Designers Walter M. Herip &
             John R. Menter

13. Client   Dalad Group
   Designers John R. Menter &
             Walter M. Herip

14. Client   Bioproducts, Inc.
   Designers Walter M. Herip, John R.
             Menter, & Rick Holb

15. Client   Stark Enterprises
   Designers Walter M. Herip, John R.
             Menter, & Rick Holb

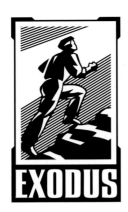

1.

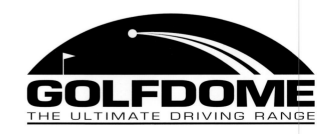

2.

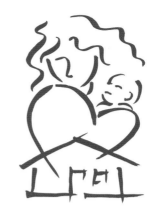

3.

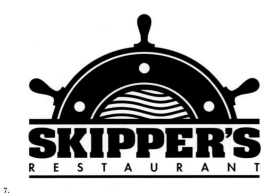

4.

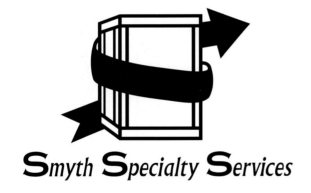

Smyth Specialty Services

5.

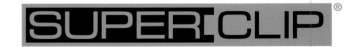

6.

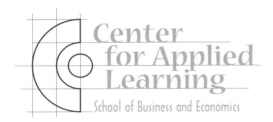

SKIPPER'S
RESTAURANT

7.

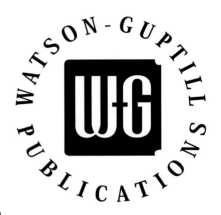

GOLFDOME
THE ULTIMATE DRIVING RANGE

8.

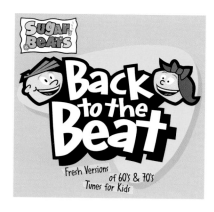

9.

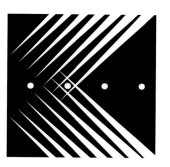

10.

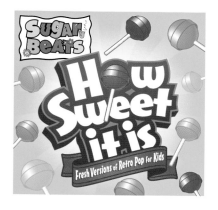

11.

12.

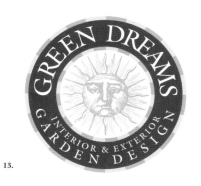

13.

14.

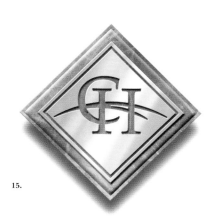

15.

1 - 3		
Design Firm	**Ray Braun Graphic Design**	
4		
Design Firm	**Farenga Design Group**	
5		
Design Firm	**Graphx Design**	
6 - 13		
Design Firm	**Todd Nickel**	
14, 15		
Design Firm	**Herip Associates**	

1.	Client	Exodus International
	Designer	Ray Braun
2.	Client	Everett Gospel Mission
	Designer	Ray Braun
3.	Client	Seattle Pacific University
	Designer	Ray Braun
4.	Client	Watson-Guptill Publications
	Designer	Anthony Farenga
5.	Client	Smyth Specialty Services, LLC
	Designers	Patrick Smith & Alex Sobie

6.	Client	North Atlantic Services
	Designer	Todd Nickel
7.	Client	Skipper's Restaurant
	Designer	Todd Nickel
8.	Client	GOLFDOME
	Designer	Todd Nickel
9 - 11	Client	Sugar Beats
	Designer	Todd Nickel
12.	Client	MS. PC
	Designer	Todd Nickel
13.	Client	Green Dreams
	Designer	Todd Nickel
14.	Client	Herip Associates
	Designer	Walter M. Herip
15.	Client	The Richard E. Jacobs Group
	Designers	Walter M. Herip & John R. Meter

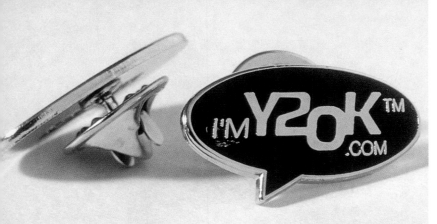

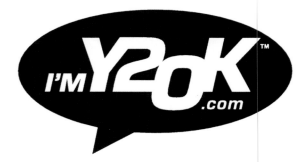

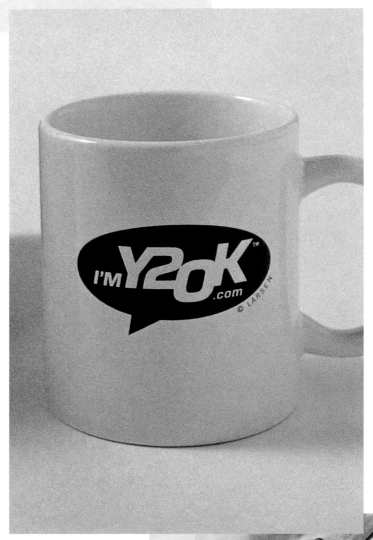

THE HEARING Advocate

1.

THE HEARING ADVOCATE

2.

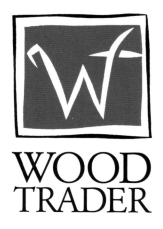

WOOD TRADER

3.

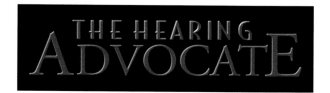

4.

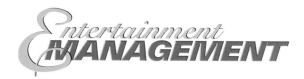

5.

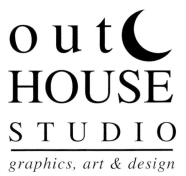

out ☾ HOUSE STUDIO

graphics, art & design

6.

SUCCESS at FELICIAN

ACCELERATED DEGREE PROGRAMS

7.

1, 2, 4 - 7		5. Client	Pulse Plastic Products, Inc.
Design Firm	**Outhouse Studio**	Designers	Alex Lindquist & Jolanta Hyjek
3			
Design Firm	**Nesnadny + Schwartz**	6. Client	Outhouse Studio
		Designer	Alex Lindquist
1, 2			
Client	Ingroup Networking	7. Client	Ingroup Networking
Designers	Alex Lindquist & Jolanta Hyjek	Designer	Alex Lindquist
3. Client	WoodTrader	**(opposite)**	
Designers	Timothy Lachina, Gregory	**Design Firm**	**Larsen Design + Interactive**
	Oznowich, & Brian Lavy		
		Client	Larsen's I'm Y2OK Campaign
4. Client	Entertainment Management	Designers	Tim Larsen, Sascha Boecker,
Designers	Alex Lindquist & Jolanta Hyjek		& Elise Williams

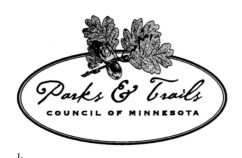

1.

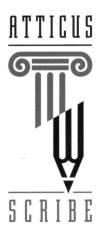

2.

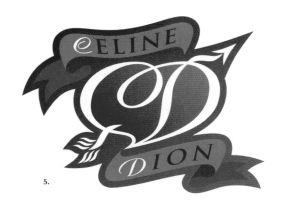

3.

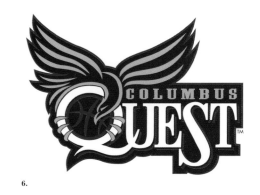

4.

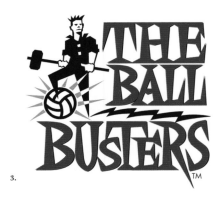

5.

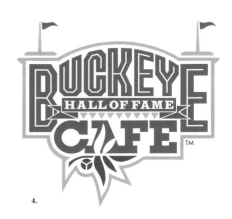

6.

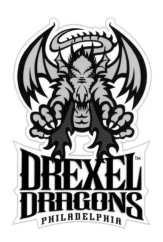

7.

8.

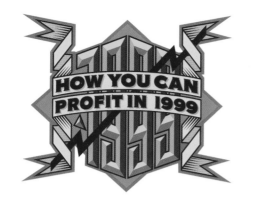

9.

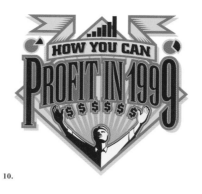

10.

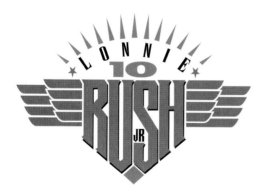

11.

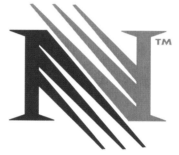

12.

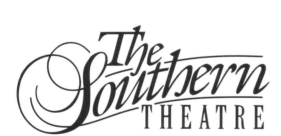

13.

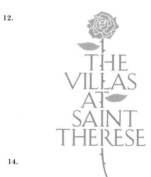

14.

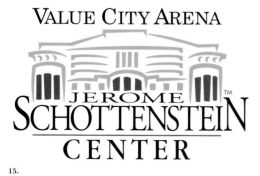

15.

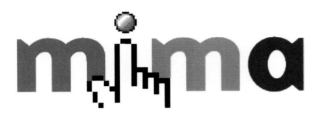

1.

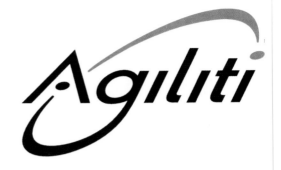

2.

nexen ™

3.

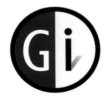

Gartner**Institute**

5.

6.

GREAT PLAINS

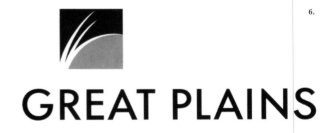

7.

1 - 7

Design Firm	**Larsen Design + Interactive**

1.	Client	Minnesota Interactive Marketing Association
	Designers	Richelle J. Huff, Emily Eaton, & Peter Langlais
2.	Client	Agiliti
	Designers	Paul Wharton & Brad Serum
3.	Client	Nexen
	Designers	Jo Davison & Bill Pflipsen
4.	Client	The Minneapolis Institute of Arts
	Designers	Todd Nesser, Peter de Sibour, Todd Mannes, Pepa Reimann, & Mark Wagner
5.	Client	Gartner Institute
	Designers	Paul Wharton & Todd Mannes

6.	Client	Great Plains Software
	Designers	Richelle J. Huff, Mike Haug, Bill Pflipsen, Sascha Boeker, Chad Amon, & Michael Hersrud
7.	Client	21 North Main
	Designers	Jo Davison, Mark Saunders, & Todd Nesser

(opposite)

Design Firm	**Larsen Design + Interactive**
Client	Target
Designers	Paul Wharton, Peter de Sibour, & Chris Zastoupil

314

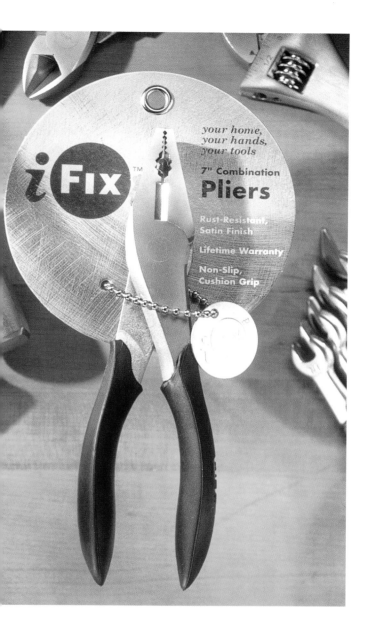

*your home,
your hands,
your tools*

7" Combination
Pliers

**Rust-Resistant,
Satin Finish**

Lifetime Warranty

**Non-Slip,
Cushion Grip**

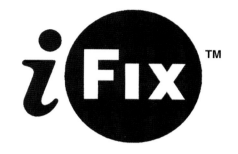

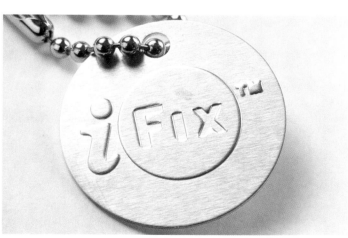

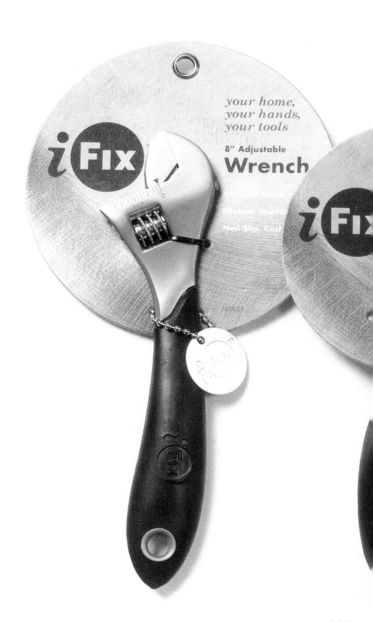

*your home,
your hands,
your tools*

8" Adjustable
Wrench

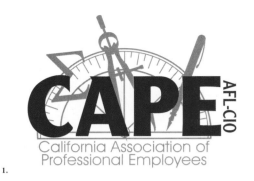

1.

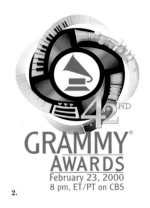

42ND GRAMMY AWARDS
February 23, 2000
8 pm, ET/PT on CBS

2.

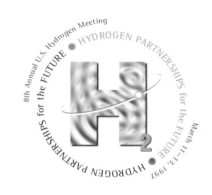

8th Annual U.S. Hydrogen Meeting
HYDROGEN PARTNERSHIPS for the FUTURE
March 11–13, 1997

3.

TAIX

French
Country
Cuisine
Established 1927

4.

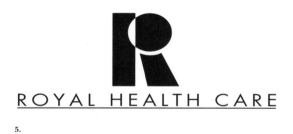

ROYAL HEALTH CARE

5.

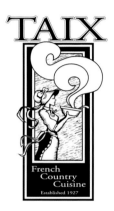

EASTERN WOMEN'S CENTER
security, sensitivity, support...

6.

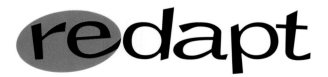

7.

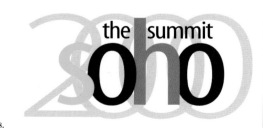

the summit
soho
2000

8.

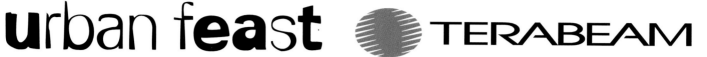

9.

10.

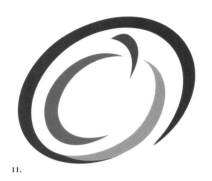

11.

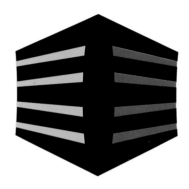

12.

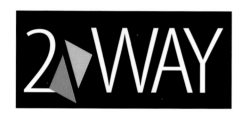

13.

14.

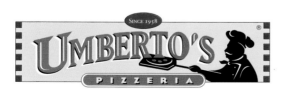

15.

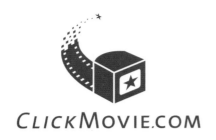

1. CLICKMOVIE.COM

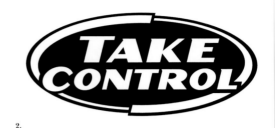

2.

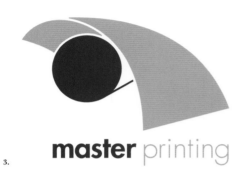

3. master printing

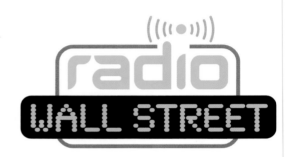

4. radio WALL STREET

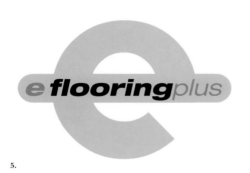

5. e flooring plus

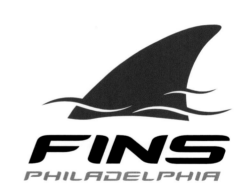

6. FINS PHILADELPHIA

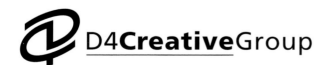

D4**Creative**Group

7.

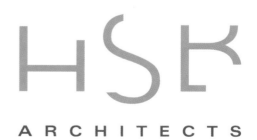

8. HSK ARCHITECTS

WYSE·LANDAU

9.

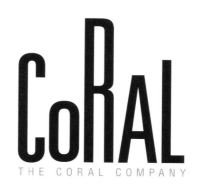

THE CORAL COMPANY

10.

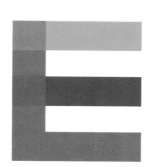

11.

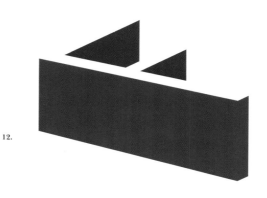

12.

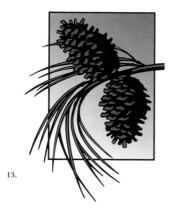

13.

SMITH+Co

14.

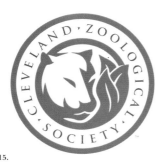

15.

1, 2
    Design Firm Derek Yee Design
3, 8 - 11, 15
    Design Firm Nesnadny + Schwartz
4 - 7
    Design Firm D4 Creative Group
12 - 14
    Design Firm Michael Courtney Design

1. Client   Click Movie.com
   Designer   Derek Yee

2. Client   Oracle
   Designer   Derek Yee

3. Client   Master Printing, Inc.
   Designers Cindy Lowrey & Stacie Ross

4. Client   Radio Wall Street
   Designer   Wicky W. Lee

5. Client   E Flooring Plus
   Designer   Wicky W. Lee

6. Client   Fins Philadelphia
   Designer   Wicky W. Lee

7. Client   D4 Creative Group
   Designer   Wicky W. Lee

8. Client   Hengst Streff Bajko Architects
   Designers Timothy Lachina, Michelle
               Mohler & Gregory Oznowich

9. Client   Wyse Landau Public Relations
   Designers Joyce Nesnadny &
               Michelle Mohler

10. Client   Coral Company
   Designers Cindy Lowerey & Stacie Ross

11. Client   Crossey International
   Designer   Joyce Nesnadny

12. Client   Fleischmann Office Interiors
   Designers Michael Courtney, Dan Hoang,
               Heidi Favour, & Brian O'Neill

13. Client   Evergreen Printing
   Designer   Michael Courtney

14. Client   Smith & Co.
   Designers Michael Courtney &
               Brian O'Neill

15. Client   Cleveland Zoological Society
   Designers Timothy Lachina &
               Gregory Oznowich

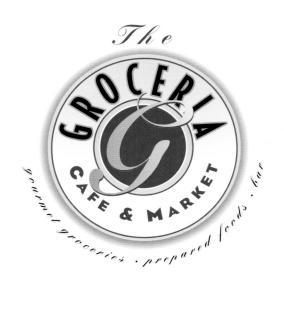

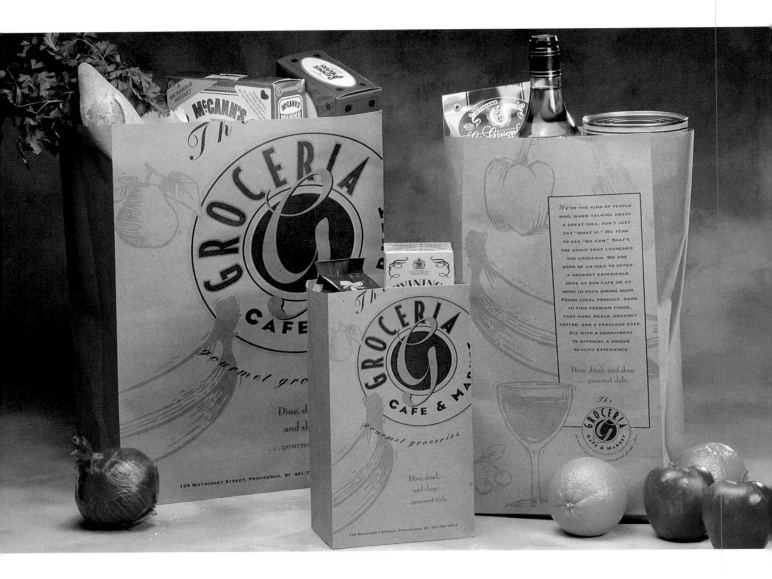

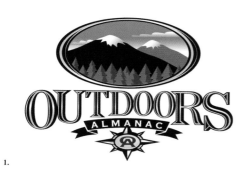

1.

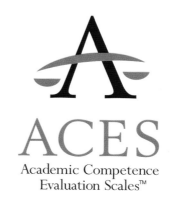

ACES
Academic Competence
Evaluation Scales™

2.

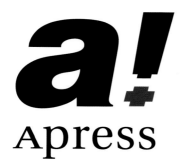

3.

Derek Yee Design

4.

a!
Apress

5.

MY NEWS

6.

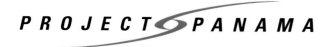

7.

(opposite)
Design Firm **Adkins/Balchunas**

Client   The Groceria
Designers   Jerry Balchunas &
            Michelle Phaneuf

1, 2
Design Firm **Clockwork Design**
3 - 7
Design Firm **Derek Yee Design**

1. Client   Outdoors Almanac
   Designers   Steve Gaines & Terri Gaines

2. Client   The Psychological Corporation
   Designers   Steve Gaines & Terri Gaines

3. Client   Symmorphix
   Designers   Derek Yee, Elysia Chuh,
               & Philip So

4. Client   Derek Yee Design
   Designer   Derek Yee

5. Client   Apress
   Designers   Derek Yee, Elysia Chuh,
               & Seiko Nozaki

6. Client   America Online
   Designer   Derek Yee

7. Client   Oracle
   Designers   Elysia Chuh & Derek Yee

CLOCKWORK DESIGN

1.

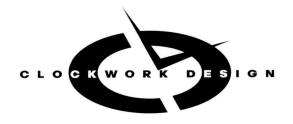

2.

GlobaNet

3.

NM

4.

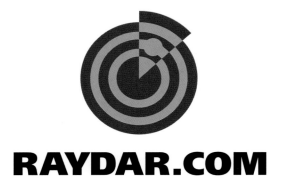

RAYDAR.COM

5.

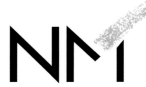

6.

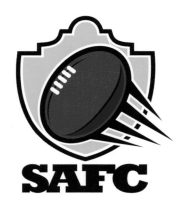

SAFC

7.

Velotools

8.

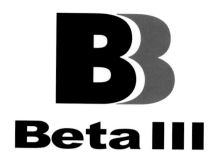

Beta III

9.

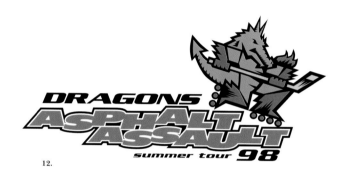

10.

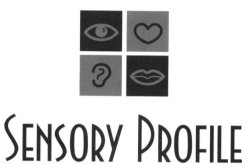

SENSORY PROFILE

11.

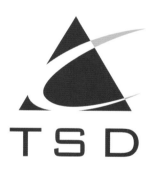

DRAGONS ASPHALT ASSAULT summer tour 98

12.

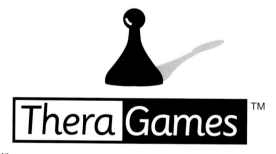

Thera Games ™

13.

TSD

14.

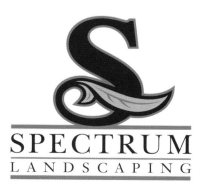

SPECTRUM LANDSCAPING

15.

1 - 9, 11 - 15			8. Client	Velotools
Design Firm	Clockwork Design		Designers	Steve Gaines & Terri Gaines
10				
Design Firm	Look		9. Client	The Psychological Corperation
			Designers	Steve Gaines & Terri Gaines
1. Client	Clockwork Design			
Designers	Steve Gaines & Terri Gaines		10. Client	Look
			Designer	Betsy Todd
2. Client	Foresight Consulting Inc.			
Designers	Steve Gaines & Terri Gaines		11. Client	The Psychological Corperation
			Designers	Steve Gaines & Terri Gaines
3. Client	GlobalNet			
Designers	Steve Gaines & Terri Gaines		12. Client	San Antonio Dragons
			Designers	Steve Gaines & Terri Gaines
4. Client	New Millennium Consulting			
Designers	Steve Gaines & Terri Gaines		13. Client	The Psychological Corperation
			Designers	Steve Gaines & Terri Gaines
5. Client	Raydar.com			
Designers	Steve Gaines & Terri Gaines		14. Client	Total Systems Development
			Designers	Steve Gaines & Terri Gaines
6. Client	San Antonio Chamber			
	of Commerce		15. Client	Spectrum Landscaping
Designers	Steve Gaines & Terri Gaines		Designers	Steve Gaines & Terri Gaines
7. Client	San Antonio Football Club			
Designer	Steve Gaines			

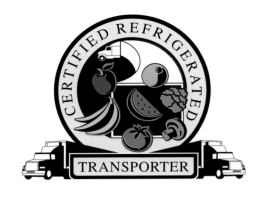

1.

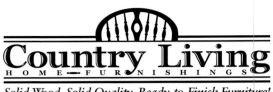

2.

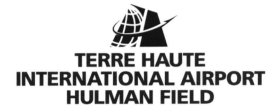

3.

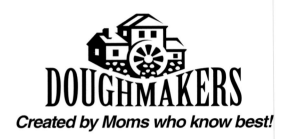

4.

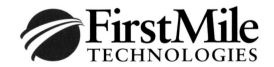

5.

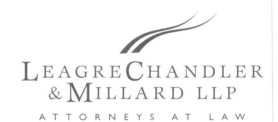

6.

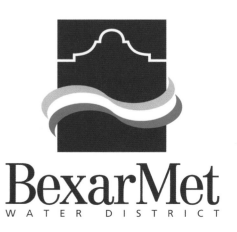

7.

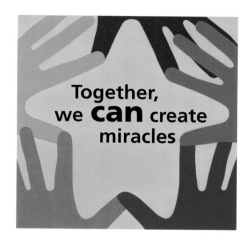

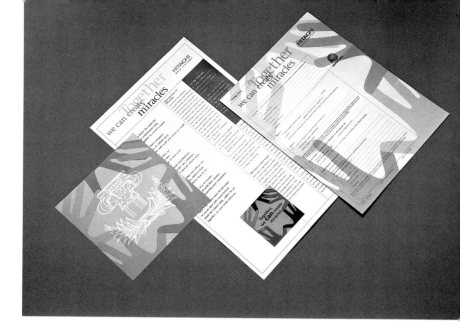

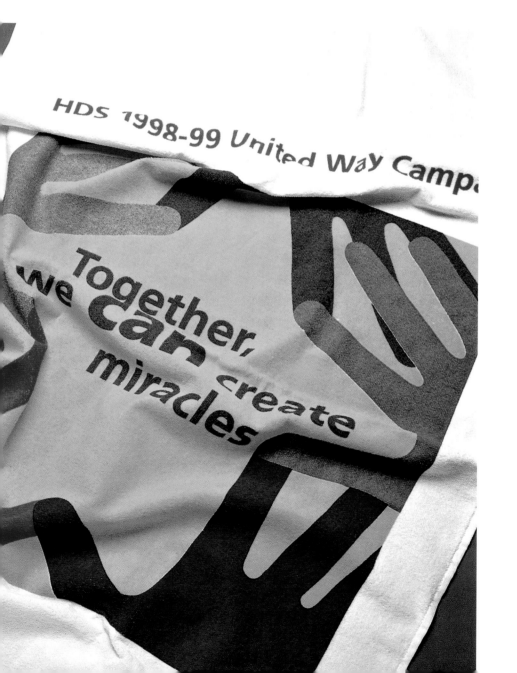

SNAPP
& ASSOCIATES
ARCHITECTURAL DESIGN TEAM

1.

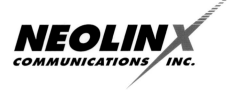

neolinx.com

2.

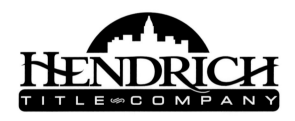

3.

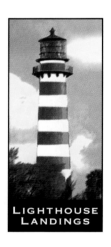

**A PARTNER IN THE
UNION HOSPITAL HEALTH GROUP**

4.

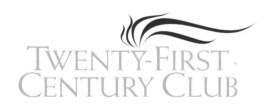

5.

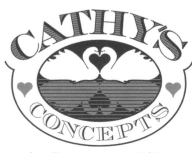

6.

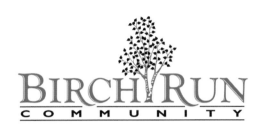

7.

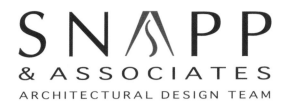

An Expression of You

8.

326

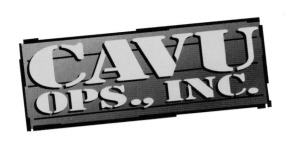

9.

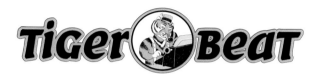

10.

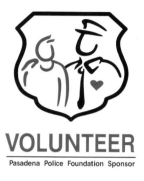

VOLUNTEER
Pasadena Police Foundation Sponsor

11.

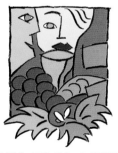

12.

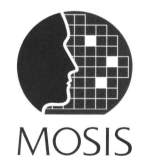

MOSIS

13.

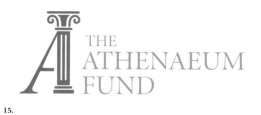

FALL FOOD & WINE

14.

THE ATHENAEUM FUND

15.

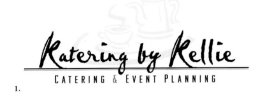

Ratering by Rellie

CATERING & EVENT PLANNING

1.

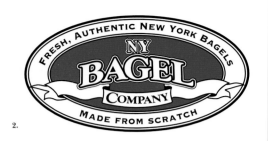

FRESH, AUTHENTIC NEW YORK BAGELS

NY
BAGEL
COMPANY

MADE FROM SCRATCH

2.

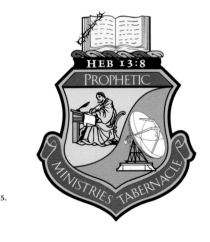

Help

OnCall

personal **computing**

3.

SWAN'S PLACE

4.

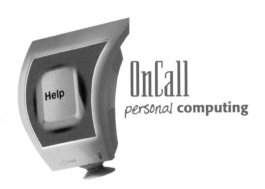

HEB 13:8

PROPHETIC

MINISTRIES TABERNACLE

5.

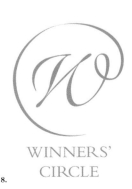

xchange
product replacement card

6.

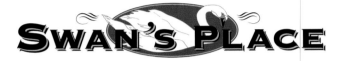

Commun**ITy**

The power of sharing

7.

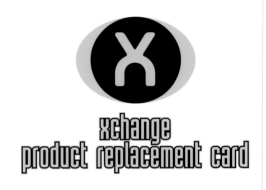

WINNERS'
CIRCLE

8.

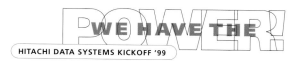

9.

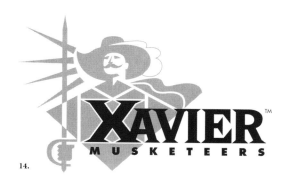

10.

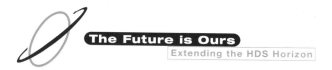

HITACHI DATA SYSTEMS KICKOFF '99

11.

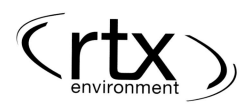

12.

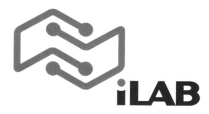

iLAB

13.

XAVIER™
MUSKETEERS

14.

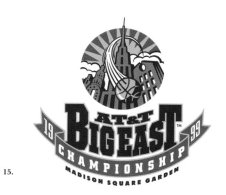

15.

1 - 6		
Design Firm	Up All Night	
7 - 13		
Design Firm	Hitachi Data Systems	
14, 15		
Design Firm	Rickabaugh Graphics	

1.	Client	Katering By Kellie
	Designer	Rich Owens

2.	Client	NY Bagel Company
	Designer	Rich Owens

3.	Client	Warrantech
	Designer	Rich Owens

4.	Client	Swan's Place
	Designer	Rich Owens

5.	Client	Prophetic Ministries Tabernacle
	Designer	Rich Owen

6.	Client	Warrantech
	Designer	Rich Owens

7, 8		
	Client	Hitachi Data Systems
	Designer	Kim Ocumen

9.	Client	Hitachi Data Systems
	Designer	Carolyn Rosenberg

10 - 12		
	Client	Hitachi Data Systems
	Designer	Kim Ocumen

13.	Client	Hitachi Data Systems
	Designer	Barry Chan

14.	Client	Xavier University
	Designer	Eric Rickabaugh

15.	Client	The Big East Conference
	Designer	Eric Rickabaugh

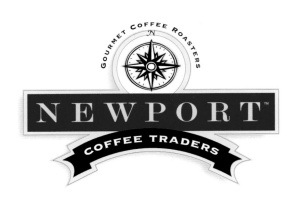

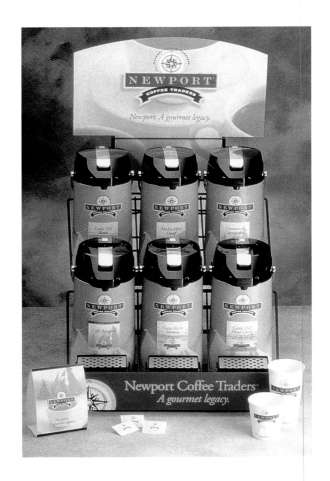

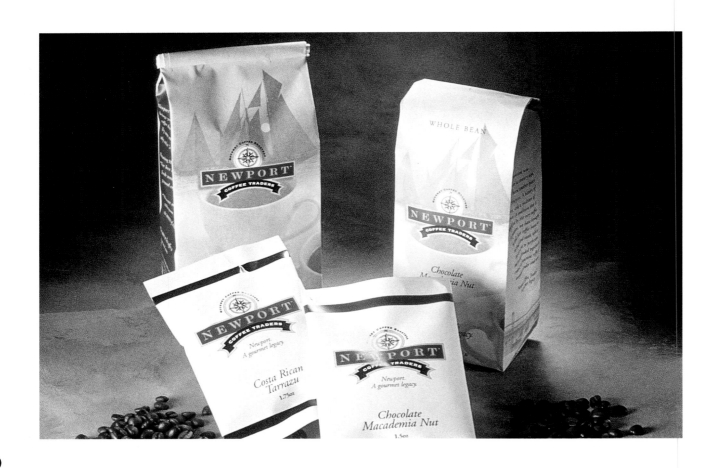

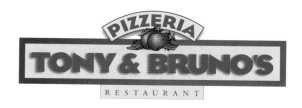

1.

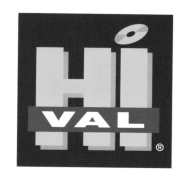

2.

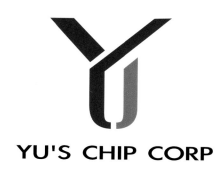

3.

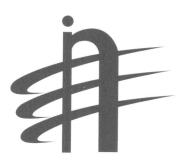

4.

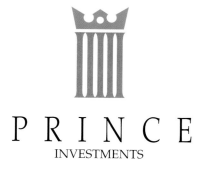

5.

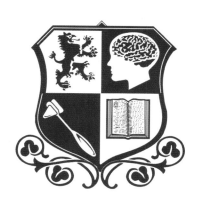

6.

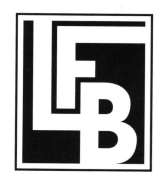

7.

1
Design Firm **Adkins/Balchunas**
2 - 5
Design Firm **Vivatt Design Group**
6, 7
Design Firm **Mark Deitch &**
Associates, Inc.

1. Client   Sbarro
   Designers   Jerry Balchunas &
                     Michelle Phaneuf

2. Client   HI-VAL
   Designer   Dan Wen

3. Client   Yu's Chip Corp.
   Designer   Dan Wen

4. Client   Inwin Development, Inc.
   Designer   Dan Wen

5. Client   Prince Investments
   Designer   Dan Wen

6. Client   UCLA Medical School
   Designers   Lisa Kokenis & Joe Ibarra

7. Client   Landsman, Frank & Bloch
   Designer   Raoul Pascual

(opposite)
Design Firm **Adkins/Balchunas**

   Client   Autocrat, Inc.
   Designers   Jerry Balchunas, Michelle
                     Phaneuf, & Susan DeAngelis

DIAMANTI

1.

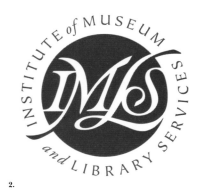

2.

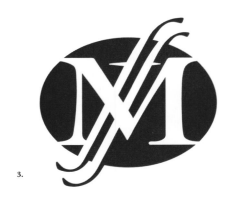

3.

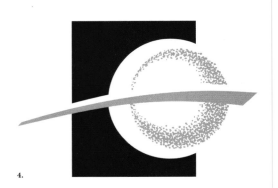

4.

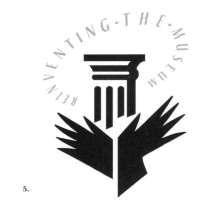

5.

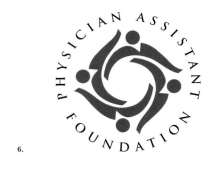

6.

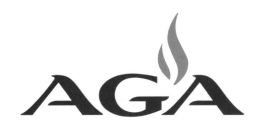

7.

8.

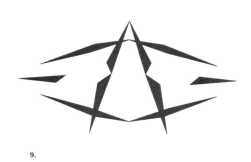

9.

10.

11.

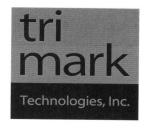

tri
mark
Technologies, Inc.

12.

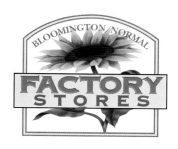

13.

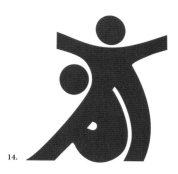

14.

actos™

15.

1 - 7		
Design Firm	**Dever Designs**	
8 - 15		
Design Firm	**CMC Design Associates**	

1. Client   Diamanti
   Designer Jeffrey L. Dever

2. Client   Institute of Museum &
              Library Services
   Designer Jeffrey L. Dever

3. Client   Martin's Furniture
   Designers Emily Martin Kendall &
              Jeffrey L. Dever

4. Client   Carnegie Endowment for
              International Peace
   Designers Jeffrey L. Dever &
              Emily Martin Kendall

5. Client   American Association
              of Museums
   Designer Jeffrey L. Dever

6. Client   American Association of
              Physician Assistants
   Designer Jeffrey L. Dever

7. Client   American Gas Association
   Designer Jeffrey L. Dever

8. Client   Abelson-Taylor, Inc.
   Designer Chris Cacci

9. Client   Spectrum Research &
              Development
   Designer Chris Cacci

10. Client   Center for Fertility &
              Reproduction
    Designer Chris Cacci

11. Client   Heart Source
    Designer Chris Cacci

12. Client   Trimark Technologies
    Designer Chris Cacci

13. Client   B & M Management
    Designer Chris Cacci

14. Client   Center for Speech &
              Language Disorders
    Designer Chris Cacci

15. Client   Abelson-Taylor, Inc./Lilly
    Designer Chris Cacci

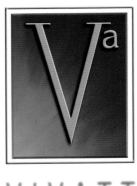

VIVATT
design group

1.

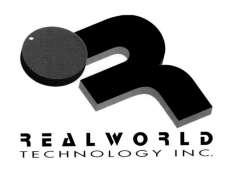

REALWORLD
TECHNOLOGY INC.

2.

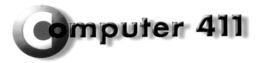

3.

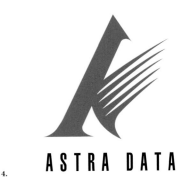

ASTRA DATA

4.

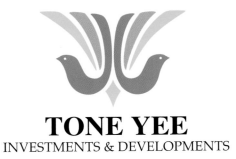

TONE YEE
INVESTMENTS & DEVELOPMENTS

5.

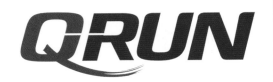

6.

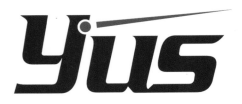

7.

1 - 7
Design Firm Vivatt Design Group
8, 9
Design Firm Hornall Anderson
Design Works

1. Client   Vivatt Design Group
   Designers   Dan Wen & Steven Wei

2. Client   Realworld Technology, Inc.
   Designer   Eric Woo

3. Client   Computer 411
   Designer   Eric Woo

4. Client   Astra Data
   Designer   Dan Wen

5. Client   Tone Yee
   Investment & Developments
   Designer   Dan Wen

6. Client   QRUN
   Designer   Dan Wen

7. Client   Yus Group
   Designer   Dan Wen

8. Client   Food Services of America
   Designers   Jack Anderson, Cliff Chung,
   Heidi Favour, Debra McCloskey,
   & Julie Lock

9. Client   Tigerlily
   Designers   Jack Anderson, Lisa Cerveny,
   Sonja Max, & Mary Hermes

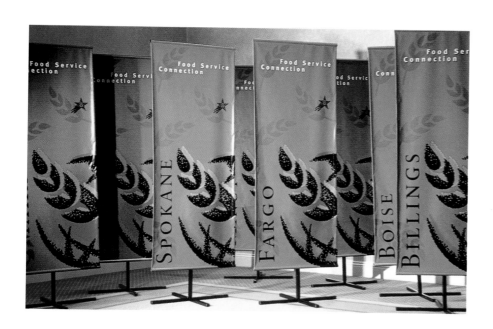

8.

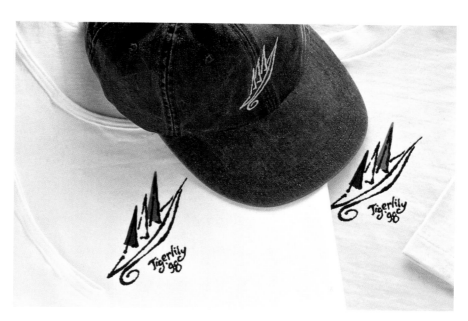

9.

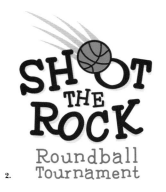

Hallin

CONSTRUCTION CONSULTING

1.

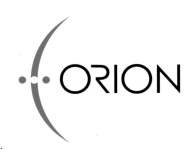

2.

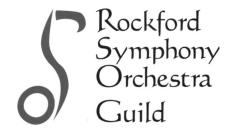

Rockford
Symphony
Orchestra
Guild

3.

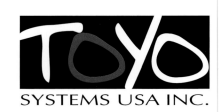

ORION

4.

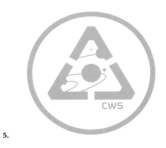

CWS

5.

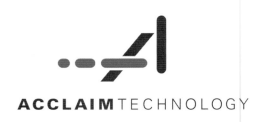

ACCLAIM TECHNOLOGY

6.

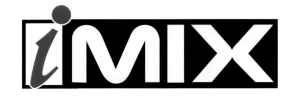

7.

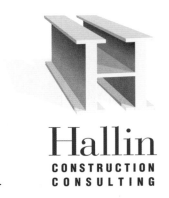

SYSTEMS USA INC.

8.

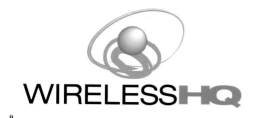

WIRELESSHQ

9.

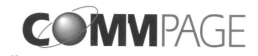

COMMPAGE

10.

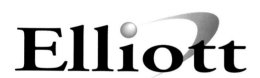

SUNPOWER

11.

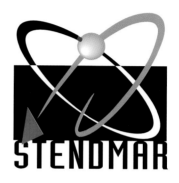

STENDMAR

12.

Elliott

13.

Dēglass furniture

14.

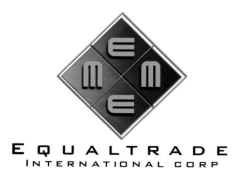

EQUALTRADE
INTERNATIONAL CORP

15.

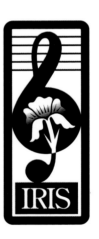

1.

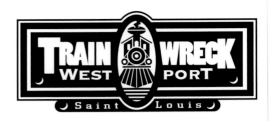

2.

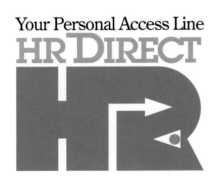

3.

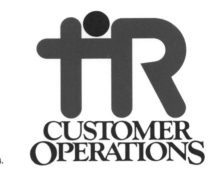

4.

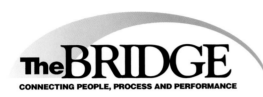

5.

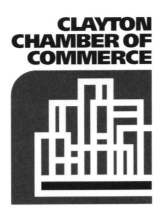

6.

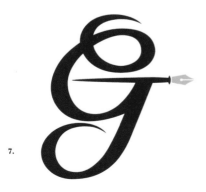

7.

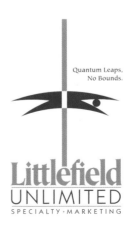

8.

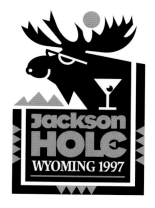

9.

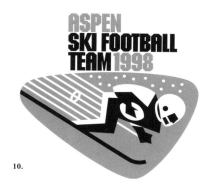

10.

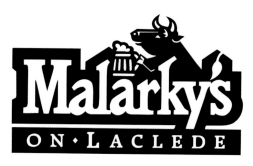

11.

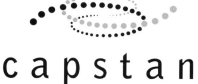

14.

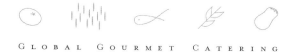

GLOBAL GOURMET CATERING

13.

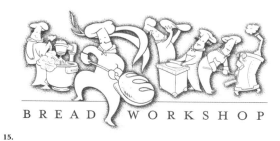

15.

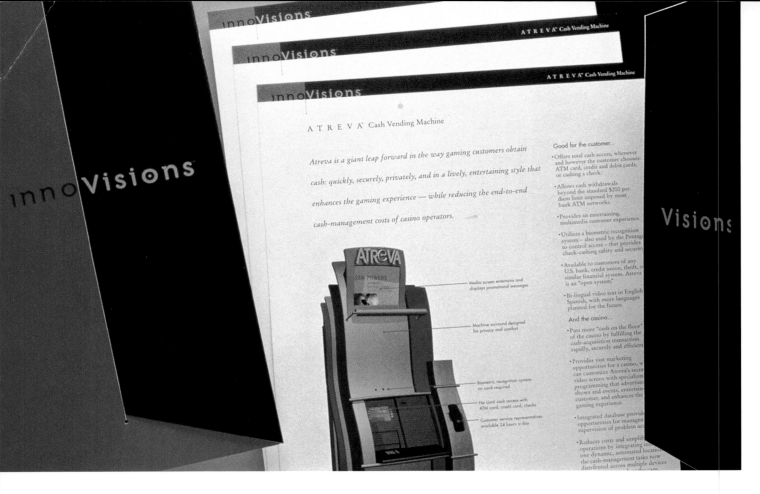

innoVisions™

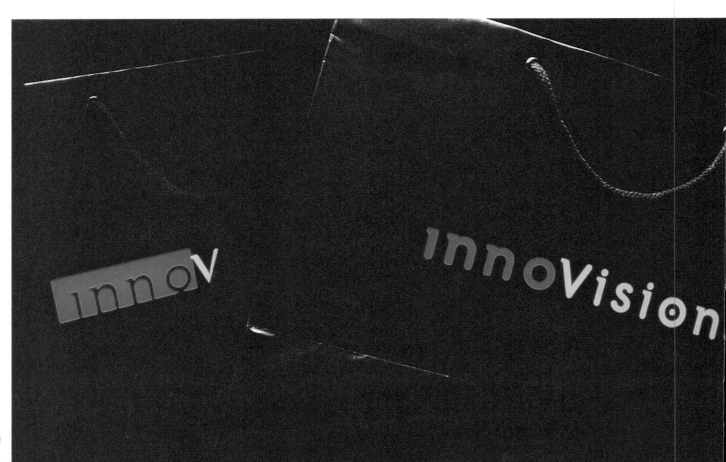

Hellmann Photography

1.

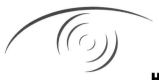

2.

school of information studies

3.

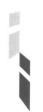

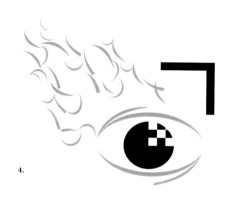

4.

**ALTERNATIVE
HEALING
CENTER**

5.

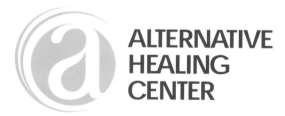

6.

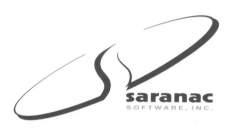

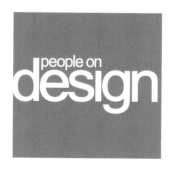

7.

(opposite)
Design Firm   **Hornall Anderson
Design Works**

Client   Wells Fargo "innoVisions"
Designers   Jack Anderson, Kathy Saito,
                Alan Copeland, &
                Cliff Chung

1 - 7
Design Firm **Adam Design**

1. Client   Hellmann Photography
    Designer   Adam Rozum

2. Client   BookQuest
    Designer   Adam Rozum

3. Client   School of Information Studies
    Designer   Adam Rozum

4. Client   Photofusion
    Designer   Adam Rozum

5. Client   Alternative Healing Center
    Designer   Adam Rozum

6. Client   Saranac Software
    Designer   Adam Rozum

7. Client   People on Design
    Designer   Adam Rozum

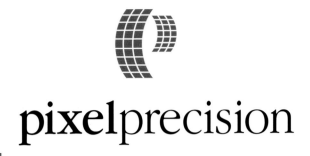

pixelprecision

1.

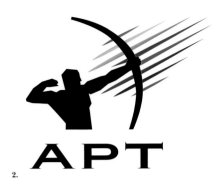

APT

2.

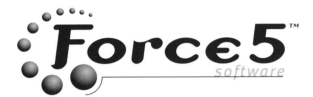

Force5™

software

3.

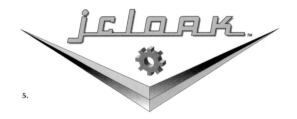

PanelLink®

DIGITAL

4.

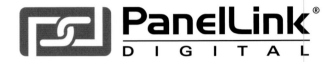

jcloak™

5.

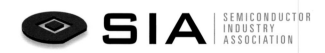

SIA

SEMICONDUCTOR
INDUSTRY
ASSOCIATION

6.

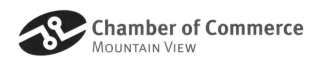

Chamber of Commerce
MOUNTAIN VIEW

7.

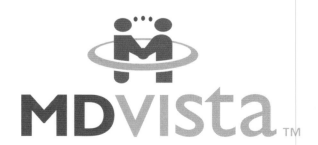

MDVista™

8.

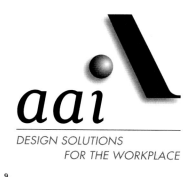

aai
DESIGN SOLUTIONS
FOR THE WORKPLACE

9.

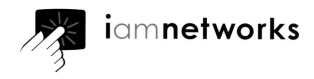

SINCE 1960 **PFG**™
POLLOCK FINANCIAL GROUP

10.

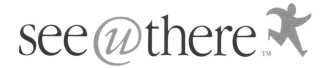

see@there™

11.

iam networks

12.

ebalance™

13.

power client™

14.

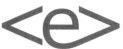

en Vision identity, inc.

15.

(all)

Design Firm	**en Vision Identity, Inc.**	
1. Client	Pixel Precision	
Designer	Karl Kromer	
2. Client	APT	
Designer	Vadim Goretsky	
3. Client	Force 5 software	
Designer	Shepherd Brown	
4. Client	PanelLink Digital	
Designer	Erin Mathis	
5. Client	Force 5 software	
Designer	Shepherd Brown	
6. Client	Semiconductor Industry Association	
Designer	Karl Kromer	
7. Client	Mountain View Chamber of Commerce	
Designers	Nicole Bloss & Iva Dasovic	
8. Client	MD Vista	
Designer	Nicole Bloss	

9. Client	aai	
Designer	Karl Kromer & Shepherd Brown	
10. Client	Pollock Financial Group	
Designer	Vadim Goretsky	
11. Client	See U There	
Designer	Karl Kromer	
12. Client	i am networks	
Designer	Karl Kromer	
13. Client	eBalance, inc.	
Designer	Nicole Bloss	
14. Client	PowerClient	
Designer	Nicole Bloss	
15. Client	en Vision identity, inc.	
Designer	Nicole Bloss	

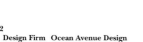

1.

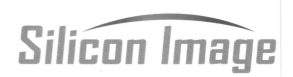

2.

DIVERSITY FORUM

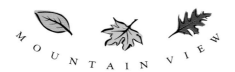

MOUNTAIN VIEW

3.

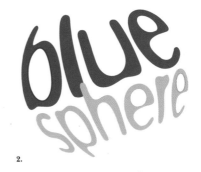

4.

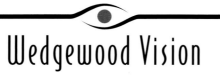

Wedgewood Vision

RANGES & COOKTOPS

5.

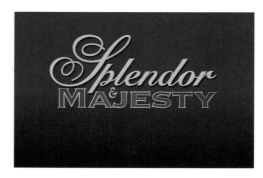

Atwood
Compliance
Systems

6.

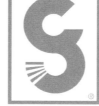

7.

1, 2
Design Firm Ocean Avenue Design
3, 4
Design Firm en Vision identity, inc.
5 - 7
Design Firm Conflux Design

1. Client   Howlett Surfboards
   Designer   Lynn E. Phillips

2. Client   Blue Sphere
   Designer   Lynn E. Phillips

3. Client   Diversity Forum
                 Mountain View
   Designer   Shepherd Brown

4. Client   Silicon Image
   Designers   Nicole Bloss &
                 Shepherd Brown

5. Client   Atwood Mobile Products
   Designer   Greg Fedorev

6. Client   Atwood Mobile Products
   Designer   Greg Fedorev

7. Client   Starlight Theatre
   Designer   Greg Fedorev

(opposite)
Design Firm Squires & Company

Client   Fast Park
Designer   Veronica Vaughn

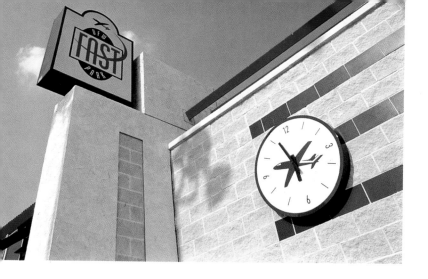

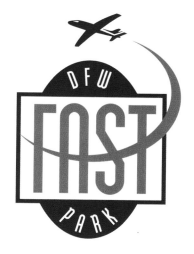

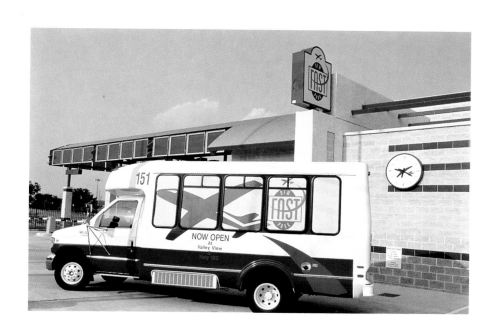

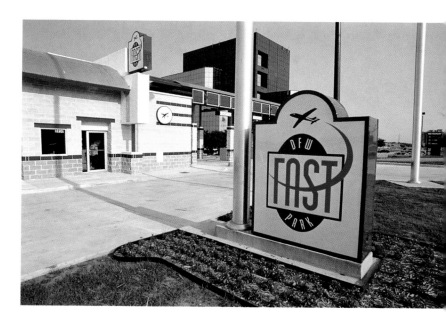

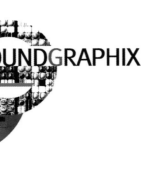

1.

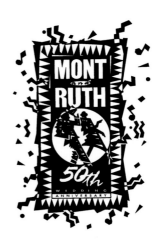

2.

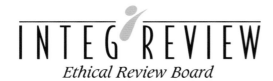

3.

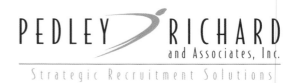

4.

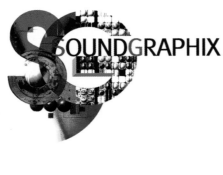

5.

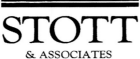

6.

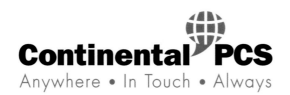

7.

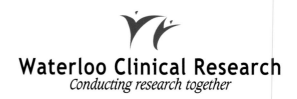

8.

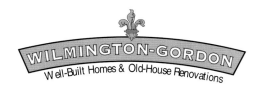

9.

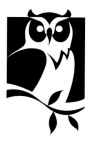

10.

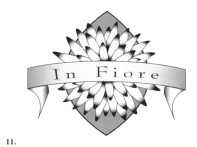

11.

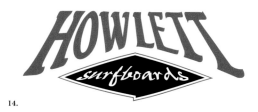

12.

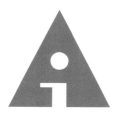

13.

14.

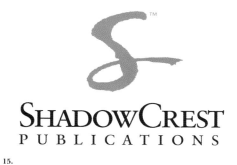

15.

1		
Design Firm	Interactive media	
2, 3		
Design Firm	Mickelson Design	
4 - 10		
Design Firm	Lewis Design	
11		
Design Firm	Aslan Graphics	
12		
Design Firm	Wild Onion Design, Inc.	
13		
Design Firm	Squire & Company	
14, 15		
Design Firm	Ocean Avenue Design	

1.	Client	SOUNDGRAPHIX
	Designer	Catsua Watanabe
2.	Client	Mont & Ruth
	Designer	Alan Mickelson
3.	Client	Stott & Associates
	Designer	Alan Mickelson
4.	Client	qd Solutions
	Designer	Larry Lewis
5.	Client	IntegReview
	Designer	Larry Lewis

6.	Client	Pedley Richard
	Designer	Larry Lewis
7.	Client	Continental PCS
	Designer	Larry Lewis
8.	Client	Waterloo Clinical Research
	Designer	Larry Lewis
9.	Client	Wilmington-Gordon
	Designer	Larry Lewis
10.	Client	Cycle Solutions
	Designer	Larry Lewis
11.	Client	In Fiore
	Designer	Dayala Levenson
12.	Client	Midwest Banc Holdings, Inc.
	Designer	Barbara Inzinga
13.	Client	Inter Audit
	Designer	Brandon Murphy
14.	Client	Howlett Surfboards
	Designer	Lynn E. Phillips
15.	Client	ShadowCrest Publications
	Designer	Lynn E. Phillips

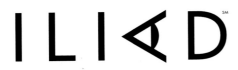

1.

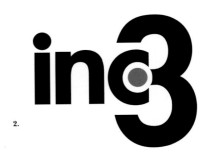

2.

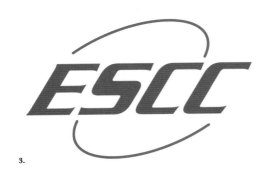

3.

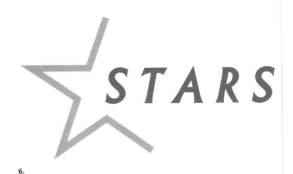

M.A. Weatherbie & Co., Inc.

4.

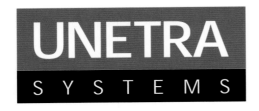

5.

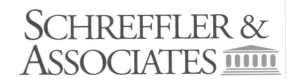

6.

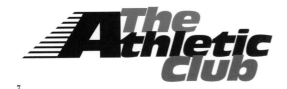

7.

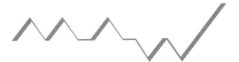

8.

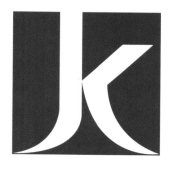

9.

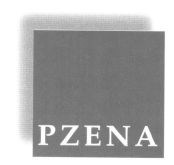

10.

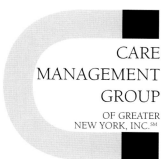

CARE
MANAGEMENT
GROUP
OF GREATER
NEW YORK, INC.ᔆᴹ

11.

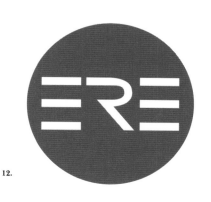

12.

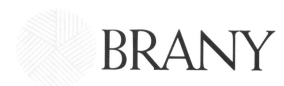

BRANY

13.

GRACEHOPPER

14.

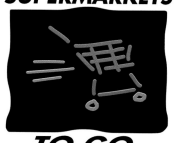

15.

1		
Design Firm	**Sibley Peteet Design**	
2 - 15		
Design Firm	**inc3**	

| 1. | Client | Chase Bank |
| | Designer | Tom Hough |

2.	Client	inc3
	Designers	Harvey Appelbaum &
		Nick Guarracino

3.	Client	ESCC
	Designers	Harvey Appelbaum &
		Nick Guarracino

4.	Client	M. A. Weatherbie & Co.
	Designers	Harvey Appelbaum &
		Nick Guarracino

5.	Client	Unetra Systems
	Designers	Harvey Appelbaum &
		Nick Guarracino

6.	Client	North Shore
	Designers	Harvey Appelbaum &
		Nick Guarracino

7.	Client	The Atheletic Club
	Designers	Harvey Appelbaum &
		Valerie Viola

8.	Client	Schreffler & Associates
	Designers	Harvey Appelbaum &
		Nick Guarracino

9.	Client	J - K Orthotics & Prosthetics
	Designers	Harvey Appelbaum &
		Nick Guarracino

10.	Client	Pzena Investment Management
	Designers	Harvey Appelbaum &
		Nick Guarracino

11.	Client	Care Management Group
	Designers	Harvey Appelbaum &
		Nick Guarracino

12.	Client	ERE
	Designers	Harvey Appelbaum &
		Nick Guarracino

13.	Client	Biomedical Research Assoc.
		of NY
	Designers	Harvey Appelbaum &
		Nick Guarracino

14.	Client	Gracehopper
	Designers	Harvey Appelbaum &
		Nick Guarracino

15.	Client	Supermarkets To Go
	Designers	Harvey Appelbaum &
		Nick Guarracino

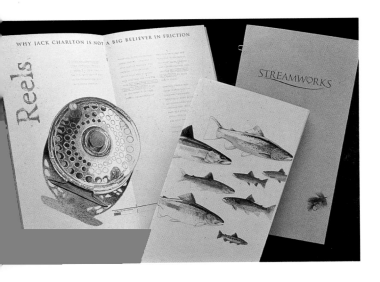

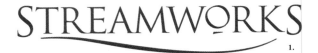

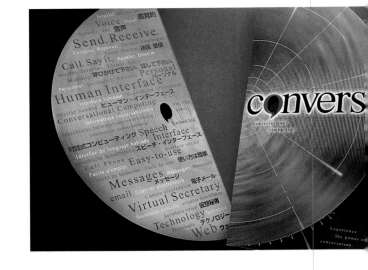

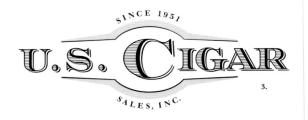

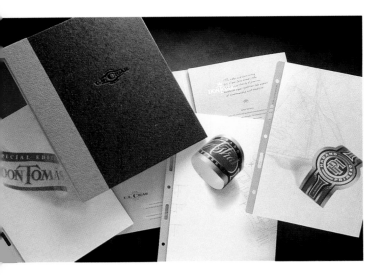

1.

2.

3.

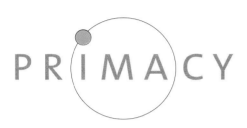

4.

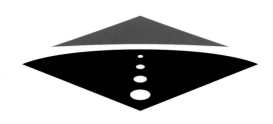

5.

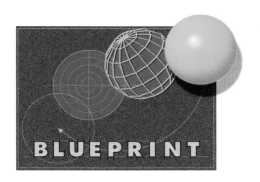

6.

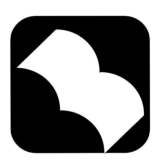

7.

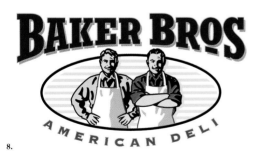

8.

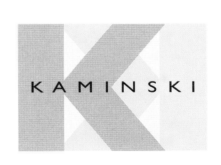

9.

10.

1 - 3		
Design Firm	**Hornall Anderson**	
	Design Works	
4 - 10		
Design Firm	**Sibley Peteet Design**	

1.	Client	Streamworks
	Designers	Jack Anderson, Belinda Bowline, Andrew Smith, & Ed Lee
2.	Client	Conversa
	Designers	Jack Anderson, Kathy Saito, & Alan Copeland
3.	Client	U.S. Cigar
	Designers	Jack Anderson, Larry Anderson, Mary Hermes, Mike Calkins, & Michael Brugman

4.	Client	THE SABRE GROUP
	Designer	Brent McMahan
5.	Client	Trans Solutions
	Designer	Joy Price
6.	Client	Skin Ceuticals
	Designer	Joy Price
7.	Client	Bentonville Public Library
	Designer	David Beck
8.	Client	Baker Bros
	Designer	Tom Hough
9.	Client	Karen Kaminski
	Designer	Roger Ferris
10.	Client	John Hutton
	Designer	Brent McMahan

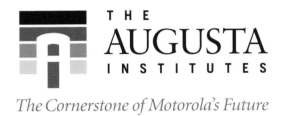

THE AUGUSTA INSTITUTES

The Cornerstone of Motorola's Future

1.

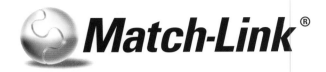

Match-Link®

2.

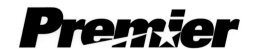

MOONLIGHT AT MEDINAH

A gala evening to benefit the American Cancer Society

3.

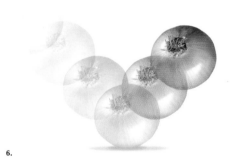

MAGNOLIA STREET KITCHEN

4.

b

BaerDesignGroup

5.

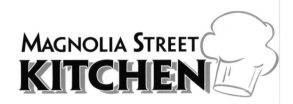

6.

Premier

7.

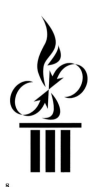

8.

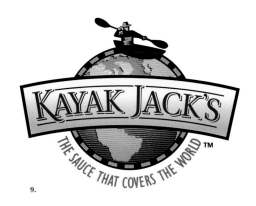

9.

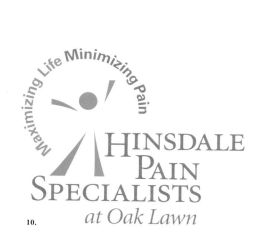

10.

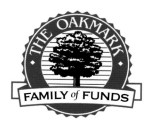

THE OAKMARK FAMILY of FUNDS

11.

HARLOW & ASSOCIATES P.C.

Certified Public Accountants • Tax Consultants

12.

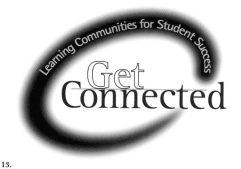

13.

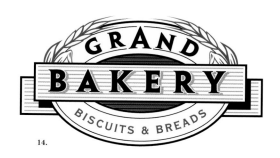

14.

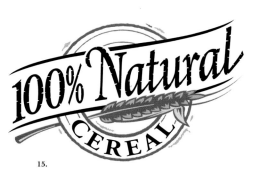

15.

1 - 5, 9 - 15
Design Firm Baer Design Group
6 - 8
Design Firm Wild Onion Design, Inc.

1.	Client	Motorola University
	Designers	Todd D. Baer, Dominy
		Burkhart, & Julie Rigby

| 2. | Client | Cendant |
| | Designer | Todd D. Baer |

| 3. | Client | American Cancer Society |
| | Designer | Todd D. Baer |

| 4. | Client | Haagen Grocers |
| | Designer | Todd D. Baer |

5.	Client	Baer Design Group
	Designers	Geoff Stone, Dominy
		Burkhart, & Todd D. Baer

| 6. | Client | Wild Onion Design Inc. |
| | Designer | Barbara Inzinga |

| 7. | Client | Premier Auto Finance, Inc. |
| | Designer | Barbara Inzinga |

8.	Client	Professional Organization for
		Association Executives
	Designer	Barbara Inzinga

| 9. | Client | Kayak Jack |
| | Designer | Todd D. Baer |

| 10. | Client | Hinsdale Pain Specialists |
| | Designer | Toy Nakajima |

| 11. | Client | Harris Associates LLP |
| | Designer | Todd D. Baer |

| 12. | Client | Harlow & Associates |
| | Designer | Todd D. Baer |

| 13. | Client | Harper College |
| | Designer | Dominy Burkhart |

| 14. | Client | Haagen Grocers |
| | Designer | Todd D. Baer |

| 15. | Client | Food Club |
| | Designer | Todd D. Baer |

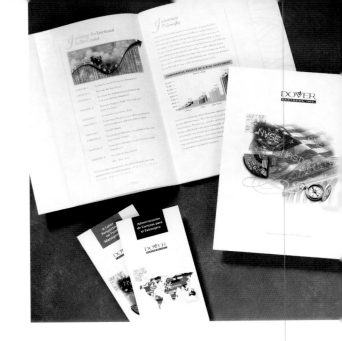

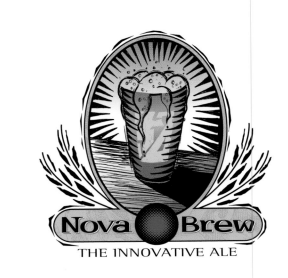

THE INNOVATIVE ALE

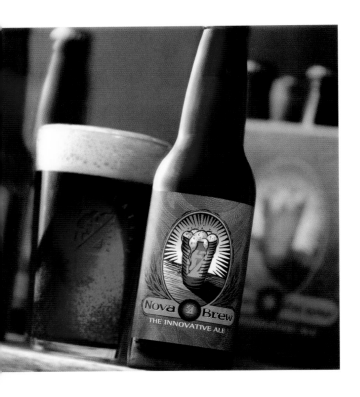

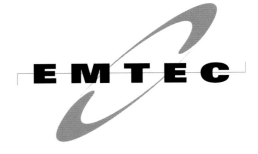

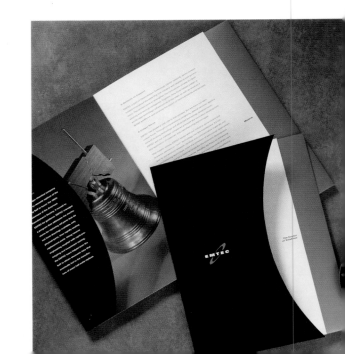

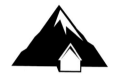

1.

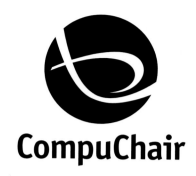

CompuChair

2.

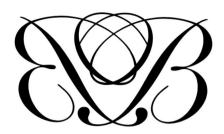

MOUNTAIN
trading co.

3.

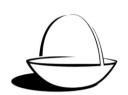

baskets
BY DESIGN

4.

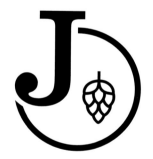

5.

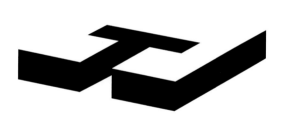

6.

7.

1 - 3		
Design Firm	**Nova Creative Group, Inc.**	
4 - 10		
Design Firm	**Graphica**	
	Communication Solutions	
1. Client	Dover Partners, Inc.	
Designer	Kris Hosbein	
2. Client	Nova Creative Group, Inc.	
Designer	Tim O'Hare	
3. Client	EMTEC	
Designer	Jack Denlinger	
4. Client	Best In Bows	
Designer	Craig Terrones	

5. Client	CompuChair	
Designers	Craig Terrones &	
	Robin Walker	
6. Client	Mountain Trading Co.	
Designer	Craig Terrones	
7. Client	Baskets by Design	
Designers	Robin Walker &	
	Craig Terrones	
8. Client	Jaenicke, Inc.	
Designer	Craig Terrones	
9. Client	Tarragon	
Designer	Craig Terrones	
10. Client	Solid Vision, Inc.	
Designer	Christa Fleming	

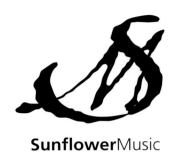

SunflowerMusic

1.

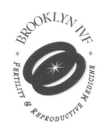

2.

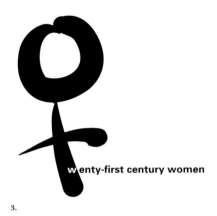

w enty-first century women

3.

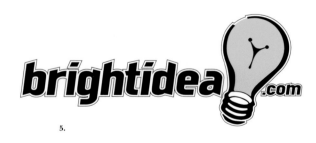

4.

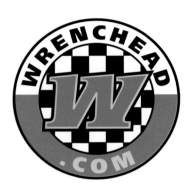

brightidea.com

5.

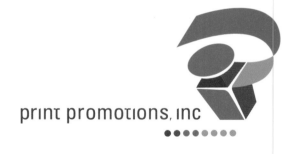

print promotions, inc

6.

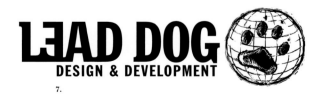

L3AD DOG
DESIGN & DEVELOPMENT

7.

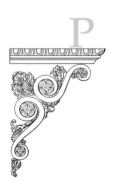

8.

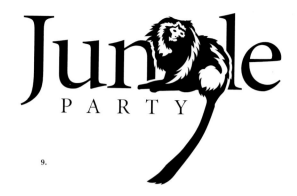

9.

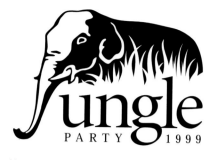

10.

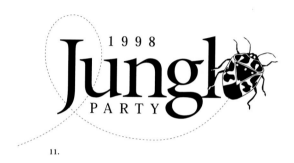

11.

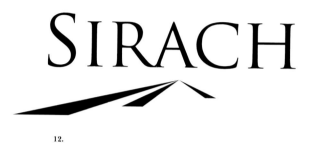

12.

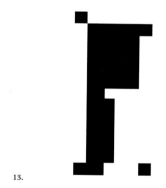

13.

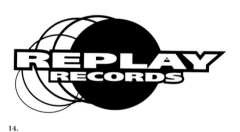

14.

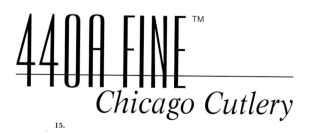

15.

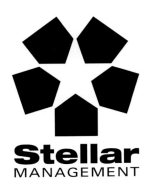

Stellar
MANAGEMENT

1.

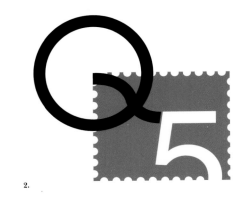

2.

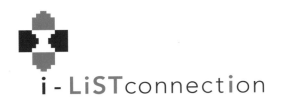

i-LiSTconnection

3.

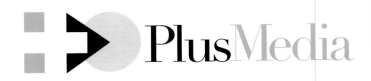

PlusMedia

4.

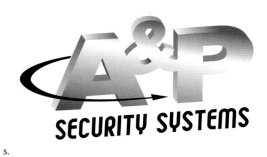

SECURITY SYSTEMS

5.

T R I
ARCH

6.

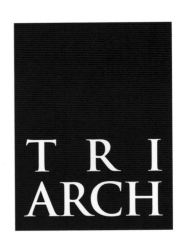

musicLens™

7.

1 - 4
Design Firm The Font Office Inc.
5 - 7
Design Firm Hassenstein Design, Inc.

1. Client   Stellar Management
   Designer   Charles S. Trovato

2. Client   Q-5 List Marketing
   Designer   Charles S. Trovato

3. Client   I-List Connection
   Designer   Charles S. Trovato

4. Client   PlusMedia
   Designer   Charles S. Trovato

5. Client   A & P Security Systems
   Designer   Susanne Hassenstein

6. Client   TriArch
   Designer   Susanne Hassenstein

7. Client   DDD Design
   Designer   Susanne Hassenstein

(opposite)
Design Firm   Hornall Anderson
**   Design Works**

Client   Foster Pepper Shefelman
Designers   John Hornall, Julie Keenan,
                Katha Dalton, & Nicole Bloss

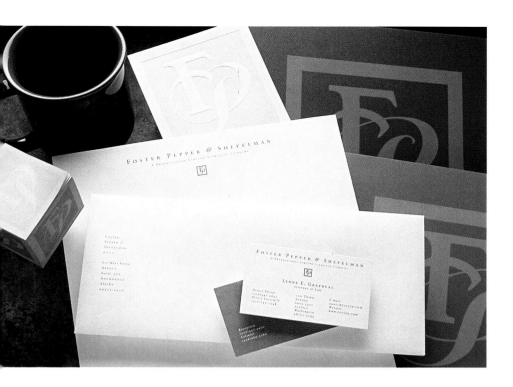

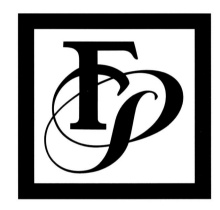

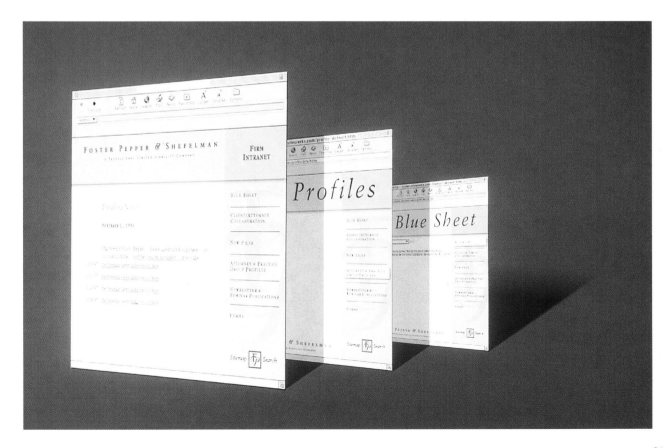

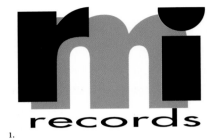

1.

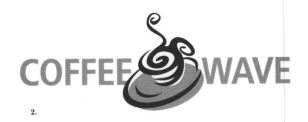

2.

3.

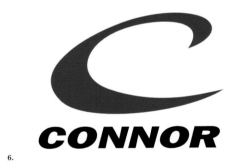

4.

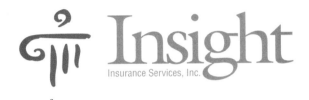

5.

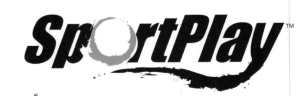

6.

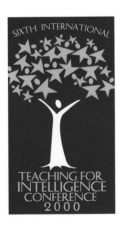

7.

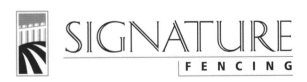

8.

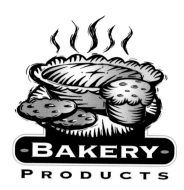

9.

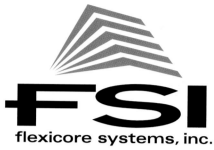

10.

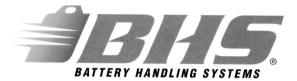

11.

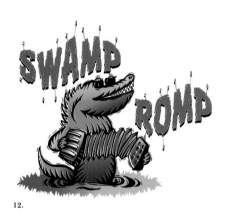

12.

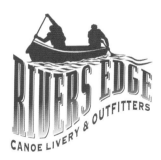

13.

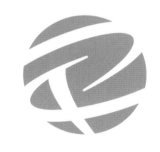

14.

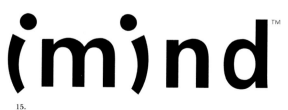

15.

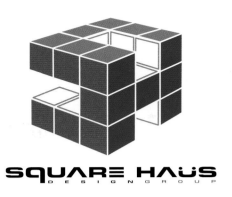

1. **SQUARE HAÜS**
   DESIGN GROUP

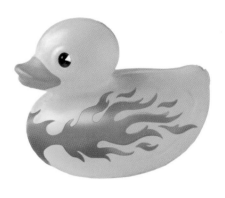

2.

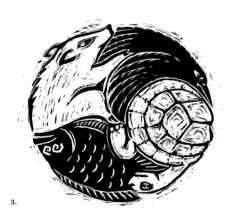

3.

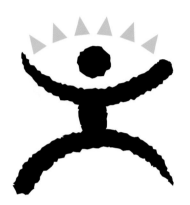

4.

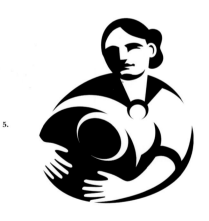

5.

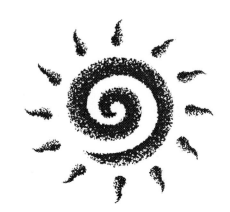

6.

7.

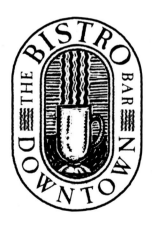

8.

ethics

9.

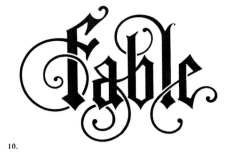

10.

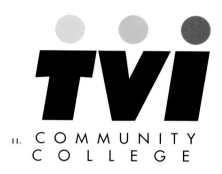

11. COMMUNITY COLLEGE

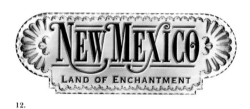

12.

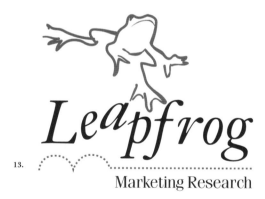

13. *Leapfrog*
Marketing Research

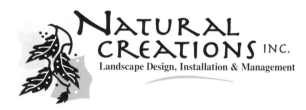

14.

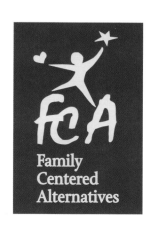

15.

1
Design Firm Square Haus Design Group
2 - 12
Design Firm Rick Johnson & Co., Inc.
13 - 15
Design Firm Design Directions

1. Client   Square Haus Design Group
   Designer   Dion M. Isselhardt

2. Client   Deming Duck Race
   Designer   Mark Chamberlain

3. Client   Rio Grande Nature Center
   Designer   Mark Chamberlain

4. Client   New Mexico Optics
                Industry Association
   Designer   Mark Chamberlain

5. Client   Albuquerque Convention &
                Visitors Bureau
   Designer   Mark Chamberlain

6. Client   Double Tree Hotel
   Designer   Mark Chamberlain

7. Client   Susan B. Fomen Foundation
                of Central New Mexico
   Designer   Mark Chamberlain

8. Client   Suncare
   Designer   Mark Chamberlain

9. Client   Samaritan Institute
   Designer   Mark Chamberlain

10. Client   Fable
    Designer   Mark Chamberlain

11. Client   TUI
    Designer   Mark Chamberlain

12. Client   New Mexico
                Department of Tourism
    Designer   Mark Chamberlain
    Tin Work   Fred Lopez

13. Client   Leapdrog Marketing
    Designer   Melissa Muldoon

14. Client   Natural Creations
    Designer   Melissa Muldoon

15. Client   Family Centered
                Alternatives Counseling
    Designers   Melissa Muldoon

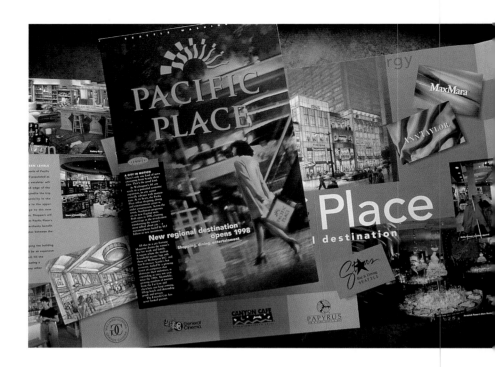

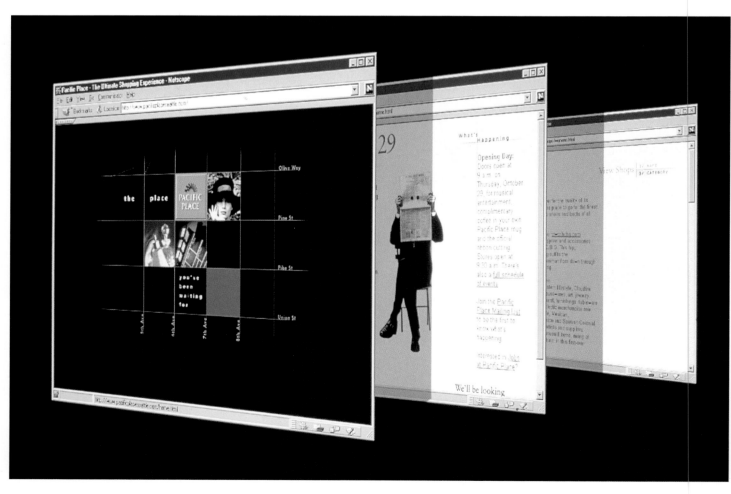

SUNFLOWER
HOLISTIC
Home Health Care, LLC

1.

HOPE
CHRISTIAN CHURCH

2.

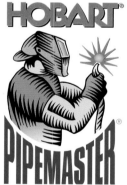

EquitySource
Innovative Capital Creation

3.

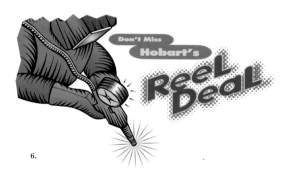

4.

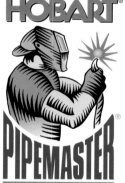

5.

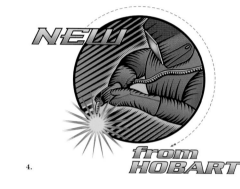

6.

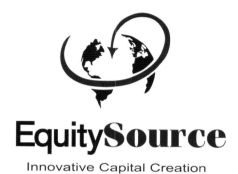

7.

(opposite)
Design Firm **Hornall Anderson**
Design Works

Client   Pacific Place
Designers   Jack Anderson, Heidi Favour,
            & David Bates

1 - 3
Design Firm **Design Directions**
4 - 7
Design Firm **Nova Creative Group Inc.**

1. Client   Sunflower Holistic
    Designer   Melissa Muldoon

2. Client   Hope Church
    Designer   Melissa Muldoon

3. Client   Equity Source
    Designer   Melissa Muldoon

4. Client   Hobart Welding Products
    Designer   Tim O'Hare

5. Client   Hobart Welding Products
    Designer   Tim O'Hare

6. Client   Hobart Welding Products
    Designer   Tim O'Hare

7. Client   Family Arena
                 Management Enterprise
    Designer   Dwayne Swormstedt

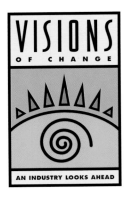

1.

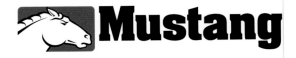

2.

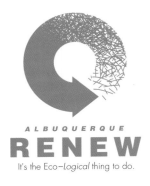

3.

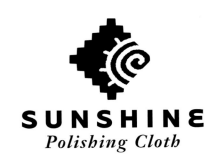

4.

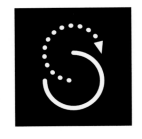

5.

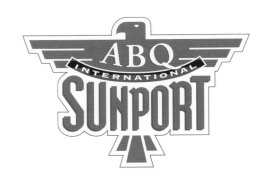

6.

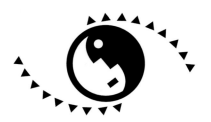

7.

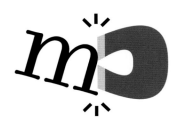

8.

9.

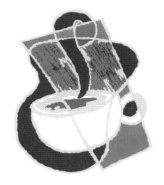

10.

11.

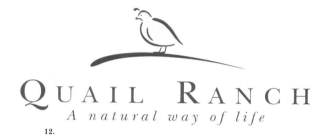

QUAIL RANCH
A natural way of life

12.

13.

14.

CHANNEL
105 ɪɴᴇ fm
all hit music

15.

(all)
Design Firm Rick Johnson & Co.

1. Client	Public Service Co. of New Mexico	
Designer	Lisa Graff	
2. Client	Giant Industries	
Designer	Molly Davis	
Illustrator	Brad Goodell	
3. Client	City of Albuquerque	
Designer	Tim McGrath	
Copywriter	Tim Pegors	
4. Client	Rio Grande	
Designer	Tim McGrath	
5. Client	New Mexico Economic Development	
Designer	Tim McGrath	
6. Client	Albuquerque International Sunport	
Designer	Lisa Graff	
7. Client	On-Site Solutions	
Designer	Tim McGrath	

8. Client	Media Dynamics
Designer	Tim McGrath
9. Client	Santa Ana Golf Club
Designer	Tim McGrath
10. Client	Gold Street Caffe
Designer	Rick Gutierrez
11. Client	Interactive Solutions, Inc.
Designer	John Reams
12. Client	Quail Ranch
Designers	Tim McGrath & Lisa Graff
Copywriter	Katie Duberry
13. Client	Albuquerque Women's Resource Center
Designer	Tim McGrath
14. Client	New Mexico Museum of Natural History
Designer	Tim McGrath
15. Client	Simmons Radio Group
Designer	Tim McGrath

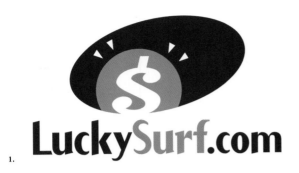

1.

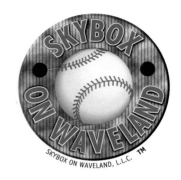

2.

flair

3.

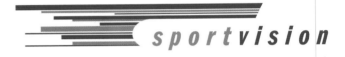

4.

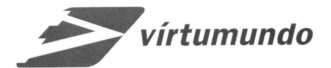

5.

NEXTPHASE

6.

1
   Design Firm Soul Studio
2
   Design Firm Indigo Design
3 - 5
   Design Firm Platinum Design, Inc.
6, 7
   Design Firm The Ideas Group
8 - 10
   Design Firm Hornall Anderson Design Works

1. Client   LuckySurf.com
     Designer   Stan Strocher

2. Client   Bear Kaufman Realty, Inc.
     Designer   Larry Kaminsky

3. Client   Hearst Magazines
     Designers Mike Joyce & Victoria Stamm

4. Client   Sportvision
     Designer   Kelly Hogg

5. Client   Virtumundo
     Designer   Alfred Assin

6. Client   Next Phase
     Designer   Heidi Davis

7. Client   ReloAction
     Designers Jeff Ivarson & Ramsey Said

8. Client   Yves Veggie Cuisine
     Designers John Hornall, Debra McCloskey,
              Heidi Favour, Jana Wilson Esser,
              & Michael Brugman

9. Client   Jamba Juice
     Designers Jack Anderson, Lisa Cerveny,
              Sonja Max, & Heidi Favour

10. Client   Cloud Nine
     Designers Jack Anderson, Jana Nishi,
              David Bates, & Sonja Max

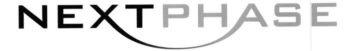

7.

8.

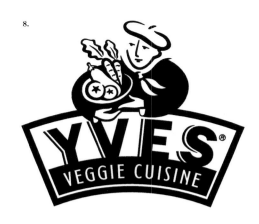

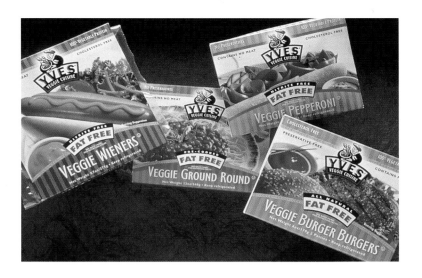

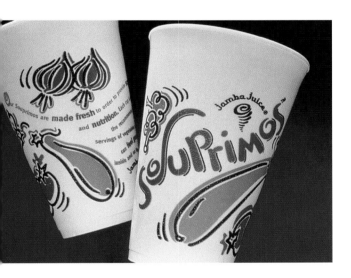

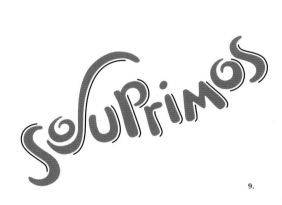

9.

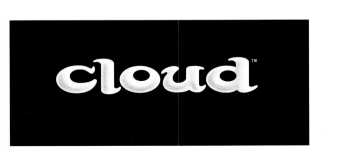

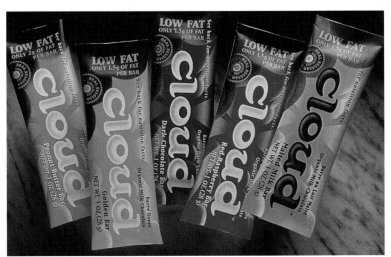

10.

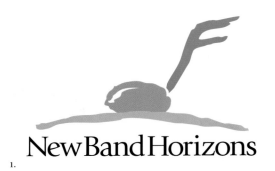

New Band Horizons

1.

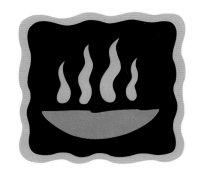

2.

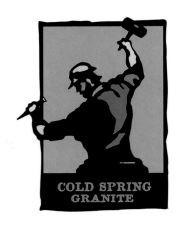

COLD SPRING
GRANITE

3.

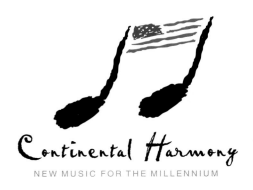

Continental Harmony

NEW MUSIC FOR THE MILLENNIUM

4.

AMERICAN COMPOSERS FORUM

5.

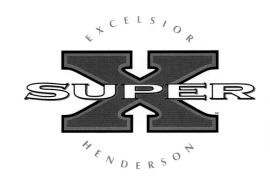

6.

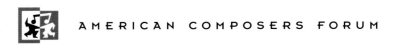

7.

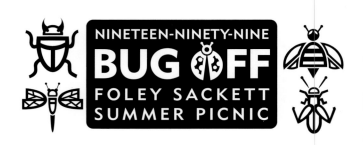

8.

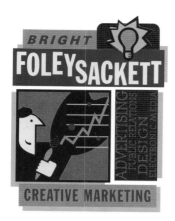

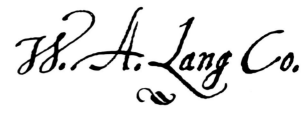

90TH ANNIVERSARY

9.

10.

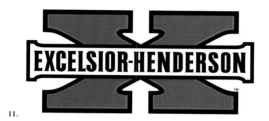

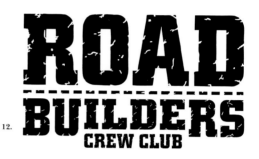

11.

12.

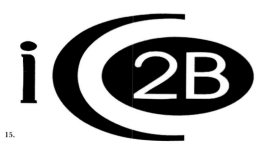

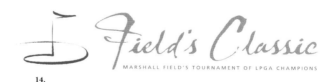

13.

14.

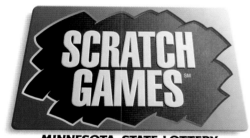

15.

1 - 14
Design Firm Foley Sackett, Inc.
15
**Design Firm Hornall Anderson
Design Works**

1.	Client	American Composers Forum	8.	Client	Foley Sackett, Inc.
	Designer	Tim Moran		Designer	Michelle Willinganz
2.	Client	Asia Grille	9.	Client	Foley Sackett, Inc.
	Designers	Michelle Willinganz		Designer	Michelle Willinganz
		& Joan Meath	10.	Client	W. A. Lang Co.
3.	Client	Cold Spring Granite		Designer	Michelle Willinganz
	Designer	Chris Cortilet	11.	Client	Excelsior-Henderson
4.	Client	American Composers Forum			Motorcycles
	Designer	Tim Moran		Designer	Michelle Willinganz
5.	Client	American Composers Forum	12.	Client	Caterpillar
	Designer	Michelle Willinganz		Designer	Wayne Thompson
6.	Client	Excelsior - Henderson	13.	Client	Minnesota State Lottery
		Motorcycles		Designer	Joan Meath
	Designers	Michelle Willinganz	14.	Client	Marshall Fields
		& Chris Cortilet		Designer	Michelle Willinganz
7.	Client	Leeann Chin, Inc.	15.	Client	IC2B
	Designer	Chris Cortilet		Designers	Jack Anderson,
					Mary Chin Hutchison,
					& Andrew Smith

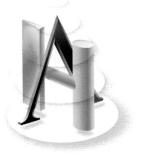

1.

ONYX

SOFTWARE

2.

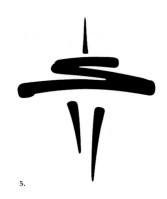

3.

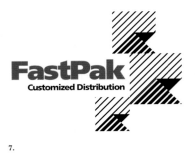

4.

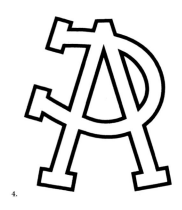

5.

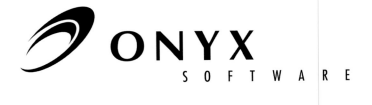

6.

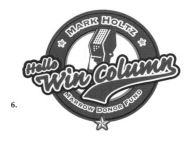

7.

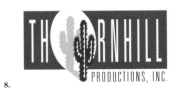

8.

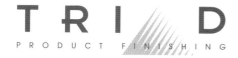

9.

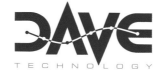

10.

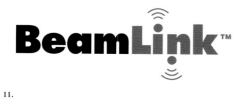

11.

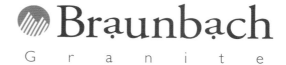

12.

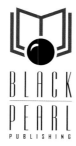

BLACK
PEARL
PUBLISHING

13.

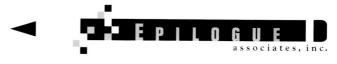

14.

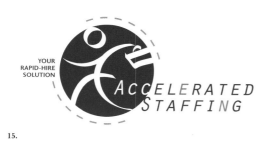

YOUR
RAPID-HIRE
SOLUTION

15.

1 - 5		
Design Firm	**Hornall Anderson Design Works**	
6 - 13		
Design Firm	**Hallmark Levy Smith**	
14, 15		
Design Firm	**White Communications, Inc.**	

1.	Client	Hornall Anderson Design Works
	Designers	Jack Anderson & David Bates
2.	Client	Onyx Corporation
	Designers	John Hornall, Debra McCloskey, Holly Finlayson, & Jana Wilson Esser
3.	Client	Ground Zero
	Designers	Jack Anderson, Kathy Saito, Julie Lock, Ed Lee, Heidi Favour, & Virginia Le
4.	Client	Anderson Pellet
	Designers	Jack Anderson & David Bates
5.	Client	Space Needle
	Designers	Jack Anderson, Mary Hermes, Gretchen Cook, Julie Lock, Amy Fawcett, & Andrew Smith

6.	Client	Mark Holtz
	Designer	Chuck Hodges
7.	Client	FastPak
	Designer	Cesar Hallmark
8.	Client	Thornhill Productions, Inc.
	Designer	Rick Levy
9.	Client	Triad
	Designer	Rick Levy
10.	Client	Dave Technology
	Designer	Rick Levy
11.	Client	BeamLink
	Designers	Rick Levy
12.	Client	Braunbach
	Designer	Sean Gregory
13.	Client	Black Pearl
	Designer	Chuck Hodges
14.	Client	Epilogue Associates, Inc.
	Designer	Karen B. White
15.	Client	Executives Network, Inc.
	Designer	Karen B. White

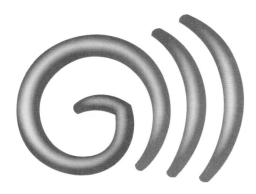

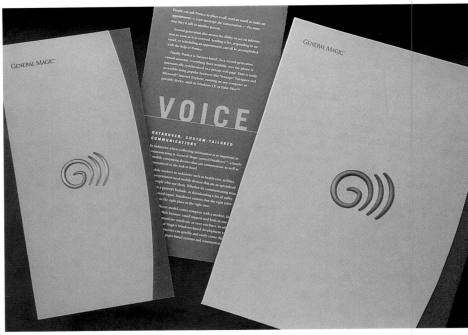

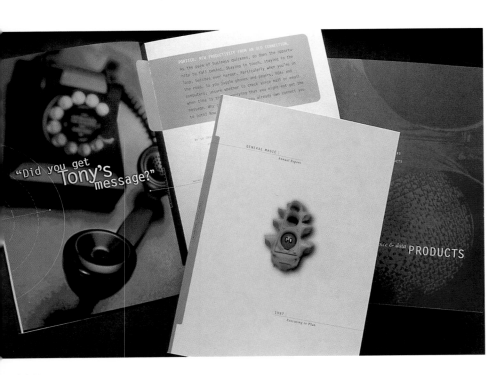

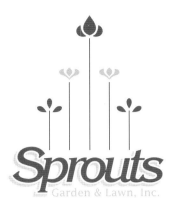

1.

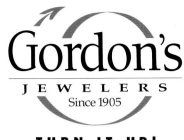

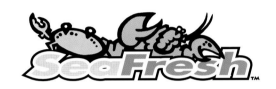

2.

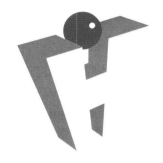

3.

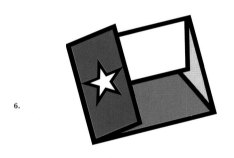

4.

5.

6.

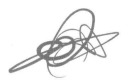

Hallmark Levy Smith
Marketing & Creative, Inc.

7.

(opposite) Design Firm	Hornall Anderson Design Works
Client	General Magic
Designers	Jack Anderson, Jana Nishi, Mary Chin Hutchison, Larry Anderson, Michael Brugman, & Denise Weir

	(all) Design Firm	Hallmark Levy Smith
1.	Client	Sprouts Garden & Lawn, Inc.
	Designer	Cesar Hallmark
2.	Client	Gordon's Jewelry
	Designer	Chuck Hodges
3.	Client	Huge Image
	Designer	Cesar Hallmark
4.	Client	Sea Fresh
	Designer	J.R. Mounger
5.	Client	Nature Growers
	Designer	Cesar Hallmark
6.	Client	Paris Packaging
	Designers	Sean Gregory & Rick Levy
7.	Client	Hallmark Levy Smith
	Designers	Cesar Hallmark

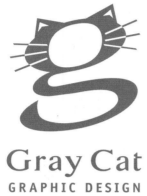

1.

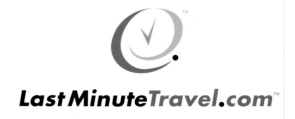

2.

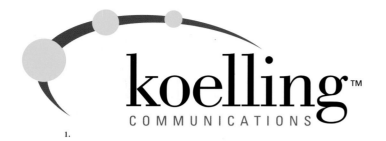

3.

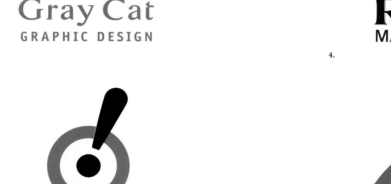

4.

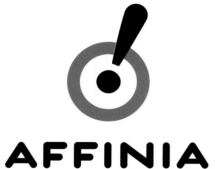

5.

6.

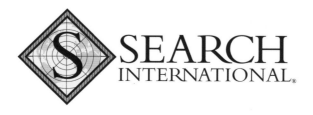

7.

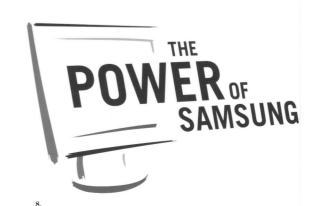

8.

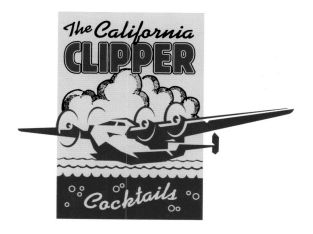

9.

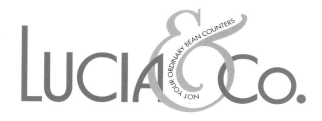

10.

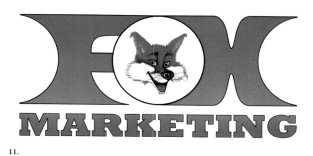

11.

COLTON FIRST BAPTIST CHURCH

12.

DAVID HOPKINS

PAINT & DRYWALL
INCORPORATED

13.

IRRIGATION TECH

14.

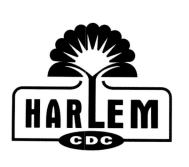

Harlem Community Development Corporation

15.

1, 2, 5, 8				
Design Firm	Muccino Design Group			
3, 9				
Design Firm	Gray Cat Graphic Design		6. Client	ePatients.com
4, 7				
Design Firm	River Marketing, Inc.		7. Client	Search International
6			Designer	Jennifer Sailer
Design Firm	The Graphic Expression, Inc.		8. Client	Samsung Electronics
10, 12, 13			Designer	Alfredo Muccino &
Design Firm	P.K. Design			Joshua Swanbeck
11, 14				
Design Firm	Fox Marketing		9. Client	The California Clipper
15			Designer	Lisa Empleo
Design Firm	Granola Graphics			
			10. Client	Lucia & Co.
1. Client	Koelling Communications		Designer	Phyllis Kates
Designers	Alfredo Muccino & Julia Held			
			11. Client	Fox Marketing
2. Client	Last Minute Travel.com			
Designers	Alfredo Muccino &		12. Client	CFB Church
	Joshua Swanbeck		Designer	Phyllis Kates
3. Client	Gray Cat Graphic Design		13. Client	Hopkins Paint & Drywall
Designer	Lisa Empleo		Designer	Phyllis Kates
4. Client	River Marketing, Inc.			
Designer	Jennifer Sailer		14. Client	Irrigation Tech.
5. Client	Affinia		15. Client	Harlem Community
Designers	Alfredo Muccino, Michael			Development Corp.
	Lee, & Colm Sweetman		Designer	Paul Howard

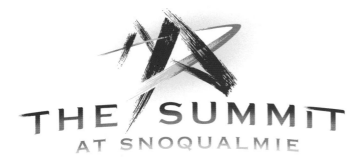

1.

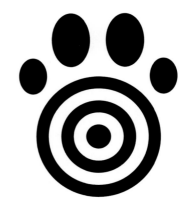

2.

workengine™

3.

gettuit.com

4.

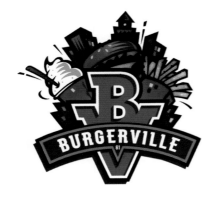

5.

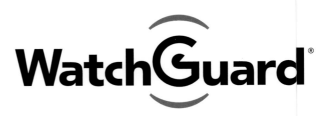

6.

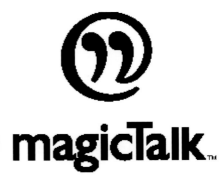

7.

(all)

Design Firm	**Hornall Anderson Design Works**	

1. Client — The Summit at Snoqualmie
   Designers — Jack Anderson, David Bates, & Sonja Max

2. Client — Hammerquist & Halverson
   Designers — Jack Anderson, & Mike Calkins

3. Client — Getuit.com "Workengine"
   Designers — Jack Anderson, Kathy Saito, Gretchen Cook, James Tee, Julie Lock, & Henry Yiu

4. Client — Getuit.com
   Designers — Jack Anderson, Margaret Long, & Jason Hickner

5. Client — Burgerville
   Designers — John Hornall, Larry Anderson, Bruce Branson-Meyer, & Jana Nishi

6. Client — WatchGaurd
   Designers — Jack Anderson, Lisa Cerveny, Mary Hermes, Kathy Saito, Michael Brugman, Holly Finlayson, & Belinda Bowling

7. Client — General Magic (MagicTalk)
   Designers — Jack Anderson, Jana Nishi, Mary Chin Hutchison, Larry Anderson, Michael Brugman, & Denise Weir

(opposite)
   Client — Boullion Aviation Services
   Designers — Jack Anderson, Kathy Dalton, Ryan Wilkerson, & Belinda Bowling

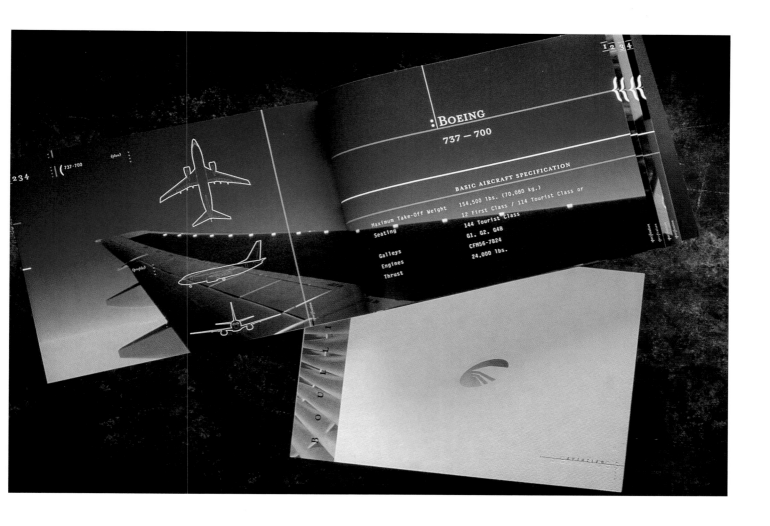

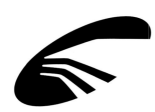

BOULLIOUN

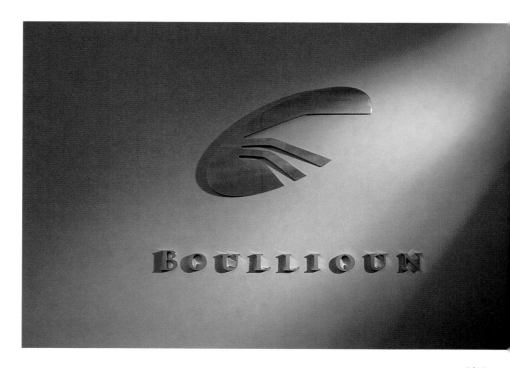

Index